# FATAL ENCOUNTER

## NICHOLAS ECKERT

POOLBEG

Published 1999
by Poolbeg Press Ltd
123 Baldoyle Industrial Estate
Dublin 13, Ireland

Photographs reproduced by kind permission of Pacemaker Press International,
Douglas Celecia, the Kane and Timmons families.

Extract from *GiB: A Modest Exposure*, 1990 by Jack Mitchell
reproduced by kind permission of Fulcrum Press, Connolly Books,
43 East Essex Street, Dublin 2, Ireland.

A catalogue record for this book is available from the British Library.

ISBN 1 85371 837 8

Cover design by Poolbeg Group Services Ltd
Set by Poolbeg Group Services Ltd in Times 10.5/14
Printed by The Guernsey Press Ltd,
Vale, Guernsey, Channel Islands.

## ABOUT THE AUTHOR

Nicholas Eckert served over five years on active duty in the United States Army as a military intelligence officer. He took part in the 1989 invasion of Panama, was decorated for outstanding performance during the Persian Gulf War, and was a member of the United Nations Protection force in the Former Yugoslavia. He has written two magazine articles about the conflict in Ireland, "Shoot to Kill" and "Death at Narrow Water: the Anatomy of an Ambush", for the United States Army periodical *Military Intelligence*.

To my mother, father, and the rest of my family. Without their constant love, patience, and willingness to listen, this book would not have been possible.

Also, to the Gibraltar Police Press Officer who refused to answer my simplest questions, saying only: "What's in the public record is in the public record, and what isn't isn't." That statement erased whatever doubts I've had about what I've written here.

Until one mild March afternoon,
As balmy as an English June,
A Sunday, full of peaceful sounds
And strolling tourists on their rounds
There came a change of quality.
The game became reality.
At sometime after three o'clock
The thing they harboured in their Rock
Descended on them; out of the blue –
Slaughter in Winston Churchill Avenue
Panic among the passers-by
As three young Irish people die,
Mown down by men with automatics
The story goes they were fanatics
Dangerous terrorists, they said.
Who, the assassins? No – the dead.

But how do we know the intention was
To shoot to kill? We know because
The SAS, to put it straight
Is that intention incarnate.

Jack Mitchell, *GiB: A Modest Exposure*, 1990

"When those who make the law break the law in the name of the law, there is no law."
                              – anonymous

# TABLE OF CONTENTS

# GLOSSARY

**active service unit**: a unit of the Provisional IRA; its size depends on the type of mission it has

**assembly area**: the car park in Gibraltar by Southport Gate where the Royal Anglian Regiment Band assembled before and after the weekly changing-of-the-guard ceremony

**blocking car**: a vehicle used to hold a parking space for a car-bomb

**button job**: a radio-signal-initiated bomb

**the Convent**: the Gibraltar Governor-General's official residence and site of the then weekly changing-of-the-guard ceremony on the Rock

**Gardaí**: members of the Republic of Ireland's police force, formally known as the Garda Síochána

**heli-tele**: the film taken of the March 19, 1988 incident at Kevin Brady's funeral

**INLA**: the Irish National Liberation Army, Republican splinter group which broke away from the Official IRA after that organization declared its unilateral cease-fire

**inquest**: the legal procedure used in Britain to establish the cause of death in cases where circumstances warrant it

**MI5**: the British domestic counter-intelligence agency, also known as "the Security Service"

**MI6**: the British foreign intelligence agency, also known as "the Secret Intelligence Service"

**MoD**: the British Ministry of Defence

**Operation Flavius**: the code name for the British SAS/MI5 operation in Gibraltar

**Provisional IRA**: the main republican paramilitary group in Ireland

**SAS**: Special Air Service, the British Army's elite counter-terrorist unit

**semtex**: the powerful, Czech-manufactured plastic explosive provided to the IRA by Libya

**UDA**: Ulster Defense Association, a Northern Ireland Protestant paramilitary group

**UDR**: Ulster Defense Regiment, a locally-raised, largely Protestant Northern Ireland militia, now defunct

**UVF**: Ulster Volunteer Force (UVF), a Northern Ireland Protestant paramilitary group

**Volunteer**: description of a member of the Irish Republican Army

# CAST OF CHARACTERS

*Provisional Irish Republican Army*

Daniel McCann: IRA volunteer killed in Gibraltar on March 6, 1988

Seán Savage: IRA volunteer killed in Gibraltar on March 6, 1988

Mairéad Farrell: IRA volunteer killed in Gibraltar on March 6, 1988

Kevin Brady: IRA volunteer killed in Milltown Cemetery on March 16, 1988

*Gibraltar*

Kenneth Asquez: witness to Seán Savage's death (retracted)

Stephen and Lucinda Bullock: witnesses to Daniel McCann's death

Josie Celecia: witness to deaths of Daniel McCann and Mairéad Farrell

Carmen and Maxie Proetta: witnesses to Daniel McCann and Mairéad Farrell's deaths

Diana Treacy: witness to Seán Savage's death

Robin Mordue: British vacationer who witnessed Seán Savage's death

Felix Pizzarello: the Gibraltar Coroner

*Operation Flavius*

Joseph Canepa: Commissioner, Gibraltar Police

Mr O: pseudonym for MI5 officer who set the counter-terrorist operation in motion

Soldier F: pseudonym for the senior SAS officer in Gibraltar, commander A Squadron, 22nd SAS

Soldier E: pseudonym for the SAS officer who controlled Soldiers A, B, C, and D

Soldiers A, B, C, D: pseudonyms for the SAS men who killed McCann, Savage, and Farrell

Soldier G: pseudonym for Operation Flavius's bomb disposal expert

Watchers H, I, J, K, L, M, N: pseudonyms for the MI5 surveillance specialists in Gibraltar

Officers P, Q, R: pseudonyms for the Gibraltar Police Special Branch officers

Patrick McGrory: Belfast solicitor who represented the McCann, Savage, and Farrell families at the Gibraltar Inquest

## Belfast

Corporal David Howes: member, British Army Signals, murdered in Andersonstown on March 19, 1988

Corporal Derek Wood: member, British Army Signals, murdered in Andersonstown on March 19, 1988

Patrick Kane: given double life sentence in 1990 for allegedly taking part in the murders of Corporals Wood and Howes, conviction quashed in 1997

Michael Timmons: given double life sentence in 1990 for allegedly taking part in the murders of Corporals Wood and Howes

Seán Kelly: given double life sentence in 1990 for allegedly taking part in the murders of Corporals Wood and Howes

Michael Stone: free-lance Loyalist paramilitary who murdered Kevin Brady and two other men at Milltown Cemetery on March 16, 1988

# PREFACE

First, I would like to stress that this book represents my viewpoints and not those of the United States Government, military, nor of my current employers.

Second, outside the movies, people rarely speak (or even write) in a consistently easy-to-understand manner. Often, they stutter, give obscure nicknames for people, places, and things, and use jargon and pronouns excessively. Where I felt the reader would be confused, I have clarified what the person, newspaper article, or document was saying (with the clarifications enclosed in brackets).

As for the book, I had always been puzzled that no one had written one before about the Gibraltar affair. After all, it had all the elements of a classic true-crime story: terrorists, car-bombs, commandos, executions, mob violence, and bloody revenge. It seemed that the many writers more established than I had failed the public by passing this one up.

Little did I know. Researching *Fatal Encounter* taught me just how hard it is to get the truth about a highly controversial series of events. At least one participant in what you are writing about will always be ready to accuse you of being his or her enemy.

That has been the case with the Gibraltar Killings. As much as my modest resources allowed, I went out of my way to speak to people with first-hand knowledge of the case. From the British side, I often received stony silences or suggestions that I must be some sort of communist to question what happened in

Gibraltar. In contrast, a relative of Mairéad Farrell told me that one reason why he would not speak with me was because I might be a British spy.[1]

With these experiences in mind, I have no doubt that there will be some who will curse this book for being "soft on terrorism" as well as some who will damn it for being biased against "the armed struggle". To them, I have only two things to say. First, they had their chance to speak to me, and they chose not to. If they believe what I say here is wrong, they should write their own books and not expect mine to parrot their viewpoints, particularly when they refused to provide them to me.

Second, I have tried my utmost to keep my book focused on the Gibraltar Killings and, to a lesser extent, related events in Casement Park. Those are single – albeit complex – incidents. My intent never was to judge the overall morality of the actions of the IRA or the British government.

That being said, I would like to thank the many who did help me write *Fatal Encounter*, particularly Yvonne Murphy and the other researchers at Belfast's Linen Hall Library for granting me access to their files, and Dr J Bowyer Bell for the invaluable assistance he gave me. I would further like to thank the Committee for the Administration of Justice, the Casement Accused Relatives' Committee, the Commission of the European Court of Human Rights, the *Irish News*, the *Sunday Tribune*, the British Broadcasting Corporation (for letting me use the excerpts from "Murder in Mind"), Channel Four Television (for allowing me to quote extensively from their transcript of the Gibraltar Inquest), The British and Irish Embassies in the United States, Station WGBH Boston of the Public Broadcasting Service (for permitting me to use material from *Death of a Terrorist*), The Gibraltar Public Archives, Reynaldo Nogueras, Elizabeth Green, Father Seán McManus,

Jim Neeson, Seán Kelly, John Kelly, James Howland, Trudy Timmons, John Burke, Brendan O'Brien, Father Tom Toner, Professor Michael Scott, Dr Loren Thompson, Jim Kelly, Bernard and Maureen Kane, Douglas Celecia, Stephen and Lucinda Bullock, Harry Debelius, Ian Jack, Jack Holland, Roger Bolton, "Strobes" at *Private Eye*, Michael F Quilligan, David Miller, Dominic Searles, Lucille Redmond, Tam Dalyell, Joe Austin, Dennis Woolfe, Mark Urban, Dr Ehud Sprinzak, Andrew Coleman, Nicole Hodson of Poolbeg, and the people in Belfast, Gibraltar, Spain, the United States, and the United Kingdom who were willing to talk about the case that I cannot name because it might cause them difficulties or embarrassment.

## Notes
1. The Gibraltarians were equally suspicious. During my visit to the Rock, whenever I brought the topic of the killings up, the natives' first question was almost always, "Are you Irish?" Some of the Colony's inhabitants gave the e-mails I sent them asking for the telephone numbers of various witnesses to the killings to the Gibraltar Police Special Branch.

# PROLOGUE

## A ROW OF DOMINOS

"[The IRA] should be wiped off the civilized world."
– Margaret Thatcher

The Prime Minister was dressed for mourning that cold, rainy day in Enniskillen, Northern Ireland. The only splash of colour in her clothes was the red poppy pinned on the left-hand side of her coat. Everyone around Margaret Thatcher, except for the soldiers standing stiffly at attention in the town square, wore similar flowers above their hearts.

Enniskillen, a small town nestled in the rolling countryside of County Fermanagh, seemed an odd place for the Prime Minister of the United Kingdom to be. On the surface, there was little to set it apart from the other villages nearby. What distinguished Enniskillen was not something visible but history, recent history.

On November 8, 1987, just two weeks before, it had been Remembrance Day, when Britons honour the dead of their nation's wars. Each year on that day, across the United Kingdom, the young and old pin on red poppies and gather at war memorials. There they pray for those who died for God, King, and Country at Flanders, Dunkirk, and other less remembered battlefields.

"Poppy Day" is a particularly sacred time for Ulstermen. During July 1916, in just two days of battle at the Somme, 5,500 members of the Protestant 36th Ulster Division died in

1

combat with the German Army. More than seventy years later, their descendants still religiously invoke the memory of the 36th Division's blood sacrifice for the Empire. Gathering on Remembrance Day at cenotaphs like the one in Enniskillen is more than just a tradition for Protestants. It is a reaffirmation of the link between Ulster and the British Crown.

So it came as a cruel shock when just before the wreath-laying ceremony at the Enniskillen Cenotaph, a fifty-pound charge of explosives planted by the IRA in a nearby social club detonated. The blast blew down the wall of the building, showering those standing next to it with rubble. Eleven people died and sixty-three more were badly hurt, crushed by tons of masonry or smashed up against a steel barrier. As one survivor put it, "the explosion . . . seemed to last about fifteen seconds. Then there was a dead silence for two seconds. Then there was sobbing and crying."[1] There had been no warning.

Thatcher learned about the atrocity at the reception following the Remembrance Day ceremonies she attended at the London Cenotaph. She immediately condemned the bombing as an act which desecrated the dead, "a blot on mankind".[2] Now, two weeks later, she had come to Enniskillen to lay a wreath for those who died in what the press was calling the "Poppy Day Massacre".

As she walked toward the marker, her face was set with dignified grief. Underneath, there may well have been one other emotion: barely controlled rage at those responsible for the slaughter.

Throughout her entire tenure as Prime Minister and for years before, Margaret Thatcher had been under what she liked to call "the shadow of the gunmen".[3] This was inevitable, simply because of her background and political beliefs. As a member of the British Conservative Party, she was profoundly committed to the union between Northern Ireland and the United Kingdom. For her, "the Province" was as "British as

Finchley", her parliamentary constituency. As a good Methodist, she could sympathize and empathize with the Protestants living there far more than she ever could with the region's Catholics. For those reasons, Thatcher never could and never would see the IRA as anything other than a collection of criminals.

Her views were not much different from those that millions of British citizens held. What set the Prime Minister apart were the personal losses and psychological wounds she had suffered because of them.

The first of these came in 1975, the year she became leader of the Conservative Party. An IRA active service unit (ASU) had been operating in London for nearly a year, conducting an attack every week, deeply disrupting the fabric of ordinary life in the capital. In an effort to put a stop to this, Ross McWhirter, the editor of *Guinness Book of Records*, bravely offered a £50,000 reward for information leading to the capture of the bombers. In response, on November 27, an IRA gunman murdered McWhirter on his doorstep. Speaking about his murder, Thatcher did not mince words. In a dramatic speech the next day before the House of Commons, she called for vengeance, saying "hang these assassins . . . they have forfeited the right to live".[4] Later, when the police finally arrested McWhirter's killers, they found Thatcher's name on a target list in one of the IRA men's safehouses. Briefed about this, Thatcher must have realised she would be spending the rest of her life looking over her should for assassins.[5]

On March 30, 1979, Irish Republican militants struck even closer at her and the heart of the British establishment. That day, a member of Parliament climbed into his car in the House of Commons' underground car park. As he drove his blue Vauxhall up the ramp to the street level, a mercury-tilt switch triggered the bomb an Irish National Liberation Army (INLA) member had hidden under the car. Legs severed by the blast, the driver died just thirty minutes later.

Thatcher learned about the explosion while visiting her constituents in Finchley. The first thought that flashed through her mind was, "Please, God, don't let it be Airey".[6] But it was. Airey Neave, Conservative Party Spokesman on Northern Ireland, her most trusted political advisor, was dead. It was an incalculable loss for the soon-to-be Prime Minister. Neave, "a short, ruddy-faced man with a big grin", had been her best friend and closest confidant, an absolutely loyal strategist who had masterminded her takeover of the Conservative Party.[7] And now he was gone, killed because of the position he had held, one that she had given him.

It did not end with Neave. Later the same year, while Thatcher was still mourning her friend's death, the Provos struck again. At 11:30 a.m. on August 27, in Sligo, Louis Lord Mountbatten, Queen Elizabeth's uncle, stepped aboard his yacht, the *Shadow 5*, and headed out to clear the lobster traps that his family had set just off the coast of Mullaghmore. A well-loved man with no connection to the violence in the North, he felt safe vacationing in the Republic with his family. That particular day, nothing seemed out of place to the Garda officers acting as the British peer's bodyguards.

Yet somehow an IRA man had managed to slip on board the yacht, perhaps the night before. When the *Shadow 5* stopped by the first line of lobster pots, a Provisional watching from the shore pressed a button on a small radio transmitter. A split second later, the boat disintegrated in a fiery blast. Mountbatten, his grandson Nicholas, and a 14-year-old deckhand were killed instantly. Lady Brabourne, one of the British lord's in-laws, died the next day from her injuries.

That was not the end of it that day. Near Warrenpoint, a few hours after Mountbatten's death, the IRA killed eighteen British paratroopers in a land-mine ambush. It was the worst defeat the British Army had ever suffered in Northern Ireland.

The press concentrated on the murder of Lord Mountbatten. A full page headline of one London paper simply read: THE

BASTARDS. But for the Prime Minister, the deaths of eighteen soldiers were worse. For her, it was a "contemptible defiance of civilized custom", to kill young men she felt had only come to Ulster to bring peace.[8] That day, Thatcher personally wrote letters of condolence to their families. It was not an easy experience for her, but it was one she would become well accustomed to in the future.

As the years rolled by, Thatcher's hatred of the IRA intensified. In 1981, when Republican prisoners in the Maze Prison went on hunger strike to win political status, she let ten starve themselves to death rather than give in to "murderers". Yet whatever victory she found in that proved a hollow one. On October 10, 1981, just a week after the protest ended, the IRA blew up a coach carrying Irish Guardsmen outside Chelsea Barracks in London. The nail-bomb killed two civilian bystanders and wounded many soldiers. Describing the incident in her memoirs, the Prime Minister wrote:

I went quickly to the scene and with horrified fascination pulled a nail out of the side of the coach. *To say that people capable of this were animals would be wrong: no animal would do such a thing* [author's emphasis].[9]

The IRA returned her hatred. For them, Thatcher – cold, haughty, imperious – was the personification of everything they loathed about Britain. In the words of Gerry Adams, by late 1981, she had become "an Irish folk memory. She will be remembered even when the names of some of the hunger strikers are forgotten. All the six and seven-year olds have the memory of Thatcher in their heads".[10] If it had not been the case before, the Prime Minister was now at the very top of the Provisionals' target list.

The question was when, where, and how to kill her. Thatcher's bodyguards were fully aware of the threat to her life and were quite watchful. Yet in 1984, the IRA scouts studying the Prime Minister's movements thought they had found the answer. That October, the leaders of the Conservative Party would gather in the Grand Hotel at the seaside resort of Brighton for their annual conference. It was an event that the Prime Minister never missed. Even better from the Provisionals' point of view was that in the past, security around the gathering had been unforgivably lax.

At 2:45 a.m. on October 12, the last day of the Conservative Party assembly, a time-bomb planted by the IRA in the hotel exploded, generating a 3000 degrees Celsius fireball that nearly collapsed the building. But Thatcher had been on a different floor from the bomb and escaped the blast unscathed. Others were not so fortunate. In all, five people died, including one member of Parliament. Thirty-two more, including some of the highest ranking figures of the Thatcher Administration, suffered serious injuries, some permanent.

The IRA had come within inches of eliminating the entire British government. In case Mrs Thatcher had any doubts about who the Brighton bomb was for, the statement the Provisionals released a day later must have answered them:

> The IRA claim responsibility for the detonation . . . in Brighton against the British cabinet and the Tory warmongers. Thatcher will now realize that the British cannot occupy our country, torture our prisoners and shoot our people on their own streets and get away with it. Today, we were unlucky, but remember, *we have only to be lucky once. You will have to be lucky always* [author's italics]. Give Ireland peace and there will be no more war.

The Prime Minister appeared in public only hours after the attempt on her life, vowing that Britain would never surrender to terrorism. But the blast had left a scar in the Iron Lady's hide. She had spent long minutes in the darkness of the ruined hotel waiting for her bodyguards to take her from the building. Hating the dark and hating the feeling of being trapped, from that day on, Margaret Thatcher would carry a flashlight in her purse, something that would give her a daily reminder of just how close she had come to sharing Airey Neave's fate.[11] At her fifty-ninth birthday party, the day after the bombing, she broke down and wept, telling her guests, "this was a day I wasn't meant to see".[12]

Perhaps she thought about all of this when she bent down and placed the wreath at the base of the Enniskillen Cenotaph. The world will never know. Yet three facts are beyond dispute. First, on October 16, 1984, still shaken from Brighton, the Prime Minister went on record as saying, "people who go out prepared to take the lives of other people, forfeit their own right to live".[13] Second, at the time of the Enniskillen bombing, her government had been receiving every indication that the IRA was on the brink of a massive escalation of violence. Third, by November 22, 1987, the Prime Minister had a report from her intelligence advisors that an IRA unit was in Spain, preparing to attack a target in the British colony of Gibraltar.[13] On March 6, 1988, just months later, three members of that bombing team, Daniel McCann, Seán Savage, and Mairéad Farrell, died at the hands of the Special Air Service (SAS), Britain's elite counter-terrorist unit.

That event triggered one of the most intense periods of violence in the recent history of Northern Ireland. During the two weeks that followed the killing of McCann, Savage, and Farrell, seven more people died horrible deaths in and around Belfast, and three young men later found themselves condemned to life in prison for murders they did not commit. And it all had begun with Gibraltar. Because for many, the way the Provos died there, given no chance to surrender, shot with their hands up, and riddled with bullets after they fell wounded to the ground, was little more than cold-blooded murder. As the vicar of a British soldier tortured and killed by the IRA in reprisal for Gibraltar said, "I do not understand what happened . . . but I can see it all goes back to Gibraltar. Gibraltar triggered it all like a row of dominos."[15]

By sending the SAS to the Rock, Margaret Thatcher knocked over the first domino. It was ironic. When she became Prime Minister of Britain in 1979, she had invoked Saint Francis of Assisi's words to describe her intentions:

Where there is discord, may we bring harmony; where there is error, may we bring truth; where there is doubt, may we

7

bring faith; and where there is despair, may we bring hope.[16]

Instead, the killings on March 6, 1988, brought fresh discord to the United Kingdom, not harmony. The concealment of the crimes committed on the Rock created error and doubt, not truth and faith. And the punishment of the innocent was a gift of despair, not hope, to those living in Northern Ireland.

Ten years have passed since the bright spring day on the Rock when McCann, Savage, and Farrell died. Yet the memory of their deaths and their bloody sequels in Belfast have not faded. Instead, the bitterness each incident created lingers on in the minds of the Catholic community. For them, the bloodshed and the men rotting away in the Maze Prison for crimes they did not commit remain the ultimate proof that the law is simply a weapon directed against them. More than anything else, more than their simple high drama and tragic nature, that is the reason why events during March 1988 make such a compelling story.

## Notes

1. Eamonn Mallie and David McKittrick, *The Fight for Peace: The Secret Story Behind the Irish Peace Process*, Heinemann, London, 1996, pp. 57-60.
2. "The World is Horrified by a 'Blot on Mankind'", *The Impartial Reporter and Farmers' Journal*, November 12, 1987.
3. Margaret Thatcher, *The Downing Street Years*, HarperCollins Publishers, New York, 1993, pp. 379-416.
4. Maurice Romily, "Hang these Assassins", *Evening News*, November 28, 1975.
5. Patrick Bishop and Eamonn Mallie, *The Provisional IRA*, Corgi Books, London, 1989, p. 256.
6. Chris Ogden, *Maggie: An Intimate Portrait of a Woman in Power*, Simon and Schuster, New York, 1990, pp. 146-147.
7. Ibid.
8. Thatcher, p. 56.
9. Ibid, p. 393.
10. Patrick Bishop and Eamonn Mallie, *The Provisional IRA*, Corgi Books, London, 1987, pp. 422-423.
11. Andrew Thomson, *Margaret Thatcher: The Woman Within*, WH Allen, London, p. 187.
12. Chris Ogden, *Maggie: An Intimate Portrait of a Woman in Power*, Simon and Schuster, New York, 1990, p. 213.
13. Ibid, p. 349.
14. "Death on the Rock", *This Week*, Thames Television, April 28, 1988.
15. Rory Godson, "The Real Face of the IRA", *Sunday Tribune*, March 27, 1988.
16. Thatcher, p. 19.

# CHAPTER ONE

## VICTIMS OF IRISH HISTORY

"For those who believe, no explanation is necessary. For those who don't believe, no explanation is possible."
— IRA graffiti

Who were the three young people who died on that sunny afternoon in Gibraltar? Margaret Thatcher had a ready answer to that question. As members of the IRA, they were "representatives of the forces of darkness" – an image that suggests the British Army is fighting Satan himself in Belfast. The view of the Republican faithful – that the trio were "people who passionately wanted change in their community" – invokes the equally absurd picture of "the Gibraltar Three" as social workers toting assault rifles.

Neither label is particularly helpful.[1] They do not explain the contradiction in Daniel McCann, Seán Savage, and Mairéad Farrell's personalities, that they could be kind and loving but capable of what many would consider mass murder in the name of their political beliefs. Yet beyond the eulogies and the condemnations, enough information exists to see a pattern in their lives, an old Irish one that the then Bishop Cahal Daly described in 1979:

It does not come naturally for young people to kill. They have to be indoctrinated, brain-washed, made cynical, hard-faced, and hard-hearted first. Something has to be killed in themselves first before they can kill others; and what is killed is what is most deeply human – compassion, sensitivity, humanity, what the older people called "nature".[2]

This process made McCann, Savage, and Farrell what they were: victims of Irish history.[3] But for the unique conditions they lived in, none of them would have become "terrorists" or "freedom fighters". Looking at each of their backgrounds, particularly Mairéad's, the truth in that becomes clear.

Thirty years old, with a medium build, Daniel McCann probably was the leader of the ASU. He was from a prominent West Belfast family. His parents, Gerry and Sheila, were the owners of a butcher's shop that had been in business since 1899.[4] McCann had been on the fringes of the IRA since his early teens. But he did not become fully involved until after serving a six-month prison sentence in 1973 for riotous conduct. Upon leaving prison, McCann became a full-fledged member of the IRA.

Early on, he showed an aptitude for "the urban guerrilla war" and was active for five years before being arrested in 1978 for possessing a detonator. While in custody, McCann underwent questioning at the infamous Royal Ulster Constabulary (RUC) Castlereagh Interrogation Centre, named in honour of Lord Castlereagh, a founder of the Protestant ascendancy and a hate figure for Catholics. As the old rhyme went:

> *I met murder on the way*
> *and he had a mask like Castlereagh.*

Castlereagh lived up to its namesake's grim reputation. In 1979, the British government would admit that in an effort to obtain confessions, the RUC had "mistreated" fifteen suspects held there during the late 1970s. Inquiries by human rights groups and the Police Surgeons' Association into seventy-eight cases (including McCann's) suggest that "torture" might be a better word for what went on there. Apart from simply beating

10

suspects, police burned their hands against radiator pipes; slammed their heads against walls; or simply held their heads under water until they talked. In some cases, female detainees were threatened with rape.

What McCann underwent at Castlereagh did not weaken his commitment to the IRA. In May 1981, just out of prison after serving a two-year sentence, he fired several shots at a RUC Land Rover that was driving through his old neighborhood. After realizing that he had missed, he tried to flee but the police quickly caught him.[5]

But not before McCann got rid of his pistol. The lack of that critical piece of evidence was enough to ensure that the charges against him failed. He spent only four months on remand in Crumlin Road Jail before going free. Almost immediately, he found himself behind bars on another weapons offense. That case against McCann collapsed as well. Another brief spell in jail came in July 1982, when the RUC arrested him for taking part in a plot to car-bomb the police band.[6] When the witness who testified against McCann retracted his evidence, the authorities – no doubt frustrated – were obliged to release him.

In the middle of all this, McCann somehow found the time to work in his parents' butcher shop, marry Margaret Doherty, and father two children. To his friends, he seemed an ordinary man, a good husband and devoted father, someone who liked nothing more than a bit of *craic* (fun) at the local pub.[7] McCann was also an extremely devout Catholic.

Yet this "ordinary man" could be quite ruthless. In July 1983, he was the driving force behind a plan to murder a judge. The scheme was clever and quite simple. Perhaps from contacts at a hospital where he briefly worked, McCann obtained an ambulance. He and several other IRA men planned to park a milk-truck laden with explosives by the judge's home. When it went off, the truck-bomb would hopefully kill the target. McCann's ambulance with a team of three gunmen onboard, dressed as medics, would be first on the scene. If by some miracle the judge survived, they would take him away and kill him.[8]

Luckily for their target, the RUC Special Branch had been watching the ASU at work for some time. When it looked like the murder bid was proceeding, they arrested a number of IRA men, including the young butcher from the Falls Road. Incredibly, that case against him collapsed like the ones before. By early 1988, McCann was still free and working at his "second career" as an explosives officers for the IRA's Belfast Brigade.[9]

For the British, "Big Dan" was a man who had become addicted to the "thrill and adventure" of killing. The fact that he could evade the law with seeming impunity must have been a source of immense frustration for them and may have been the motive behind the severe beating British soldiers allegedly gave him in October 1982. And he had other enemies as well. On one occasion, men armed with shotguns burst into the home he kept for his wife and two sons, but the family was out.[10] His would-be killers had been Protestant paramilitaries, members of groups which sometimes received intelligence files on IRA members from sympathetic police and soldiers.

Even more threateningly, in early 1988, McCann had found a cross pinned to his front door. In light of what happened to him just a few weeks later in Gibraltar, its inscription, *Danny McCann, Rest in Peace,* may have been more a promise than a warning.[11] In any case, he was not the type to be deterred. As McCann's obituary would read, "he knew no compromise and was to die as he had lived in implacable opposition to Britain's criminal presence in [Ireland]."[12]

The second man in the ASU was Seán Savage, an explosives expert the RUC had briefly held along with McCann in 1982. Born on Kashmir Street, Savage, at the age of twenty-three, was the youngest member of the Gibraltar team as well as its least

12

well known. Dark-haired and slightly built, he was the child of "religious, respectable" parents, John and Lily, who both held jobs (an unusual distinction given the level of Catholic unemployment in West Belfast).[13]

After his death, *An Phoblacht/Republican News* eulogized him as someone whose "dedication to the struggle was total and unswerving". Described there as "a quiet and single-minded individual who neither drank, nor smoked and rarely socialized", he attended Mass regularly and often helped his mother and father take care of his brother Robert who had Down's Syndrome. The sight of them riding their bikes together was a familiar one to Falls Road residents.[14]

According to Savage's family, even though Billy McKee, a Provisional IRA founder and onetime commander of its Belfast Brigade, was his uncle, Savage had little interest in politics.[15] He seemed to find cooking, cycling, photography, and the study of the Irish and French languages far more interesting.

One formative experience of Savage's short life appears to have come when he was just four. In August 1969 after a long hot summer of bitter confrontations between the police and civil rights demonstrators, Loyalist rage over "IRA subversion" began to boil over. Often drunk and sometimes supported by the RUC, Protestant mobs invaded Catholic parts of West Belfast, putting hundreds of homes to the torch. Before British soldiers could intervene, the rioters reduced Savage's neighborhood to a smouldering pile of rubble. For an impressionable child like him, it would have been a traumatic experience.

Another one came in 1976. That year, like thousands of other eleven-year olds, Savage took the "eleven plus", the national qualifying exam that determines which children are eligible to attend academically-oriented grammar schools. In the 1970s, eighty percent of those taking the tests received neat little notes from the Ministry of Education informing them that they had "failed to satisfy the Inspectorate". Apparently, Seán

Savage was among their number, for he was shunted off to a less prestigious secondary school. According to Tom McAnulty, a childhood friend, Savage's experience with the eleven plus left a mark on the young man. Already painfully shy – McAnulty's mother called him "the quiet fella" – he became "more so, the kind of kid who hides upstairs when visitors call . . . an unlikely 'hero' for Ireland".[16]

Seeing her son get involved in the conflict was the last thing his mother wanted As Savage grew up, Lily tried hard to keep him from being drawn into the violence that was sweeping West Belfast. She never let him go out and throw stones at British soldiers like the other kids of the neighborhood did. Yet she could not completely shield her young son. She discovered that when she found a picture he had drawn. It showed a British soldier pointing a gun at a child on the street. Underneath it, Seán had written, "Why is this gun pointing at me?"[17]

What Savage lived through and probably the influence of his uncle led him to join the IRA in 1982 at the age of seventeen. He quickly became known to the authorities as an explosives officer who often worked with McCann. Apparently, Savage was quite good at his job and lucky as well. Except for the arrest in 1982 which derailed his plans for attending university, he somehow managed to avoid prison.[18] And his parents remained oblivious to his involvement. Asked about it once in 1989, his mother said: "I never knew. He was so quiet."[19]

"Small, determined, angry, ready to sacrifice her life or anyone else's to her cause, ready for whatever comes her way," was how one reporter remembered Mairéad Farrell, the final member of the ASU.[20] Just over five feet tall in height with pert features and brown hair she wore with curls or straight, she was the oldest of the trio at thirty-one. She was also the best known. Both in life and death, Farrell's intelligence, good looks, and middle class background ensured far more media scrutiny of her IRA career than she would have received based on her

14

operational record. In fact, in 1989 she was the subject of an American television documentary, *Death of a Terrorist,* which apparently received cooperation from the Farrell family. Drawing on this documentary and several interviews Farrell gave before she died, it is possible to chart her drift toward violence with more detail than that of McCann or Savage.[21]

Farrell was the youngest child of prosperous shopkeepers who owned a hardware and drapery store on Grosvenor Road, a major artery in Belfast's shopping district. After having five boys, her parents celebrated Mairéad's birth with pink champagne. As their only daughter, she was special to her mother and father and had an idyllic early childhood in the comfortable home in Andersonstown that the family moved to in the mid-1960s.[22] The Farrells' home movies show her as a toddler in a yellow sun dress dancing with her teddy bear, all smiles and giggles, and bear out her mother's memories of Mairéad as a "very placid, very good child".[23]

While sympathetic to the nationalist cause, none of Farrell's immediate family had any involvement with the violence that swept Northern Ireland in the late 1960s. Apart from dabbling in the civil rights movement and the Campaign for Nuclear Disarmament, her brothers (with one exception) found reaching the middle-class status of their parents a more appealing goal.[24] Yet looking back another generation, her family was split between Ireland's two warring traditions. A number of Farrell's mother's relatives were officers of the Royal Irish Constabulary, the predecessor of the RUC and bitter opponents of the IRA during the War of Independence. But her maternal grandfather, a railway worker named John Gaffney had belonged to the IRA and been imprisoned by the British in 1920 for refusing to work on trains that carried soldiers. Released after a year in jail, he remained a life-long supporter of the Republican Movement and briefly served as a senator in the Irish parliament.[25]

Mairéad adored her grandfather and treasured the times

when her family visited him at his home in Leitrim, just across the border in the Republic of Ireland. She spent hours listening to the old man's tales about heroic IRA men of the Civil War era. She also enjoyed splashing in the chilly Atlantic Ocean under his watchful gaze. Or sometimes, as the home movies show, Mairéad and her grandfather simply kicked a football back and forth.[26]

Childhood ended early for her. Farrell became involved with the IRA at the age of fourteen. She liked to say that the British Army's killing of thirteen unarmed people on Bloody Sunday had made her pick up the gun. What seems more likely is that the influence of John Gaffney and her personal experiences led her to that choice.

Those experiences were far from pleasant. Each year, the violence overtaking the North had cast a progressively longer shadow over Farrell's life. By 1968, she could no longer bicycle to school with her friends because Protestant youths would attack them simply for wearing Catholic school uniforms. When she began riding a bus to classes, it had to take longer and longer detours to avoid stone-throwing Loyalist mobs.[27]

Then in 1970 came the Falls Road curfew and the series of searches and house raids that turned many apolitical Belfast Catholics into supporters of the IRA. Half-way through the thirty-five hour curfew, the British Army announced that it would give the residents two hours to buy groceries and other necessities. In response to this, Farrell and her parents drove to their shop to open it, but a soldier stopped them, saying that they couldn't go any further. As Mrs Farrell recalled:

Dan (Mairéad's father) had an argument with him. In the end, he let us through but insisted on coming down in the car with us. When we reached the shop, he put us in and closed the door . . . One girl put her head right out to see what was going on. The soldier turned and shouted, 'If you

16

don't take your head in, I'll blow it off!' . . . Mairéad was horrified. She always talked about that – how horrible it was the way the [soldiers] spoke to people.[28]

On November 4, 1971, the war in Belfast invaded Farrell's life in an even uglier way. That day, troops from the Parachute Regiment cordoned off and searched Tulleymore Gardens for weapons. In that housing estate, just a few blocks away from the Farrells' house, lived Emma Groves and her daughter Eithne, who was one of Mairéad's best friends. Angry at being confined to her home during the search, Mrs Groves told Eithne to play a nationalist ballad, "Four Green Fields", on the family's record-player. Then as Emma stood by her window listening to the music, a passing soldier shot her in the face with a rubber bullet which smashed into her face at 160 miles an hour, permanently blinding her. In Mrs Farrell's opinion, what had happened to Emma Groves "didn't leave Mairéad's mind". It marked the point of no return in her drift toward the IRA.[29]

Despite her involvement with the IRA, Farrell continued to attend Rathmore Convent School where her friends remembered her as a bright, vivacious girl whose only clash with authority came when she laughed at a nun who had fallen to the ground. She remained an avid reader and loved to dance, sing, and swim. Yet at the same time, Farrell was becoming increasingly involved with the Provisionals. Like Savage's mother and father, her parents never realized that their daughter was leading a double life. Yet the signs were clear. When British soldiers entered the neighborhood, Mairéad would be out with the other Republican women banging trash-can lids on the street to warn the local IRA of the danger. Every Easter Sunday, she would march down the Falls Road in the Republican parade to Milltown Cemetery in the white blouse and black skirt that identified her as a member of Fianna Éireann, the youth wing of the Provisionals.[30]

By the age of sixteen, Farrell graduated from this casual

involvement to what the IRA calls "military activities". She was never particularly forthcoming about what these were, but she probably carried messages, helped move weapons, and acted as a scout. As a school girl, she would have looked quite innocent to the police and soldiers on the street. Only a small circle of IRA members know whether Farrell ever killed anyone, but her statement years later to a journalist that she would "bomb or kill again in a minute" if she had to indicates that she may indeed have taken life in the "armed struggle".[31]

Farrell's active service with the IRA was interrupted on April 5, 1976. That day, she, Kieran Doherty, and Seán McDermott entered the Conway Hotel in Dunmurry. After overpowering the hotel's security men, they planted three five-pound bombs throughout the building. The trio warned the patrons to flee the hotel and raced out the front door. Farrell had just gotten into the bomb team's getaway car, when McDermott shouted *"It's the cops. Run!"* Jumping out of the car as a RUC van pulled up beside it, she fled toward the swimming pool by the hotel, dropping her pistol as she ran. But Farrell's high heels slowed her down and she heeded a warning to stop or be shot and was placed under arrest.[32]

Meanwhile Doherty and McDermott tried to hijack the car parked in front of a nearby house. Unfortunately for them, the owner was a reserve RUC officer who shot McDermott dead instead of handing over his keys as demanded (Doherty escaped but would later die on hunger strike in prison). According to the police, upon being shown a picture of McDermott's corpse on the footpath, Farrell broke down and sobbed, "How did I ever get involved in all of this?"[33] Yet her lapse was momentary, and she refused to say anything further to her RUC interrogators. Farrell continued her silence on December 9, 1976, the day of her trial for destroying the hotel. It was a one-day affair, and it ended with the judge giving her a fourteen-year sentence.[34]

Farrell proved more valuable to the IRA in jail than out of it. 1976, the year she entered Armagh Women's Prison, saw the beginning of a new phase in the struggle between the Republican Movement and the authorities. Recognizing that it had been a mistake to give jailed paramilitaries virtual prisoner-of-war status, the British government decided that it would begin treating them as ordinary criminals. They would wear prison uniforms and do work like any other inmates. Naturally, the IRA refused to accept this policy change. Scores of its members went naked rather than wear "a monkey suit" (a prison uniform). Relationships between the prisoners and prison officers deteriorated sharply.

Yet the beatings and privation the activists suffered only reinforced their determination not to give in. By the late 1970s, many inmates had moved far beyond simply refusing to wear clothing. Instead, they escalated the confrontation into the "dirty protest", refusing to wash themselves and smearing the walls of their cells with excrement.

In her position as "officer commanding" of the thirty-two Provo women in prison, Farrell emerged as a major leader of the protest. She and her fellow inmates spent months locked up for up to twenty-three hours a day in tiny cells swarming with vermin. During this time, Tim Pat Coogan interviewed Farrell. He remembered her as being caked in dirt looking like a filthy scarecrow after losing twenty-six pounds while on a nineteen-day hunger strike, with menstrual blood smeared on the walls of her cell.[35] Throughout the strike, she struck a defiant note, proudly declaring:

> I am a Volunteer in the Irish Republican Army, and I am a political prisoner in Armagh Jail. I am prepared to fight to the death if necessary to win recognition that I am a political prisoner and not a criminal.[36]

Farrell and her friends' willingness to inflict such extreme misery upon themselves appears bizarre at first. Indeed, many

Britons came to view the dirty protest as just one more proof that the Provisionals who are not criminals are lunatics. Yet there was a method to the madness. Such total defiance of authority gave the prisoners a sense that the system had not broken them. As Farrell put it, "your mind's your strongest weapon. That's how we always counteract whatever [the authorities] do, because they can't control our minds, and they can't get inside of them, and that's their failure".[37]

When set down on paper, that sort of statement makes Farrell and her fellow inmates look like single-minded fanatics or IRA saints, in either case people devoid of any human character. Yet as Father Raymond Murray, the Armagh prison chaplain at the time, recalled, prison life was not entirely cheerless. Instead, it was a place where there were "shared joys and sorrows, ups and downs, hardships and friendships for ten years."[38] Throughout all of this, Farrell never seemed to lose her sense of connection with the outside world, something born out by her interest in dressing well. After the hunger strike effectively won the inmates the right to wear their own clothes, she routinely instructed her mother through the prison social worker about what clothing she wanted bought for her, and the fussy young woman did not hesitate to send back garments she did not like.[39]

After serving ten-and-a-half years of her sentence, Farrell was released from prison on September 19, 1986. She cried over leaving her friends in jail behind, and her long-suffering mother wept tears of joy that her daughter was free. Worried that Farrell might fall back in with the IRA, she urged her to enroll at Belfast's Queen's University and put her life in order. But to Mrs Farrell's regret, Mairéad chose to take the year off and "adjust" to being free. During the next twelve months, she made frequent appearances at Republican functions and unsuccessfully stood for election for Sinn Féin in the Republic. Enjoying the political work, she decided she would study politics at Queen's, a decision that made her mother hope that she would at least not be on the sharp end of the IRA campaign.

Before her release, Farrell's friends had worried that prison might have changed her, but apart from her pallor from years out of the sunlight, there was little mark of it on her. Along with her interest in political work, Farrell was determined to make up for all the time she had missed during her years in prison. In the words of her brother Niall, "she was into high heels, fancy clothes, disco dancing, earrings, perfumes, hair perms, and really loved life."[40]

Yet Farrell had already resumed IRA activities. Her day-to-day behavior gave that away. While out shopping with her mother, she would suddenly dart in a doorway, explaining that she thought they were being followed. On other occasions, Farrell would warn her family not to say anything about her movements because the police could monitor conversations in the house through the telephone and the television set. The identity of her boyfriend with whom she lived for five months after her release was an even stronger clue. He was Seamus Finucane, named in the House of Commons in 1994 as the intelligence officer of the Provos' Belfast Brigade.[41]

Mairéad finally entered Queen's University in the autumn of 1987 and, as planned, began taking classes in political science and economics. Her hard work and enthusiasm for her courses no doubt made Mrs Farrell breath a little easier about her daughter's future. Yet on January 29, 1988, at Daniel Farrell's birthday party, there was an incident that seemed eerily prophetic, given what would happen just five weeks later. After wishing him a happy birthday, Mairéad embraced her father and told him that she loved him. Then, almost as an afterthought, she added, "You know, Daddy, I could be shot dead". Taken off guard by the remark, Mr Farrell joked that she better not get killed because funerals were expensive. To which she solemnly replied, "You needn't worry. If I'm shot dead, the IRA will bury me".[42]

McCann, Savage, and Farrell were among the best IRA operatives in 1988. Each had skills and experiences that made them activists the movement could hardly afford to lose. Farrell was particularly valuable because she made a mockery out of the British government's claim that members of the IRA were mindless thugs and psychopaths. Indeed, she had become a hero for radical feminist groups in Europe. Yet McCann, Savage, and Farrell shared a liability. The authorities knew them for what they were. Everywhere they went, there were eyes on them, watching them, recording and analyzing their every move. Farrell herself said it: "They all know who I am."[43]

Yet this did not matter to the IRA. What counted was that McCann, Savage, and Farrell were "sound" (i.e. absolutely trustworthy and dedicated to Republican ideals). After the series of catastrophes the IRA suffered in 1987, they were among the small number available to conduct the planned campaign against British facilities on the European mainland. If the trio could play their part, the IRA would reap the benefits. Yet the odds were heavily against them. At least Farrell – if not McCann and Savage – understood this. In one of her last interviews, she said, "You have to be realistic. You realize that ultimately, you're either going to be dead or end up in jail. It's either one or the other. You're not going to run forever".[44]

## Notes

1. Despite several requests, the McCann, Savage and Farrell families declined to be interviewed for this book.
2. Tim Pat Coogan, *On the Blanket: The Inside Story of the IRA Prisoners' "Dirty" Protest,* Robert Rineharts Publisher, Boulder, Colorado, 1997, p. 191.
3. Bill Cran, *Death of a Terrorist*, Frontline, WGBH, Boston, 1989.
4. *An Phoblacht/Republican News*, March 10, 1988.
5. Peter Taylor, *Families at War*, BBC Books, London, 1989, pp. 49-50.
6. Ian Jack, "Gibraltar", *Granta*, Winter 1988, pp. 33-34.
7. Interview with one of McCann's friends, Belfast, June 1996.
8. Jack Holland and Susan Phoenix, *Phoenix: Policing the Shadows*, Hodder and Stoughton, London, 1996, pp. 112-113.

9. Ibid, pp. 134-135. Although listed on the IRA's Roll of Honour as "GHQ Staff", I believe he remained in the Belfast Brigade and was simply seconded (like Savage and Farrell) to the GHQ.

10. *An Phoblacht/Republican News*, March 10, 1988.

11. Ibid.

12. Ibid.

13. Ibid.

14. Ibid.

15. Tim Pat Coogan, *The Troubles: Ireland's Ordeal 1966-1995 and the Search for Peace*, Hutchinson, London, 1995, p. 290.

16. Tom McAnulty, "Back Home in Belfast", *Virginian Pilot-Ledger Star*, March 19, 1995. The fact that Savage went to a secondary school does not definitely mean that he failed. However, the language of McAnulty's article (I could not locate the author) as well as Savage's obituary strongly implies that he did.

17. "British Cabinet Ordered Killings", *An Phoblacht/Republican News*, May 19, 1988.

18. This is some question about Savage's encounters with police. When I spoke with Jack Holland, co-author of *Phoenix: Policing the Shadows*, he told me that Phoenix's diaries showed that Savage was also arrested in December 1983 for possession of explosives and once in 1984 under the Prevention of Terrorism Act. Yet there is no other record of this. Several people have suggested to me that the fact Savage managed to avoid going to prison indicates he may have been an informant. This seems unlikely.

19. Tom McAnulty.

20. Elizabeth Shannon, *I am of Ireland*, Little, Brown, and Co, Boston, 1989, pp. 123-126.

21. Or as her brother Niall put it, how she went in "just three years from handing out cups of tea to the British Army" to being a member of the IRA.

22. Taylor, p. 32.

23. Ibid.

24. With the exception of her brother Niall who was a member of the Irish Communist Party for a time. Interestingly enough, I first heard this from a professor that Niall, Mairéad, and I took classes from, albeit at different times and locations.

25. Taylor, pp. 31-32.

26. Cran.

27. Taylor, p. 33.

28. Ibid, pp. 35-36.

29. Ibid, pp. 36-36.

30. Cran.

31. Shannon, pp. 123-126.

32. Jenny McGeever, "The Story of Mairéad Farrell", *Magill,* October 1986, p. 8.

33. Cran.

34. McGeever, pp. 12-13.

35. Tim Pat Coogan, *The IRA: A History*, Roberts Rinehart, Niwot, Colorado, 1993, p. 372.

36. Eileen Fairweather, *Only the Rivers Run Free*, Pluto Press, London, 1984, p. 224.

37. Cran.

38. Raymond Murray, *The SAS in Ireland*, Mercier Press, Cork, 1990, p. 428.

39. Taylor, p. 39.

40. Cran.

41. Kevin Toolis, *Rebel Hearts: Journeys Within the IRA's Soul*, Picador, London, 1995, pp. 182-183.

42. Taylor, p. 41.

43. Ibid.

44. Jack, p. 34.

# CHAPTER TWO

## THE ROAD TO THE ROCK

"It only just seems to me that there aren't many towns like this . . . But one town like it is enough. Because I think something kind of bad happened here . . . I know this much. The rule of law has left here, and the guerrillas have taken over."
   – Spencer Tracy, from the film *Bad Day at Black Rock*, 1955

In the year 974, an Arab poet stood on the shores of Morocco and gazed north across the sea at what is now known as Spain. Transfixed by the sight of the gaunt limestone bastion that loomed before him, on the eastern edge of a narrow peninsula just nine miles away, he felt moved to write a simple poem:

*Uproot the mountains of the world, save this. This one retain,*
   *But free from fear and misery; Here let peace reign.*

This was not to be. Far from watching over peace, the small town of Gibraltar has witnessed war, time and time again, for hundreds of years. Its commanding position over the straits that connect the Atlantic Ocean with the Mediterranean Sea has ensured that. For centuries, empire after empire has played an all too real game of King of the Hill with rivals on the Rock's craggy slopes.

Although historical accounts make reference to a great rock guarding the approaches to the Atlantic almost a millennium before the birth of Christ, it was not until the eighth century that events thrust Gibraltar into the foreground of world events. That was the time of the Muslim conquest of Spain. Legend has it that the Arab warriors landed on the shores of the great limestone formation in 711 and named it Djabal Tarik (Mount of Tarik) in honour of their commander. Over the years, this gradually became corrupted to its present name.

In 1713, after years of war with Spain, Britain seized the Rock. Ever since then, the Gibraltarians, a people of Spanish, Maltese, Genoese, and Jewish ancestry, 29,000 strong, have proudly regarded themselves as British. Since most have names like José or Conchita and prefer speaking Yanito (a dialect very close to ordinary Spanish) to English, their identification with Britain seems puzzling.

But when Gibraltarians look north across their border at Spain, they see a state with a history of authoritarian rule (e.g. Franco) quite alien to them. Madrid's attempts to coerce the Rock's inhabitants into union with Spain have not helped matters. In 1969, angry over a British guarantee that Gibraltar would never be transferred to Spain without its population's consent, the Spanish sealed the border. This peaceful siege, the fifteenth the Rock has endured, did not end until 1985. Its memory lives on. And because of that, the Gibraltarians fear and look down on the Spanish (calling them "slops" or "sloppies"). Just in case the casual tourist might miss this sentiment, murals of Union Jacks and proclamations of the Colony's "Britishness" cover the town's walls much like Protestant neighborhoods in Belfast.

But the Gibraltarians are not content with symbols; they carry their sense of identity into their ordinary lives, at great inconvenience to themselves. Today, even though Spanish bakeries are just minutes away by car, the Gibraltarians eat *British* frozen bread brought in at great expense from Bristol. In the Colony's shops, Spanish newspapers are absent. Instead, there are *British* papers flown in from London. In fact, some of the Rock's inhabitants feel so separate from Spain that they refer to the border with that country as being the "garlic curtain".[1]

This manic nationalist feeling led to one of the more bizarre incidents in the recent history of Gibraltar. It began in the wake of the 1967 referendum held in the Colony to determine whether its inhabitants wished to be under British or Spanish rule. On September 10, by a vote of 12,138 to 44, the Rock rejected the Spanish option. On March 15, 1968, the "Doves", a small group of citizens unhappy with the landslide, were unwise enough to publish a letter in the *Gibraltar Chronicle* recommending that Gibraltar negotiate its eventual return to Spain.

Such a suggestion did not sit well with the patriotic citizens of Gibraltar, particularly on April 4, when the Doves revealed in another letter to the *Chronicle* that they had been secretly negotiating with Madrid on the Colony's behalf. They claimed that the Spanish had accepted their proposals. On April 5, Spanish television broadcast a government commentary that this was not true, that the Doves' plans for Gibraltar would be implemented only after the Rock came under Spanish rule.[2]

The next day, "a spontaneous and unpremeditated eruption took place".[3] In other words, a riot broke out but quite a peculiar one. The property of Doves was the one and only target of the violence. Events took on a comical note when the tear-gas the police used to disperse the mob overpowered the policemen instead. The constables, more used to handling drunken sailors than mobs, were out of their depth (as they would be in 1988). The Colony's Governor had to threaten to use troops to restore order on the streets. No one was hurt – badly that is – but the pro-British riot had served its purpose. It sent a clear signal that those who made statements that threatened the Colony's Britishness would do so at their own risk.

Yet despite its oft-proclaimed loyalty to that symbolic object, the British Crown, and boasts of being "Free Since

1713", Gibraltar is not particularly noted for observing British laws. Instead, the Colony has always had a reputation for being a haven for smugglers and a pirate's cove. Each night, black-painted speedboats piloted by "the Winston Boys", enterprising local smugglers, flit back and forth across the Gibraltar Straits. Sometimes the load they carried is cigarettes and sometimes it is *kif*, Moroccan hashish. Hampered by their dispute over the ownership of Gibraltar, Britain and Spain have been unable to completely halt the illegal traffic. A 1996 effort to crack down on the smuggling sparked riots on the Rock even more violent than those in 1967.[4] And as events that same year proved, the Royal Gibraltar Police Force "the oldest in the United Kingdom" has not been immune to serious corruption.[5]

One final distinguishing characteristic of Gibraltar in 1988 is that for territory belonging to a modern democracy, it was hardly a monument to the principle of self-determination. Supreme executive power in the Colony rested in the hands of the Governor-General, a retired military man appointed by the British Foreign Office. This official held sole responsibility for the Rock's defense and security, and the Gibraltar Police Commissioner reported to him. Not allowed any say in Parliament, the Gibraltarians were entitled to elect a House of Assembly that supposedly determines their domestic affairs. However, the Governor-General (Sir Peter Terry) had the power to overrule this legislative body if he believed its policies threatened the Rock's security. Given this state of affairs and the British military's position as the largest employer in the Colony, "democracy" in Gibraltar was a trifle tenuous.

Those are just a few details that one is not likely to read about Gibraltar in the quaint tour books on sale in the shops there. Yet they go a long way in explaining why so many people saw "absolutely nothing" on March 6, 1988, or decided "not to get involved" in a matter involving the police and British military. And those details do raise questions about just how much value the word of a Gibraltar Police officer should have had over the few completely independent civilian witnesses brave enough – or foolish enough – to talk about what they saw that bright, spring day on the streets of their town.

The Rock is unique. Its only similarity to Northern Ireland is the fierce nationalism of its inhabitants and that is a vague parallel at best. Because of that, it seems a strange place for people like McCann, Savage, and Farrell to try to stage a "spectacular". But after a second glance at the fortress, it becomes quite obvious why they came there.

First, while its strategic significance has faded in recent decades, Gibraltar is still a military town. During the 1982 Falklands War, it served as a critical link in the long logistical chain connecting the British fleet off Argentina with the United Kingdom. Using the forest of antennas on its crest, the Colony acts as a listening post for the Government Communications Headquarters, Britain's signals intelligence agency. It also plays host to a NATO storage depot and a number of facilities used by the British military's special forces.

For the IRA, an added attraction was the Colony's link to the Irish conflict. British Army units routinely shuttle back and forth between it and Northern Ireland. Hidden away in one of the Rock's caverns, closed off to the public, there is a life-sized replica of a West Belfast neighborhood complete with streets, shops, a school, and a Roman Catholic Church named Saint Malachi's.[6] No doubt it is there that raw recruits practise confronting simulated mobs, pretend snipers, actors playing angry priests, and fake bombs before going on to the real thing some hundreds of miles away. It had all been written about in the *Observer* in 1984, a newspaper certainly on the reading list of the IRA's intelligence officers.

Yet these were only the immediate reasons for operating in a place so distant from Northern Ireland. By far, the overriding factor that drove the Provisionals to strike at the Rock was the ebb and flow of the conflict in Ireland and Northern Ireland. More than anything else, events there were what led to what some would call the "suicide mission" in Gibraltar.

One of the most important of these took place on a cold day in October 1986, when the a ship tied up at Roadstone Pier, a jetty by a remote beach on the east coast of Ireland. Aboard was the biggest consignment of weapons the Republican Movement had ever smuggled into the country, all courtesy of Colonel Muammar Quadaffi, dictator of Libya.[7]

. On the beach, waiting for the weapons, was a team of thirty men, brought together by the quartermaster of the IRA GHQ. By the end of the day, they had transferred the ship's cargo – hundreds of assault rifles, heavy anti-aircraft machine guns, flame throwers, ammunition, and a ton of semtex plastic explosive– into a waiting convoy of trucks and vans. By next morning, the arms were dispersed throughout the Republic in bunkers specially dug to hide them. Meanwhile in Dublin and London, the authorities remained blissfully unaware that in the space of twenty-four hours, the Provisional IRA, in the words of one of its leaders, had become "the most dangerous and committed revolutionary force in Ireland".[8]

It was not as if the British and Irish governments had no advance warning about what had taken place at Roadstone Pier. They knew that the IRA had an on-off relationship with Quadaffi. As early as March 1973, the Irish Navy had intercepted a Cypriot coaster, the *Claudia*, loaded with five tons of Libyan weapons off County Waterford, bound for Northern Ireland. Six men, including IRA veteran, Joe Cahill, were arrested for conspiracy to import arms. That brought a temporary halt to the Colonel's efforts to sponsor the Provisionals. But unlike the British and Irish intelligence communities, the Provos never lost interest in the possibility of another Libyan donation.

The first clear indications that Libya was getting ready to

renew its support to the Provisionals came in early 1984. On April 17, a diplomat inside the Libyan Embassy in London allegedly shot at a crowd of anti-Quadaffi demonstrators outside the building, killing policewoman Yvonne Fletcher. Five days later, an infuriated Margaret Thatcher ordered the expulsion of every Libyan diplomat in Britain. The same day, in Tripoli, the state-run radio station, "Voice of the Homeland" made an emphatic threat:

> The People's Committees will form an alliance with the secret IRA in view of the fact that it champions the cause of liberating Ireland and liberating the Irish nation from the tyranny of British colonialism . . . If Britain tries to use any means to pressurize and oppress Libyan Arabs, the revolutionary committees will enable the IRA to do whatever it wishes in Britain and to retaliate twice as strongly [author's italics].[9]

Besides dispatching a ship, Quadaffi translated these words into action by organizing three smaller arms shipments to the Provisionals between August 1985 and July 1986. All three, a total of thirty-four tons of state-of-the-art weaponry, arrived safely in Ireland, under the noses of the Gardaí. The Libyans also gave the IRA several million dollars, funds the movement badly needed to fuel its political and military activities. By then, Quadaffi had a very personal motive for providing this support. In April 1986, Prime Minister Thatcher had permitted the United States to use its bases in Britain to stage air strikes on Tripoli. After nearly being killed in his bed by that particular "oppression", the Colonel must have found sponsoring the Provisionals a particularly satisfying form of revenge.

What made it all incredible was that by the beginning of 1986, the British knew that the IRA had reactivated the Libyan pipeline. They had received clear proof of that in January when the Irish police discovered ammunition boxes with Libyan Army markings on them in an arms cache in the Republic.[10] Yet somehow, all the intelligence resources Britain and the United States deployed around and against Libya missed the IRA's little ships.

Perhaps the lack of activity in Northern Ireland had put the British to sleep. The same time Quadaffi was packing the Provisionals' arsenals to bursting point, their armed campaign had wound down to a near all-time low. In 1985, the IRA killed just two soldiers and fourteen police.[11] The next year, only four soldiers and ten police died at the hands of the IRA. It was not like 1972, when they had sent over a hundred British soldiers home in coffins.

Yet appearances can be deceiving. While the Libyan arms flowed into Ireland, the Provisional IRA was undergoing a profound series of internal changes, changes that in the years ahead would lead to the deaths of hundreds more soldiers, police, civilians and hundreds of millions of pounds in damage to British property.

It could be traced back to 1981 and the hunger strikes. The sympathy these martyrdoms won for the Republican Movement was extensive. Using it, the IRA had been able to get Bobby Sands, the leader of hunger strikers, elected to Parliament before he died. In 1983, its political support was strong enough to win a Westminster seat for Sinn Féin's leader, Gerry Adams. He and other Sinn Féin candidates polled a total of 100,000 votes, a very far cry from the negligible support they had received in past.[12] In the next three years, they made significant gains in local elections in the North and in the Republic of Ireland as well. With that kind of success, the IRA did not need to kill Brits to get their message across. It seemed as if its members were well on their way to making good on a past promise to take power in Ireland with "an armalite in one hand and a ballot paper in the other".[13]

But there was a problem. For decades, the IRA had been wedded to abstentionism, the policy which forbade Republicans to occupy the seats they won in any elections in "the 26 county

32

regime in the south". For the faithful, the reason for this was clear, taking seats meant swearing allegiance to institutions that the IRA, by definition, considered illegitimate, but it was absolute madness to Adams and his supporters. People in the Republic would not vote for candidates who refused to take office and help their constituents. It was as simple as that.

Beginning in June 1985, the debate over abstentionism led to internal divisions. In Belfast, Ivor Bell, the Provos' link man with the Libyans, emerged as the leader of a group which tried to oust Adams and his supporters from the positions they allegedly held in the IRA's Army Council. Yet from all reports Adams moved quicker and had Bell expelled after court-martialling him in absentia. Daniel McCann and some of the Belfast Brigade's most valuable activists followed him, leaving that key unit in some disarray.[14]

Political infighting in the Republican movement peaked in 1986 when Adams began his push to formally end abstentionism. In the end, the politically-minded Republican leader allegedly had to strike a bargain with some of the most hard-line elements within the IRA to achieve this goal. These individuals provided him with the support he needed to get this policy change. But in return the IRA leadership had to concede key positions on the Army Council to militants committed to escalating the group's armed campaign, give the local IRA units more autonomy, and allow McCann and his friends to return to the fold.

It was dangerous for the Army Council to slacken its control over operations. That became blindingly apparent during two events in 1987 which the Provisionals remember with anger and shame even today.

The first took place in County Tyrone where for the previous three years, the local IRA brigade had been attacking government facilities in the countryside. Using large groups of volunteers armed with automatic rifles and explosives, it had brazenly destroyed two RUC barracks in broad daylight. On May 8, East Tyrone Brigade planned to do the same thing in Loughgall, a small Protestant village in the heart of Tyrone.

The day began promisingly enough. Eight IRA men hijacked a mechanical digger, packed it full of explosives, and set off for the Loughgall Barracks. As they had done before at the RUC base at the Birches, the IRA men planned to smash the digger through the fence guarding the building and detonate the bomb.

Little did they know. Loughgall was a trap. By concentrating on RUC facilities, East Tyrone Brigade had made the mistake of falling into a predictable pattern of operations. That and information provided by an informant who had wormed his or her way deep into the Provisionals' command structure were all the authorities needed. Ringing the town were hundreds of police and British soldiers. They waited patiently until the ASU approached the police barracks and opened fire on it. Then without warning, from every direction, hundreds of bullets ripped into the Provisionals. One of the soldiers there later joked that he had tap-danced as he poured fire from his belt-fed machine-gun into the IRA's van. In a matter of seconds, all the Provisionals were dead along with a Protestant workman unlucky enough to have strayed into the killing zone.[15]

For the Republican Movement, it was a staggering blow. Eight veteran activists, who the RUC would later estimate had killed a total of forty to fifty men between them, were dead. For the time being, the East Tyrone Brigade had been shattered. Speaking at one of the "Loughgall Martyr's" funerals, Gerry Adams could only say: "Margaret Thatcher and all the other rich and powerful people will be sorry in their time for what happened."[16] It seemed a hollow threat, one drowned out by the triumphant news stories celebrating the authorities' not so clean kill.

Yet while Loughgall was a defeat, it was one where the

Republican faithful could draw consolation from the fact that their loved ones had died in combat with the British Army. The massacre caused by the IRA's bomb at Enniskillen on November 8, 1987, which claimed eleven lives, brought no such comfort. The indiscriminate results of that attack made a joke out of the notion that they were fighting a non-sectarian war. Condemnations rained down on the Provisionals' heads. Even Libya condemned the bombing as an act that "does not belong to legitimate revolutionary operations in the fight for liberation".[17]

Making a bad situation even worse, the Provisionals tried to blame the British Army for the tragedy, claiming that it had been the soldiers' electronic countermeasures that had set the bomb off. That was a lie – the bomb had been timer-detonated – that fooled no one, not even their bedrock supporters.[18] In the words of a senior Republican, interviewed a few days after the blast, "People in the IRA just feel sick. This is probably the worst year the IRA has had for five years".[19]

As the IRA reaped the consequences of allowing the supremely reckless bombing at Enniskillen to take place, another debacle of equal magnitude had been unfolding. It began on November 1, when French customs officials boarded the *Eksund*, a tramp steamer which had lost power and drifted into France's territorial waters. Aboard was a Provisional quartermaster team and over 120 tons of weapons and explosives, the final shipment from Libya. Under police interrogation, the captain of the ship, Adrian Hopkins, disclosed the fact that four arms shipments had already gotten through. Aghast at the fact that the IRA now possessed military hardware in sufficient quantity and quality to mount a serious challenge to its police and Army, the Irish government mounted an intense search for the Libyan arms. They recovered only a fraction, but dozens of IRA safe houses were uncovered and many of the group's activists had to go on the run.[20]

The events at Loughgall, the seizure of the *Eksund*, and Enniskillen had made 1987 into one of the worst years in the history of the Provisional IRA. But the men on the Army Council saw these events as only momentary setbacks. The "big push" would come in 1988. Using the enormously powerful weapons the Libyans had provided, they planned to raise the tempo of the armed struggle to a level beyond what had been previously seen in Northern Ireland. With the semtex explosives that had come with the firearms, they would strike hammer blows at their oppressors in London and other major British cities. Finally, the movement would launch a furious assault against British facilities on the European mainland. The tens of thousands of British soldiers and civilians living there in a great arc from southern Spain to northern Germany would not be expecting this. By blowing them up and shooting them by the dozen, the Provisional IRA would drive the point home: as long as Britain continued its "criminal" occupation of Northern Ireland, she would count the cost around the world.

In line with that objective, Gibraltar was an obvious target. It not only had military value but was virgin territory where the Provisionals could expect the same lax security they had exploited with such devastating effect in Brighton in 1984. Furthermore, as one of the last remnants of the Empire, the Rock was a symbol of British prestige. Every year, thousands of vacationers from the United Kingdom came in from the Costa Del Sol to savor a little bit of their own country's great history before resuming their holidays in Spain. The tourists would drive to the frontier, and after passing through customs, cross into the Colony proper. It is a small place, only two and a half square miles in area, so it takes only a few minutes by car to get to the town centre. After parking, if they were lucky enough to find a space, visitors could tour Gibraltar's several museums, take in the sights, or photograph the small apes that are native to the Colony. Or they could simply enjoy the atmosphere of what many consider, despite its location, to be a typical English seaside village.

Finally, every Tuesday at 11:00 a.m., there was the weekly changing-of-the-guard outside the Convent, the Governor-General's residence, to watch. While not on the same scale as the ceremonies at Buckingham Palace, the soldiers of the Royal Anglian Regiment, the local garrison unit, still managed to put on a majestic ceremony. To the tune of a fifty-piece military band, they would march into the square by the residence and exchange salutes and other courtesies before crowds of admiring tourists. While the parade lasted just a few minutes, it conjured up Britain's past imperial glory for those sorry about losing it and reassured the Rock's natives that – for at least another week – they need not fear a Spanish invasion. Once it was over, the bandsmen would reassemble at a nearby car park to wait for the bus that took them back to their barracks. It was there, while the Royal Anglians were tightly packed together, that the IRA planned to set off a massive car-bomb and kill them all.

What the Provos did not know was that by early March 1988, several dozen employees of Her Majesty's Government were waiting for them in the Colony. Some were surveillance experts from the Security Service (MI5), but others were soldiers, despite their longer than regulation haircuts and civilian clothes. Had they been in uniform, anyone could have seen by their sand-coloured berets and regimental patches on their sleeves that they belonged to the Special Air Service (SAS).

**Notes**

1. Personal observations I made in June 1996 during my visit to Gibraltar.
2. Sir William GF Jackson, *The Rock of the Gibraltarians*, Associated University Press, Toronto, 1987, pp. 315-316.
3. Ibid.
4. Tim Brown, "Smuggling Curb Starts Rioting in Gibraltar", *Electronic Telegraph*, July 10, 1995.
5. Chester Stern, "Action Police Chief in Drug Probe", *Mail on Sunday*,

November 5, 1995. This scandal involved the disappearance of a large amount of cash from a police evidence safe and allegations that corrupt Gibraltar police had been bugging the telephones of their honest colleagues.

6. "What Goes on Inside the Rock", *Panorama*, March 15, 1988.

7. "Arming the IRA", the *Economist*, March 31, 1990.

8. Eamonn Mallie and David McKittrick, *The Fight for Peace: The Secret Story Behind the Irish Peace*, Heinemann, London, 1996, pp. 44-46.

9. Voice of the Arab Homeland, Tripoli, Libya, April 22, 1984.

10. Brendan O'Brien, *The Long War*, O'Brien Press, Dublin, 1995, p. 139.

11. WD Flackers and Sydney Elliot, *Northern Ireland: A Political Directory 1968-1993*, The Blackstaff Press, Belfast, 1994, p. 467.

12. Ibid, p. 393.

13. Ibid, p. 239.

14. Ibid, p. 130.

15. Mark Urban, *Big Boys' Rules: the Secret Struggle Against the IRA*, Faber and Faber, London, 1992, pp. 227-237.

16. Mallie and McKittrick, p. 57.

17. Denzil McDaniel, *Enniskillen: the Remembrance Sunday Bombing*, Wolfhound Press, Dublin, 1997, p. 83.

18. Mallie and McKittrick, p. 58.

19. Ibid, p. 59.

20. O'Brien, pp. 142-143.

# CHAPTER THREE

## A KILLING FORCE

"If you get into SAS country, you are saying the end justifies the means . . . the SAS are trained to shoot first and ask questions later."
– Anonymous British politician, *Death on the Rock and Other Stories*

The SAS, the IRA's nemesis, first attracted worldwide attention at the Iranian Embassy in London. On April 30, 1980, six men advocating independence for the Arabistan region of Iran had broken into that elegant mansion and taken the embassy staff and three British citizens there hostage. At first, the Metropolitan Police had been confident that they could talk the terrorists into surrendering. But at 6:50 p.m. on May 5, the gunmen, tiring of negotiations, shot an Iranian diplomat and dumped his body out the front door. Then they threatened to kill another in forty-five minutes. A massacre like that of the Israeli athletic team at the 1972 Munich Olympics seemed only hours away. Only it would be Britain, not Germany, that would suffer the humiliation of failing to prevent the slaughter.

Then at 7:23 p.m., the SAS launched Operation Nimrod, a desperate bid to save the hostages. From the roof of the Embassy, eight soldiers began to lower themselves by rope down the rear side of the building. Their descent was not silent for long. One of the lead men became tangled in his harness. Struggling to free him, several soldiers accidentally broke a window.[1]

Things happened quickly after that. An explosive charge let down on a line from the roof until it was just above the Embassy's glass stairwell detonated with an earth-shattering roar, stunning those in the building. Seconds later, marksmen in front of the house fired a series of tear-gas canisters into its second floor. Meanwhile, a team of SAS men on the roof smashed a skylight and jumped down into the fourth floor of the Embassy. Simultaneously, members of another assault group climbed down a ladder and stormed into its third floor.

Then, four more soldiers climbed out of the first floor windows of the house next door. Captured on film by the television cameras trained on the front side of the Embassy, they had an unearthly look, clad in black, their faces hidden by masks. Each man quickly crawled over to the first-floor balcony of the Embassy. From there, they could see Sim Harris, a BBC man and one of the hostages, staring at them through a window with a look of amazement on his face.

The SAS men shouted at Harris to get down, and he dropped out of sight. The soldiers set to work attaching explosives charges to the bullet-proof glass that fronted the room where the reporter was. Engrossed in this task, they did not see the window directly above them open and a terrorist lean out. Clutching a submachine-gun, the wild-eyed figure hurled a grenade down at the soldiers.

The SAS men were lucky. Their would-be killer forgot to pull the pin. The grenade hit the balcony and rolled harmlessly away. The terrorist was not so fortunate. From across the street, an SAS sniper shot him dead, the force of the shot throwing him away from the window.[2]

Seconds later, the demolition charges exploded, shattering the window. Stepping inside the room, the soldiers could hear shouts from the adjoining secretary's office. Entering there, they saw Trevor Lock, a London police officer taken hostage along with the Iranian Embassy staff, struggling with Awn Ali

Mohammad, the terrorists' leader. Awn was armed with grenades and the pistol with which he had murdered the Iranian diplomat just thirty minutes before. Leaping forward, a soldier shoved Lock to the ground, shouting "Trevor, leave off!"[3] He then fired a fifteen-round burst into Awn with his sub-machine gun, killing him instantly.

For the next ten minutes, those waiting in the street heard screams, gunfire, and explosions as the soldiers raced through the smouldering building, shooting off the locks of each room's door, searching for the terrorists. In the telex room where the male hostages were held, they found a scene of utter chaos. After killing two of their prisoners and wounding two more, two of the gunmen there had dropped their weapons and mingled in with the crowd of men on the floor.[4] Unable to identify them, the soldiers shouted, "The terrorists! Where are the terrorists?" After one Iranian timidly pointed out his former captors, the SAS men shot both "where they sat with their backs to the centre of the room and their hands on the wall."[5]

Still frantically looking for the missing gunmen, the commandos began to quickly hustle the terrified Iranian Embassy staff to safety. It was at this point that one of the terrorists, hiding in the middle of the crowd moving down the hallway, tried to flee. The fact that he had a grenade clutched in his hand sealed his fate. A soldier smashed the stock of his sub-machine-gun over the man's head and shot him as he lay twitching on the ground.[6]

Finally, in front of television cameras transmitting live coverage worldwide, the hostages spilled out of the building, many hysterical with fear and deafened by the stun grenades that had been detonating throughout the assault. Bringing up the rear were the SAS men, holding the one gunman who had survived, his face dazed from being hurled down the stairs by his captors.[7]

So ended the soldiers' public debut. In less than twelve

minutes, they killed five of the six terrorists and saved all but three hostages. It was a tremendous accomplishment, on par with the 1976 Israeli raid on Entebbe Airport.

However, fame has a price. The events on May 5, 1980 effectively brought the SAS out of the shadows and into the public eye. And while the Regiment had many fans, there were many who felt that it was no coincidence the letters S-A-S appeared in the middle of the word "assassins."

Yet the Regiment is not a death squad. It is one of the finest military special operations groups in the world, one that lives by the motto: *Who dares, wins.* It can trace its history back to the desert war fought between the German and British armies in North Africa during World War II. In July 1941, at the onset of that conflict, its "founding father". David Stirling, received permission from his superiors to form a unit of commandos to operate behind the German lines, attacking their supply convoys and air bases. Working in small groups, no more than four or five men strong, the raiding parties would hopefully achieve surprise far more easily than the larger groups of soldiers previously used for the same type of missions.[8]

After a lacklustre beginning, Stirling's men came into their own when the Germans began driving the British Eighth Army deep back into Egypt in late 1941. Emerging from hiding after Rommel's combat troops moved on, they raised havoc with the logistical units following in the panzers' wake. Among other things, the SAS soldiers destroyed over a hundred Nazi aircraft, prompting the comment that they had more aces in their ranks than the Royal Air Force (RAF).[9]

In the present-day British Army, the 22nd SAS is the only active duty SAS unit. It consists of four "Sabre Squadrons, A, B, D, and G, each with approximately seventy-five men (a squadron further breaking down into four sixteen-man "troops"). Also within the Regiment are a number of "wings":

training, counter-revolutionary warfare (CRW), operational research, demolitions, and operations planning/intelligence.

Anyone in the British Army can join the SAS – cooks, riflemen, mechanics – anyone, provided they pass the exhausting series of tests designed to weed out the mentally and physically unfit. After a few days of relatively tame treatment from the experienced sergeants of the SAS's Training Wing, the demands placed on applicants steadily increase. They spend days on land-navigation exercises, carrying heavy rucksacks, marching through the British countryside. Throughout it all, the training sergeants test their charges' endurance, ability to adapt to changing situations, and problem-solving skills. In the past, a typical challenge for the recruits undergoing selection came in the form of having to march for miles to a designated rendezvous point only to see the trucks waiting to pick them up drive away at the last moment. Nowadays, at the end of a march, the instructors are more likely to ask the trainees to solve mathematical problems or assemble foreign-made weapons they have never seen before.[10]

If they pass the initial selection phase, the candidates move on to "continuation training". In climates ranging from desert to jungle, they learn to use standard SAS weapons and demolitions, patrol, give first aid, and employ a host of other skills that are the stock and trade of special forces soldiers.

After twenty weeks of this, the soldiers undergo Combat Survival and Interrogation Training. After being dropped off in the middle of a wilderness, they have to live off the land and evade the patrols sent out for them by an infantry battalion. Whether they avoid capture or not, each candidate gets the "privilege" of being questioned by expert interrogators from MI5 and the Military Intelligence Corps. During these sessions, they undergo intense psychological pressure. The recruits are hooded, forced to stand or squat for hours in freezing pools of water, or stripped naked and questioned by interrogators, some of whom are women. A number of candidates recalled being tied to a wooden plank and repeatedly submerged into a pool of water to encourage them to talk. One trainee later said, "I wasn't always certain who was being trained: us or the interrogators. I think it was a bit of both really."[11]

Throughout it all, the SAS training sergeants continue to evaluate the candidates. It is only after their final approval that a soldier receives the coveted beret and a posting to one of the Regiment's operational squadrons.

The 22nd SAS Regiment conducts military counter-terrorism operations for the United Kingdom. Each of its four squadrons take turns pulling that duty from the regimental headquarters, which in 1988 was at Hereford. The Special Projects Team, the alert troop of the designated "counter-revolutionary warfare" (CRW) squadron, is subject to recall at any time and can fly to anywhere in the world in a matter of hours from the RAF base at nearby Lyneham.

Authority for the Special Projects Team to deploy comes from the Joint Operations Centre (JOC), a military command post which includes representatives from the intelligence community and Foreign Office. In the case of overseas missions like Gibraltar, the Prime Minister must personally sanction the operation.[12] Once in the field, a satellite communication system enables the Special Projects Team to remain in constant touch with London. This allows senior British officials to exercise an extraordinary amount of control over the soldiers' activities. Supposedly, sometimes, government ministers have given "SAS ambush commanders in the field their orders to proceed with an operation. In this way, it is possible for political authority to be confirmed right up to the last minute."[13]

While waiting for action that may never come, soldiers on CRW duty hone their skills at what they call close quarters battle (CQB) in the "killing house." This is a unique shooting course where the soldiers practice entering and clearing buildings or confined areas full of hostile targets. During the six weeks of the school, the soldiers fire their pistols hundreds of times in simulations where they must shoot quickly and accurately at terrorist targets without hitting nearby hostages (in the past, the instructors would play the role of the captives and stand only inches away from the "terrorist" dummies).[14] This training allows the SAS men to perfect their marksmanship, instantly identify targets, clear jams, and fire while on the move.

Besides its practical purposes, CQB training is visually impressive and is responsible for a large part of the SAS mystique. Yet in the late 1980s, for all its capabilities, the Regiment suffered from a surprising and very basic flaw for an organization often engaged in undercover work. Simply put, SAS men wearing civilian clothes tended to look like SAS men wearing civilian clothes. James Rennie, a military intelligence officer who often worked with the soldiers, described the problem this way:

> To a man, they liked to dress in tight blue jeans, trainers, sweatshirts and bomber jackets; and their notion of a civilian hair style invariably matched that of the average professional [rugby] player. The whole effect was in many cases neatly pulled together by the addition of a fierce-looking, droopy Mexican moustache.[15]

Another questionable part of the SAS mystique is that the soldiers have higher ethics than mortals in lesser organizations. That was a viewpoint expressed by a reporter who met several (carefully screened) SAS veterans of the Falklands War. In a gushing article about the obviously choreographed encounter, he wrote:

> We live in an age of selective cynicism, in which to admit a strong belief in anything . . . is deeply unfashionable . . . These men . . . seemed entirely unaware of the conventions of their age.[16]

45

The reporter should have said "some SAS men" were "unaware of the conventions of their age." Others have proven quite in tune with them. In 1974, two soldiers from the Regiment received six-year prison sentences for attempting to rob a bank in Londonderry, Northern Ireland. Other SAS men shunned that particular form of self-enrichment and sold their skills to the highest bidder instead. One of these was a man, described as having been "obliged to leave the Regiment because of his uncontrolled violence". He wound up in Angola in 1976 along with similar British Army rejects fighting for the FNLA, a local insurgent group. Meanwhile, a security company, with at least one member of an SAS reserve unit on its rolls, achieved notoriety for training the bodyguards of Libya's Colonel Quadaffi, arguably the IRA's biggest supporter. While such incidents prove little about the Regiment as a whole, they do illustrate that belonging to it does not guarantee honest or "idealistic" conduct. The latest reminder of that came in 1996 when Scotland Yard arrested an SAS man in Hereford for firearms offences.[17]

For the SAS, Northern Ireland has always been a major theatre of operations. While the Regiment has covertly operated there since 1969, a series of particularly hideous crimes during January 1976 triggered its official presence in the North. On the fourth of the month, Loyalist terrorists killed six innocent Catholic men in two separate incidents in South Armagh.[18] The next day, twelve masked gunmen from the "South Armagh Republican Action Force" (a flag of convenience for the IRA) stopped a coach full of Protestant workers on their way home from work in the small town of Kingsmills. Making their Catholic driver stand to one side, the IRA men lined up the bus's occupants and machine-gunned them, killing ten of them.[19]

What came to be known as the Kingsmill's Massacre triggered an uproar in Britain and appeals for more protection, from Protestants living in Northern Ireland's countryside. Once again, the region appeared to be on the brink of civil war. So on January 6, the British government announced that a unit of SAS would begin operations in South Armagh. In an article in the *Guardian*, a soldier-turned-journalist wrote, "They will be told to do what the Army has so far failed to do – *kill terrorists* [original italics]."[20]

In seeming response to the SAS's arrival, killings in "bandit country" dropped dramatically for the remainder of the year. That accomplishment would be one of the very few bloodless ones the Regiment achieved in Northern Ireland. During the next two decades, its members would kill over thirty members of the IRA and INLA at the cost of two SAS men's lives.

From a strictly military standpoint, that is an enviable rate of exchange. However, the one-sided nature of the Regiment's kills and its tactics offset much of the damage it did to the Provisionals. Catholics living in Northern Ireland noted that the SAS shot only IRA and INLA men. Members of the larger and at times equally murderous Protestant paramilitary groups survived the few encounters they had with the Regiment. Furthermore, the bulk of the shooting incidents involving the SAS resulted from advance warning provided by informants. In a number of cases (like Gibraltar) the authorities had known for months what the IRA men hoped to do and when they planned to do it. Instead of arresting the gunmen on conspiracy charges that might not hold up in court, the SAS ambushed them instead. If they could catch the Provisionals with weapons in their hands – the reasoning apparently went – few would protest about their being shot dead. Yet in some cases, this strategy resulted in the death of innocent civilians.

One of these unfortunates was William Hanna. By the early morning of June 21, 1978, British intelligence had learned that the IRA planned to fire-bomb the Post Office transport and engineering depot on Ballysillan Road in North Belfast. In anticipation of this attack, a team of five SAS men and one

47

police officer hid around the compound and settled down to wait for the bombers. Early next morning, they saw three IRA men, James Mulvenna, Denis Brown, and William Mailey, approach the depot. They did not have firearms but were carrying incendiaries in satchels. Two other men, William Hanna and David Graham, were also in the area. Both of them were Protestant civilians walking home after a night at the local pub.

The IRA men never got the chance to use their bombs. One of the soldiers at Ballysillan later claimed they opened fire after he shouted for them to surrender, an interesting statement since the Provos did not have guns. In a matter of seconds, the SAS/police stakeout team shot Mulvenna, Brown, and Mailey to pieces.

That accounted for three gunmen. The SAS men had been expecting four (a fourth man who remained in the car that the Provos used for the operation, panicked when he heard the gunfire, and fled on foot). Not knowing this, the soldiers decided Graham or Hanna might be the fourth bomber.

Those two men had no idea that they had inadvertently walked into an ambush and become suspected terrorists by default. When the shooting started, they dove to the ground to get out of the line of fire. A few moments later, several SAS men rushed up to where Graham lay, flung him against a wall, and hastily searched him.[21] Taken to a police barracks, he was released later unharmed.

Hanna did not survive. According to depositions made by the soldiers, his own foolishness caused his death. Told to raise his hands over his head, he instead made "a sudden twisting motion" so two SAS men shot him.

The killing of William Hanna made headlines, soured the triumph of killing three IRA men, and caused a year-long rupture between the SAS and the RUC in Belfast. It also prompted fresh accusations from Republicans that the Regiment

48

was nothing more than a "killer squad." Yet Hanna's death could have been a genuine mistake or the result of actions by two trigger-happy soldiers. After all, if the SAS had intended to kill everyone at Ballysillan, Graham, the only civilian witness to the ambush, would not have lived.

But the behavior of the soldiers when they ran after Graham and Hanna was not accidental in the slightest. At least one of them paused by the corpses of Mulvenna and Brown and shot both once in the head. The powder burns found on the IRA men's bodies suggest this was done at point-blank range. The SAS's unofficial biographer, Tony Geraghty, loftily chose to rationalize this step:

> On the battlefield, it is not unusual to make sure an apparently dead enemy really is no danger before turning one's back on him . . . At Ballysillan, someone had followed battlefield practice without comprehending the legal implications of it in Ireland where the use of force is limited.[22]

A statement like that calls into question whether Geraghty is aware that the "battlefield practice" of finishing off the wounded is a war crime, specifically a "grave breach" of the Geneva Convention. One also might wonder how Geraghty would view the IRA's use of this "battlefield practice" against British soldiers.

In any case, according to Geraghty, after Ballysillan, the soldiers received new guidance about shooting at the prone bodies of wounded men and women: "Don't do it." Yet events in Gibraltar would make some wonder whether that order had sunk home – or been given at all.

Nineteen days after Ballysillan, there was another SAS "mistake". This time the victim was John Boyle, the son of a Catholic farmer in County Antrim. On July 10, John, who was just sixteen years old, was exploring a small graveyard near his home. His attention was drawn to a stone marker, perhaps by fresh earth that indicated someone had buried something under the slab. Lifting it up, he discovered a small plastic bag with an armalite rifle, pistol, and other paramilitary gear inside it. Excited by his find, John ran home and told his father, Cornelius Boyle, who called the RUC. After some deliberation, the police and the Army decided that the SAS would stake out the area and "arrest" whoever came to collect the weapons.

By 3:00 a.m., July 11, there were four soldiers in the graveyard in two observation posts. Sergeant Allan Bohan and Corporal Ron Temperley were nearest to the arms cache.[23] According to Robert Millar, a police officer involved in the operation, the RUC warned the soldiers three times that the Boyle family had young children who might return to the site to see what was going on.

At 9:40 a.m., Millar telephoned the Boyles to tell the family to stay away from the cemetery, but he was too late. Cornelius Boyle, John, and his brother Hugh had already set off to work in the fields. At 10:00 a.m., overcome with curiosity, John Boyle entered the cemetery and walked toward the stone marker.

A moment later, working nearby, Cornelius and Hugh heard gunshots. Bohan and Temperley were the ones firing them. The Boyles rushed to the graveyard, where two soldiers threw them to the ground. Cornelius remembered hearing one of the SAS men say, "The other bastard's lying dead."[24] It was only later that he would realize that they were talking about his son John.

What happened next would be remembered by those critical of the SAS's actions in Gibraltar. A helicopter landed near the shooting scene and took Bohan and Temperley away. Then, the Army released a statement to the press saying a patrol had stopped three gunmen. When it was pointed out that the Boyles were not affiliated with any paramilitary group, the story quickly changed. It was given out that John Boyle had pointed the armalite at the soldiers and there had been a magazine in the rifle "and a round in the breech ready to fire". As the RUC officers investigating the shooting discovered, this was a lie. According to a forensics report that leaked out, Boyle had been shot in the back, and his fingerprints were not on any of the weapons in the cache.[25]

On February 1, 1979, the RUC formally charged Bohan and Temperley with the murder of John Boyle. Their subsequent trial revolved around the question whether the pathologist's report was true, that Boyle had been shot first in the back. In the end, the judge trying the case accepted the soldiers' arguments that one of their bullets had struck Boyle in the face, indicating he might have been looking at them when they opened fire. Yet while acquitting the two men, Justice Lowry did find that Sergeant Bohan lied when he said Boyle had pointed the armalite at him. He concluded his judgment by saying:

nothing would have been easier with better planning than to capture the deceased alive always *assuming that to be the primary objective* [author's italics]."[26]

After the trial, the soldiers returned to active duty and, as of 1990, were still members of the SAS. Interviewed years later about his son's death, Cornelius Boyle told the *Belfast Telegraph* that he felt no bitterness toward John's killers because, "They were doing their job, which was to kill whoever entered the graveyard. That is what the SAS are employed to do."[27]

In just three weeks, the SAS managed to kill two civilians and three Provisionals (mutilating two of their bodies). Had they been receiving orders from the IRA Army Council, the soldiers could not have done a better job at generating propaganda for the Republican Movement. The IRA would argue that the Ballysillan and Boyle episodes were simply the consequences of a standard operating procedure the commandos worked by, where they shoot suspected gunmen on sight. But if that was the case, if there really was a "shoot-to-kill" policy in constant operation, the several hundred men and women known to be IRA members would have rapidly become extinct. Clearly, there must be a more complicated explanation for the soldiers' actions.

Part of that explanation comes from the fact that just like in any government, British policy is not permanent. It has its shifts, even on matters pertaining to Northern Ireland. Sometimes, the government feels pressure to show that it is doing something about Provisional IRA outrages there. This is done by killing IRA men. On other occasions, it has tried to show that the region is becoming more and more "normal." Gunning down terrorist suspects without warning does not fit in with this picture so it does not occur.

At other times, Army and police officers appear to have unleashed the SAS simply because getting a few kills in made them feel better. In one case, officers running a centre that coordinated special operations remembered a British Army general promising, "A crate of champagne to the first man who puts a body in my in-tray".[28]

Still another reason for ambushes is the belief that they provide a quick and easy way to dispose of particularly dedicated and dangerous gunmen. Closely related to that is the view some British intelligence officials hold that the tactic raises the level of fear and paranoia within the IRA to the point where its members are afraid to mount operations.

Then there is the psychology of the SAS. In recent years, at the enlisted level, the unit has become increasingly dominated by recruits from the Parachute Regiment. More than any others in the British Army, the Paras encourage aggressive behavior and the use of force. One veteran from that regiment and the SAS, Harry McCallion, remembered the following conversation with an instructor after he had finished interrogating a "terrorist" he had captured during a training exercise:

"What are you going to do to him?" asked the training major.
I hesitated and he kicked me in the ribs so hard I was bruised for weeks.

52

"You kill him. Do you understand? Kill him. We'll have no squeamishness here."

I shot him with my blank ammunition. It was a lesson I learned well.[29]

The presence of that mentality within the SAS's enlisted ranks is significant because, since the mid-1980s, its officers began to play a minimal role in conducting counter-terrorist operations. It is the senior sergeants of the Regiment who exercised the most control over the soldiers' actions on the ground. In some of the most significant incidents involving the unit in Northern Ireland, SAS officers were not even on the scene.[30] In the words of one former SAS officer, the SAS "has become Animal Farm – run by the pigs".[31]

The best explanation, though, for the SAS's behavior is that they are *soldiers* not police. In contrast to the RUC, they do not spend their days policing a community and learning how to deal with ordinary citizens in a restrained and tactful manner. Far from it, their training is focused on the main task of soldiers, *killing*. Killing without warning is not only acceptable in wartime; it is the preferred option. And in Northern Ireland, where the SAS men confront opponents with military organization and a sense of mission far greater than "ordinary, decent criminals", it is quite natural for them to think they are at war, no matter what the politicians say. In their view, the "yellow card", the document prohibiting use of deadly force by military personnel in Northern Ireland unless soldiers or civilians are in imminent danger, is a sick joke. In a letter written in 1976, Lieutenant Colonel JC Wakerley, former assistant director of Army Legal Services in Belfast, expressed the soldiers' attitude perfectly:

Such a concept may be fine for dealing with bank robbers in Battersea or even with hijackers at Heathrow. As interpreted [here], it is utterly out of place to support an Army fighting a *seven year war* [author's italics] with no end remotely in sight.[32]

In the past, some members of the Regiment have taken that view to the point of arguing that they should be immune to criminal prosecution, in other words, given a licence to kill.[33] To date, the British government has refused to grant this to the SAS. After all, the soldiers hardly need one with jurists like Lord Justice Maurice Gibson expressing opinions like "shooting can be justified as a method of arrest". Given the nature of the SAS, it is not surprising that many consider a decision to send in the SAS as something more than law enforcement. As Paddy McGrory, a Belfast solicitor destined to become deeply involved in the Gibraltar case, commented:

> the SAS is designed as a killing force. It is not there to capture people. It is not there to arrest people. It is there as a cutting edge. If you bring the SAS [into the equation] to my mind, you intend to do what the SAS does and that is kill people.[35]

## Notes

1. Tony Geraghty, *Who Dares Wins*, Warner Books, London, 1993, pp. 446-447.
2. Ibid, pp. 448-449.
3. Ibid.
4. Murray, *The SAS in Ireland*, p. 9.
5. *Siege*, Hamlyn Paperbacks, London, 1986, pp. 126-127 (written by *Sunday Times* insight team). In the 1980 edition of Tony Geraghty's widely-acclaimed book *Inside the SAS* (retitled and updated in 1993 as *Who Dares Wins*)), the author justifies the killing of the three terrorists in the telex room as necessary because the soldiers could not have known they were trying to surrender. In the 1993 edition, Geraghty presents an entirely new version of events – namely that one terrorist was still armed and shot by the soldiers as they entered the room, another slipped away and was shot moments later making a run for it, and the third was shot while being searched because he made a sudden movement. Geraghty's 1993 account of the first and third deaths is at odds with that of several of the hostages, and he gives no explanation for presenting a radically different version of events in his earlier book.
6. Michael Paul Kennedy, *He Who Dares*, Pocket Books, New York, 1989, pp. 231-232.
7. Geraghty, 1980 edition, p. 208.
8. Peter MacDonald, *The SAS in Action*, Sidgwick and Jackson, London, 1993,

pp. 8-19. Paddy O'Daire, a man with impeccable Republican credentials, was an early member of the SAS. A veteran of the War of Independence he also fought on the Republican side in the Civil War. He was a member of the International Brigade in Spain and enlisted in the British army as a private at the outbreak of World War II, rising to the rank of major.

9. Ibid.

10. Geraghty, pp. 225-251.

11. Ibid.

12. "Knocking on the door of the Secret World", *The Guardian*, September 5, 1988; "IRA Hunts for Top Level Mole, *Observer*, March 13, 1988; and "A Job for the SAS", *Sunday Telegraph*, March 13, 1988.

13. Mark Urban, "SAS 'Go Anywhere' Satellite Communications System", *Independent*, May 13, 1988.

14. This practice ended after the accidental death of an SAS man playing the hostage role.

15. James Rennie, *The Operators: On the Streets with 14 Company*, Century, London, 1996, p. 200.

16. Geraghty, 1993, p. 17.

17. "Elite Troops Held on Arms Sales Charges", *Belfast Telegraph*, October 31, 1996.

18. Malcolm Sutton, *An Index of Deaths from the Conflicts in Ireland 1969-1993*, Colour Books, Ltd, Dublin, 1994, p. 84.

19. Gergahty, 1980 edition, pp. 172-173.

20. "Knocking on the Door of the Secret World."

21. Murray, pp. 224-225. In his statement to the authorities, Graham said that he heard no warning given, that the firing took him and Hanna by complete surprise.

22. Gergahty, p. 352, and of the Geneva Convention for the Amelioration of the Condition of the Wounded and Sick in Armed Forces in the Field, 75 UNTS 31, entered into force October 21, 1950.

23. Urban, *Big Boys' Rules*, pp. 63-66.

24. Ibid, pp. 63-66.

25. Murray, pp. 225-235.

26. Urban, *Big Boys' Rules*, p. 65.

27. Ibid.

28. Mark Urban, *UK Eyes Alpha: the Inside Story of British Intelligence*, Faber and Faber Ltd, London, 1996, p. 92.

29. Harry McCallion, *The Killing Zone: A Life in the Paras, the Recces, the SAS and the RUC*, Bloomsbury, London, 1996, pp. 28-29.

30. Urban, *Big Boys' Rules*, p. 229.

31. Mark Urban, "Silent but Deadly," *Gentleman's Quarterly*, April 1992, p. 112.

32. Pallister and Norton-Taylor.

33. Roger Bolton, *Death on the Rock and Other Stories*, WH Allen/Optomen, London, 1990, p. 225.

34. Cran.

# CHAPTER FOUR

## COUNTDOWN

"The tempting target, symbol for the IRA of British imperialism, had become a carefully prepared trap."
– Julian Manyon, *Death on the Rock*

The British authorities had known for months that the IRA was coming to Gibraltar. Just how they knew is something of a mystery. For years, the official story was that the RUC learned about the bomb plot by intercepting mail going to the homes of families of active IRA members. Seán Savage had supposedly sent a postcard to his parents while he was on the Costa del Sol in November 1987.[1] But while this may have been a clue for the MI5 and police intelligence analysts studying the Provisionals' activities in Spain, it was not the only clue, nor the first. There were other pieces to the puzzle, ones in the authorities' hands long before McCann, Savage, or Farrell ever set foot in Spain.

The first warning came from the Irish police. The Gardaí's C3 anti-terrorist unit maintained a permanent observation post at Dublin Airport. The officers manning it noted that a number of individuals with paramilitary convictions were travelling to and from Spain. This information was promptly passed to the RUC in Belfast.[2]

Alerted by the British and Irish governments, as early as 1986, the Spanish authorities saw signs that the IRA was establishing a network on the Costa del Sol. It was then that

British intelligence specialists began travelling to Spain to help the local police monitor and assess IRA activity there.

Critical intelligence about the Provisionals' intentions also appears to have come from electronic surveillance and informants within the Republican community. Confirmation of this appears in *Phoenix: Policing the Shadows,* a book based on the diaries of Ian Phoenix, a high-ranking RUC Special Branch officer who died on June 2, 1994, in the Mull of Kintyre helicopter crash. On page 135 of the book, there is a startling pair of disclosures. First, according to Phoenix, the RUC believed Daniel McCann and Seán Savage were responsible for the August 26, 1987 murders of two Special Branch detectives in Belfast. Yet despite believing this, the police did not arrest them. Second, at the time of those killings, the RUC already knew that they and Mairéad Farrell were involved in a plot to set off a bomb in Gibraltar.[3]

That the authorities had this information strongly suggests that informants tipped them off about the bomb plot.[4] In 1988, despite the Provisionals' enforcers' best efforts, there were many police spies within the Republican community. On January 26, 1989, one of them, Joseph Fenton, a workman-turned-real-estate agent, was found dead in an alleyway in a Belfast housing estate with four bullets in his head. Fenton had been a police informant for at least eight years. During this time, he allowed the IRA to make use of cars and property owned by his business. What the Provisionals did not know was that the police had wired many of them for sound. Asked to detail the scope of Fenton's "treachery", one IRA leader bluntly admitted that:

It is difficult to estimate the full extent of the damage [he did]. He had access not only to information but also to people. He provided safe-houses [that were bugged] . . . We cannot fully determine . . . what was said by volunteers who were [there] and felt . . . free to talk about operations.[5]

57

If McCann, Savage, and Farrell's superiors briefed them about Gibraltar in one of Fenton's properties, their operation would have been compromised from the very beginning.

That was just one possibility. In early 1988, tip-offs had enabled the RUC and Gardaí to seize a large number of Provisional weapons. After a lengthy investigation, the IRA's internal security unit concluded that the Belfast Brigade Quartermaster, a man who had gone into police custody, had been a police informant, for perhaps as long as eight years. A man in that position would have also been well-placed to know about overseas operations involving Belfast IRA members.[6]

There was also Brendan Davison, a top Belfast Provisional. Loyalist gunmen masquerading as police murdered him on July 21, 1988. According to senior RUC officers, Davison had been an "important informant".[7]

Finally, the British authorities did not have a monopoly on sources within the IRA. Writing in an article in the *Sunday Tribune*, Veronica Guerin described an informant working for the Gardaí as a key source of information about the activities of the IRA's "Continental Battalion". In it, she stated that the mole had passed on the first warning that McCann, Savage, and Farrell would carry out a bombing attack in Europe.[8] The spy Guerin had identified may have been the same one the IRA reportedly discovered in its Southern Command in 1997.[9]

Besides these indicators, an even sharper warning that the IRA was up to something in Spain might have come from simply watching the *Eksund*. In *The Dirty War*, Martin Dillon claims that the ship off-loaded the semtex explosives the Provisionals planned to use in Gibraltar as it passed the southern Spanish coastline on its way to Ireland.[10]

But this is speculative. The best *confirmed* indicator of IRA intentions was the movement of its personnel in Spain. On November 5, 1987, at Malaga Airport, the Spanish authorities spotted Daniel McCann travelling with a fake passport in the name of Robert Wilfred Reilly. Ten days later, they observed him and Seán Savage (who was using the name of Brendan Coyne) at Madrid Airport, disembarking from a flight from Malaga. At about the same time, a third IRA operative, a woman (but not Farrell), was seen in Malaga as well. She carried a passport stolen from Mary Parkin, the wife of a Press Association journalist. According to Spanish police, one IRA member involved in the Gibraltar operation also met with Father Patrick Ryan. Ryan, a Catholic priest long suspected by the British government as an "IRA fixer", was living in Spain at that time.[11]

Had the IRA been on its guard, it might have realized that its activities in Spain were being watched. On December 9, 1987, the British Home Secretary, Douglas Hurd, met with high-ranking security officials of the other European Community Countries in what is known as the Trevi Group on Terrorism. At that gathering, he warned his fellow ministers that the IRA was about to conduct a series of attacks against British facilities on the European mainland.

But what happened on the Rock the day before the Trevi Group met illustrates how thoroughly compromised the IRA plan for Gibraltar had been. Citing a need to repaint the guardhouse in front of the Governor General residence, the Gibraltar authorities abruptly cancelled the parade scheduled for that day. The changing-of-the-guard ceremony would only resume on February 23, 1988, eleven weeks later.

Why would the Gibraltar government need seventy-seven days to repaint a small building essential to the conduct of a major tourist event? Several weeks after the killings, Lieutenant Colonel George Styles, a retired British Army bomb-disposal expert interviewed by Thames Television, offered a theory that gave two reasons for the strange decision. First, stopping the parade took the initiative away from the IRA. With no parade, they would have no target to bomb – until the authorities were ready for them. Second, if "Mary Parkin" showed up after the parade resumed, it would confirm that the bandsmen were the Provisionals' target.[12]

This was confirmed on February 10, 1988. That day, the IRA scout returned to the Costa del Sol and checked into the Hostal Buena Vista in Estepona, just an hour's drive away from the Rock. For the next twelve days, under constant Spanish surveillance, the long-haired woman frequently travelled to Malaga, Gibraltar, and San Pedro de Alcantara, where she made calls from public telephones. One of the policemen assigned to watch "Parkin" later told a British reporter, "We knew she was timing runs to Gibraltar from different spots along the coast. Afterwards, she would go to mass at Estepona's church. She seemed very religious."[13]

On February 23, 1988, the changing-of-the-guard ceremony at the Convent resumed. Sure enough, MI5 officers spotted "Parkin" in the crowd of tourists in front of the Governor's Residence watching the band and following their route to and from the assembly area. On March 1, "Parkin" returned to the Colony to observe the parading soldiers.

The decision to defer the changing-of-the-guard ceremony also marks the time when at least some of the authorities in Gibraltar first learned about the bomb plot. Who knew what and when is unclear. Sometime, though, between December 1987 and February 1988, the Gibraltar Governor General, Sir Peter Terry, his police commissioner, Joseph Canepa, and high ranking military officers from the garrison received a briefing from MI5 about the IRA threat to the Colony. This was given by a representative of an executive from the Security Service's "G" (counter-terrorism) branch. This senior MI5 officer would appear at the inquest held over McCann, Savage, and Farrell's deaths under the pseudonym "Mr O." Strangely enough, Mr O's representation never did.[14]

Commissioner Canepa and others would later testify at that same inquest that Mr O's representative told them that the IRA planned to put a huge car-bomb in the assembly area the bandsmen used for the changing-of-the-guard parade. The intent behind this was simple, to slaughter the fifty soldiers as they marched to or from the ceremony scheduled for March 8, 1988. In a point repeatedly emphasized in the weeks to come, the MI5 officer told the Gibraltar authorities that the IRA members involved were highly skilled, ruthless, probably armed, and willing to die to accomplish their mission.

Car-bombs are the IRA's dubious contribution to conflict resolution. The fact that they look just like ordinary cars is only one of their "virtues". The other has to do with the devastating way the devices explode. In the case of the 1982 bombing of the Horse Guards in Hyde Park, London:

> The terrorists planned their attack carefully. They parked a blue Morris sedan on Carriage Road, about 600 yards along the cavalry's daily route. Hidden inside was up to 10 pounds of gelignite explosive wrapped with hundreds of 4- and 6-inch nails. As the Blues and Royals passed, an IRA member, probably hidden in the trees of Hyde Park, punched a remote controlled detonator . . . [and the bomb exploded]. Windows shattered . . . flames burst high in the air; and nails wrapped around the explosive shot out like bullets. Horses fell in a writhing mass; dying soldiers bled into the tatters of their ornate uniforms; and a woman passerby, her face shredded, screamed, 'Help me! Help me!'[15]

A year later, eight days before Christmas, the IRA used a car-bomb with deadly effect at Harrod's Department Store. The Provisionals had issued a vague telephone warning, and the blast had occurred while the police were still frantically clearing the area. A bomb-disposal officer on the scene minutes after the explosion recalled:

> Beneath the [bomb] car lay the body of a police officer. He had been trying to get people to safety when the bomb went off and blew the vehicle into the air. It had come down on

top of him. In the fierce fire that followed both car and victim had been consumed . . .

Nearby, another victim lay in the sparkling debris. He was very tall . . . with only one apparent injury, the result of a fragment striking him in the middle of his forehead . . .

The third body was a young woman. She had been blown through a plate-glass window . . . Her skirt had been blown off, and she was wearing a little pair of panties decorated with a heart which embraced the message: I LOVE YOU.[16]

This was the type of weapon the IRA – after expressing its deep regret over the massacre at Enniskillen – planned to use in the Colony.[17] Caught in the narrow confines of the town, the explosive force of a car-bomb would have ricocheted like a pinball off Gibraltar's strong stone walls. In the words of Colonel Styles, it would have "fragmented" any soldiers or tourists next to it and showered the occupants of the nearby elementary school and retirement home with rubble and shrapnel.

Such a terrifying possibility must have made a deep impression on Sir Peter, Canepa, and the rest of Gibraltar's officialdom. It was the greatest threat to the safety of the Colony since World War II. The IRA had to be stopped. Given the Gibraltar Police's total lack of familiarity with Irish terrorism (along with the less-than-inspiring way they had handled the Doves' riot twenty years before), they were quite willing to follow MI5's advice and request "special assistance" to deal with the problem.

Meanwhile, after watching the parade on March 1, 1988, "Mary Parkin" informed her IRA superiors that the changing-of-the-guard ceremonies at the Convent had resumed. Her report set the IRA's attack against Gibraltar in motion. Although many details about the IRA operation are unclear, the following facts are not.

Farrell was the first to set out for Spain. On Wednesday morning, March 2, she told her parents that there would be a three-week break in her classes at Queen's University and she would be going down to Dublin to visit some friends. When her mother asked when she would be back, the young woman said she did not know. As Mrs Farrell later recalled:

whenever [Mairéad] went down to Dublin where all her old school friends were, she always used to say if she wasn't back on Saturday night, she'd be back for her dinner on Sunday – at midday. It was a family occasion and Mairéad loved her Sunday dinner."[18]

This time, though, she told her mother not to keep any food for her.

At 2:15 p.m. the next day – it was her thirty-first birthday– Farrell left her parents' house in Andersonstown for Dublin. She got there just in time to take a flight out to Brussels (the Gardaí had stopped her driver for speeding). She then flew into Malaga on Friday, March 4. She used two false names while in transit, "Mary Johnston" and "Katherine Alison Smith".[19]

The next to move was McCann. Sometime on the afternoon of Thursday, March 3, a driver took him down to Dublin Airport. While crossing the border, a British Army patrol briefly detained and questioned him, possibly to allow the Gardaí time to get into position and take over the job of tailing the IRA man.

Then came Savage. The last in his family to see him alive was his mother. She had come home from work at about 3:00 p.m. on Thursday and found Seán in the house. He told her that he was off to spend a weekend camping out in the Gaeltacht. As Mrs Savage recalled, "He said he'd stayed back to see me to say cheerio."[20] When she asked him who was going to eat the fish she had bought for his Friday dinner, her dutiful son told her he would take it with him and cook it while on his trip. Savage had lied, of course. Instead of going to Galway, he made his way down to Dublin and met up with McCann. Together, the two men caught a flight out to Paris. They then flew on to Malaga on Iberian Airlines Flight 657. Like Farrell, both were travelling under false names and passports, the Coyne and Reilly identities they had used before.

McCann and Savage arrived in Spain on Friday and made their way down to Torremolinos, a small Spanish town not far from Gibraltar. Once there, both men booked into the Hotel Escandinavia.[21] At some point on Friday or Saturday, Farrell must have joined them since the Spanish police later found some women's clothing in their room.

Now in position, the Provisionals began the final build-up for the attack against the British garrison in Gibraltar. At midday on March 4, a man using the name "John Oakes" hired a red Ford Fiesta from a car-rental agency in Torremolinos. Several hours after the shootings, Spanish police found this car in a car park a few hundred yards from the Gibraltar border. Inside it were false documents, a money belt containing two thousand British pounds, a large suitcase covered with dirt that looked as if it had been buried for some time, several pairs of gloves, a dirty raincoat and anorak, and assorted bomb-making materials. Mud covered the Fiesta, and its odometer indicated that someone had driven it 1,594 kilometers. A Spanish policeman told the rental manager who retrieved the car that it had been to Valencia (a Spanish city along the Mediterranean coastline) and back.[22]

On Saturday, March 5, at about 11:00 a.m., someone using Savage's Coyne alias rented a second car, a white Renault 5 from the Avis agency in Torremolinos. Later that evening, using her "Smith" identity, Farrell arranged to hire a car as well, a white Ford Fiesta, from the Marbessol Agency in Marbella, another resort town on the Costa del Sol. At 10:30 a.m. on Sunday morning, March 6, she returned to the agency to pick up the car. The clerk who helped her remembered that "Smith" looked exhausted, "as if she hadn't been to bed."[23]

Two days after the shootings, Spanish police officers found the white Fiesta in an underground car park in Marbella. Inside its trunk was 141 pounds of semtex-h, the powerful Czech-made plastic explosive Quadaffi had provided to the Provisionals in 1986, twenty-two pounds of assault rifle ammunition, four electrical detonators, and two electronic timers with circuit boards that had the same "artwork" as those used in previous IRA bombs. Someone had set the timers to run ten hours and forty-five minutes and eleven hours and fifteen minutes respectively. If the timers began running at midnight on Monday, they would trigger the car-bomb at 10:45 a.m. or 11:15 a.m. on Tuesday morning, March 8. Those were the times the British bandsmen assembled and then reassembled for their parade. As for the ammunition, it would act as shrapnel when the bomb detonated.

In the weeks just after the killings, many journalists believed these scattered facts suggested the following sequence of events. Savage was the "John Oakes" who hired the red Ford Fiesta. After doing so, he gave it to Farrell who drove the car to Valencia. There, she picked up the explosives from an arms cache hidden outside the city. After returning to the Costa del Sol on Saturday evening or early Sunday morning, she parked Savage's car in the underground lot in Marbella and went to pick up the white Fiesta. Then, Farrell drove back where she left the other car and met her friends there. With McCann and Farrell standing guard, Savage, the team's explosives expert, must have transferred the semtex from the red Fiesta to the white one and rigged up the car-bomb.[24] Shortly before noon, he finished his task and climbed into the white Renault 5 that he and McCann had been using and set off for Gibraltar. The reason for Savage's excursion was simple: to put in a "blocking car". The Renault he was driving would hold a parking space in the assembly area for the car-bomb the ASU would bring into the Colony on Monday night or early Tuesday morning.

Then, perhaps an hour later, using the team's red Ford Fiesta, McCann and Farrell had driven down toward the Colony, taking the same coastal road their companion did.

Savage, after all, would need a ride back and the trip would give them a chance to reconnoitre Gibraltar.

## Notes

1. MacDonald, p. 91.
2. Interview with Brendan O'Brien, Current Affairs Correspondent, RTE, Dublin, November 1997.
3. Holland and Phoenix, pp. 134-135.
4. Oliver McGuckin, "Gardaí Tailed Gib Three: Claim," *Belfast Telegraph*, September 13, 1993. According to Garda sources interviewed by the *Sunday Tribune*, cooperation between the British and Irish authorities was comprehensive. According to Sinn Féin claims, after the shootings, the Irish authorities released the names of McCann, Savage and Farrell's before the British or the IRA did.
5. Martin Dillon, *The Dirty War*, Arrow Books, London, 1991, pp. 321-323.
6. O'Brien, *The Long War*, p. 150.
7. Jim Cusack and Henry MacDonald, *UVF*, Poolbeg, Dublin, 1996, pp. 251-252.
8. Veronica Guerin, "IRA Informer Led to SAS Killing of Gibraltar Three", *Sunday Tribune*, September 12, 1993.
9. "Mole Leads to IRA Command Change", *Jane's Intelligence Review*, November 1997.
10. Dillon, p. 442.
11. Olivia Ward and Gordon Thomas, "Vatican to Investigate Irish Priest Linked IRA Drugs-and-Arms Plot", *Toronto Star*. December 4, 1988.
12. "Death on the Rock", *This Week*, Thames Television, April 28, 1988.
13. "Intelligence Experts Stalked IRA's Movement", the *Independent*, May 23, 1989.
14. Mr O's "representative" was probably none other than Sir Peter Terry, Gibraltar's governor general. Unlike the SAS and MI5 witnesses, Terry could not have hidden a pseudonym. If he did act as O's representative.
15. "Maniacs Blowing Holes in Bandsmen by Remote Control", *Newsweek*, August 2, 1982, pp. 31-32.
16. Peter Gurney, *Braver Men Walk Away: Memoirs of the World's Top Bomb Disposal Expert*, Harper Collins, London, 1993, pp. 210-212.
17. *Death on the Rock*, Thames Television. Asked about the morality of setting off bombs in an interview before her death, Mairéad Farrell had said all such acts including Enniskillen are "political".
18. Taylor, p. 47.
19. Jack, p. 29-30.
20. Ian Jack, "Deaths that Cannot be Buried Away", the *Observer*, May 28, 1989.
21. Tim McGirk and Heather Mills, "SAS Shootings Allowed Others to Escape", the *Independent*, May 23, 1989. McCann booked in under another false passport, "Edward McCardle". Savage continued using his Coyne alias.
22. Jack, "Gibraltar," p. 30.
23. Ibid.
24. Ibid, p. 31.

# CHAPTER FIVE

## THE "MILITARY OPTION"

"There was no exchange of words on either side, no warning, nothing said; no screams, nothing; just the shots."
— Carmen Proetta, *Death on the Rock*, 1988

While the Provisionals readied for their strike in Gibraltar, the British government had been busy with preparations of its own. Since August 1987, if not before, the Joint Intelligence Committee (JIC), an analytical cell within the Prime Minister's Cabinet Office, had been receiving a steady stream of reports about the IRA's activities in southern Spain. Using information gleaned by MI5, MI6, the RUC, and the Irish and Spanish police, the JIC built up an increasingly detailed picture of the IRA's intentions, one it shared with Mrs Thatcher on a weekly basis.

By March 1, the combination of "Mary Parkin's" appearances on the Rock, the possible intercept of telephone calls she was making back to Ireland, and informant intelligence coming out of Belfast convinced the JIC that an attack in Gibraltar was imminent. With a request for assistance from the Gibraltar authorities already in hand, the security forces decided to deploy the Special Projects Team. Briefed in late February by MI5 about the plan to trap the ASU, Prime Minister Thatcher had already authorized them to do so. By March 4, 1988, at least twelve SAS men, a bomb-disposal team, and twenty to thirty MI5 surveillance specialists were on the Rock.[1] Also present were several senior MI5 officers and an Army Legal Services Corps lawyer.[2]

By then, the operation against the IRA's Gibraltar mission had acquired a code name, Operation Flavius. This was in honour of Gaius Flavius, a judge who published the rules of legal procedure for the Roman Empire. That choice supposedly reflected the desire of the counter-terrorist specialists to conduct their activities in Gibraltar in accordance with the rule of law. Later, some would come to feel the name selection reflected some MI5 or SAS man's macabre sense of humour.

Mr O remained in London, presumably helping to run that end of the operation from there. Supposedly, Commissioner Canepa was the man in charge in the Colony. As Gibraltar's senior law-enforcement official, he bore the ultimate formal responsibility for foiling the IRA. As for the SAS men, they were there to "assist the civil power" but only if Canepa made a formal, written request for them to do so. Once that happened, it would be the military, not the police that would be in control. *Military* rules of engagement would govern what the soldiers could do if they encountered the IRA team. Set out in a top-secret order given to the SAS commander by his superiors, these guidelines, which the Prime Minister personally approved, were very specific and read in part:[3]

USE OF FORCE

4. You and your men will not use force unless requested to do so by the senior police officer(s) designated by the Gibraltar Police Commissioner; or unless it is necessary to do in order to protect life. You and your men are not then to use more force than is necessary in order to protect life; and you are to comply with rule 5.

## OPENING FIRE

5. You and your men may only open fire against a person if you or they have reasonable grounds for believing that he/she is currently committing, or is about to commit, an action which is likely to endanger your or their lives, or the life of any person, and if there is no other way to prevent this.

## FIRING WITHOUT WARNING

6. You and your men may fire without a warning if the giving of a warning or any delay in firing could lead to death or injury to you or them or any other person, or if the giving of a warning is clearly impracticable.

## WARNING BEFORE FIRING

7. If the circumstances in paragraph 6 do not apply, a warning is necessary before firing. The warning is to be as clear as possible and is to include a direction to surrender and a clear warning that fire will be opened if the direction is not obeyed.

Those were the rules. Whether the SAS played by them would become one of the great controversies of the Troubles.

After the Special Projects Teams arrived, Canepa and his advisors established a command centre in a secret location in the centre of town.[4] From there, the Commissioner would control the counter-terrorist effort. As a precaution against the unthinkable, the police also drew up a plan to evacuate the area around the Convent if the situation called for it.

Meanwhile, the rank and file SAS men and designated Gibraltar Police Special Branch officers rehearsed the way they would conduct the arrest. The soldiers would work in two-man teams with an armed plainclothes police officer (which the soldiers nicknamed "Joes") assigned to each team. When the time came for action, they would approach the suspects, issue the warning the rules of engagement required, put them down on the ground while ensuring their hands were well away from their bodies. After this, the "Joes" would formally arrest the Provisionals. If everything went according to plan, no one would ever have to know the SAS had been to the Rock. They could return to England and leave the credit along with the unwelcome publicity to Canepa's men.[5]

On Saturday, March 5, with the next changing-of-the-guard ceremony just three days away, Canepa called a special meeting for Operation Flavius's participants. This took place at midnight at the command centre. There and then, the Commissioner set out his priorities. Working with the SAS and MI5, the police would arrest the IRA team, disarm them, and defuse any bomb they brought into the Colony. The events that would trigger the arrest attempt were:[6]

– if surveillance observed an ASU member drive a car across the frontier and park it at the assembly area near the Convent (or)

– if a car driven by a member of the ASU suddenly arrived without warning in the assembly area

Following this, two more events would have to take place:

– additional ASU members entered Gibraltar (and)

– having parked the car by the Convent, the ASU gave signs it was to leaving Gibraltar

MI5 officers also provided a final intelligence briefing to the soldiers, surveillance operatives, and policemen.[7] This boiled down to four points. First, they were facing three highly dangerous, dedicated, and fanatical IRA members who were willing to die to accomplish their mission. Second, on Monday night or early Tuesday morning, these individuals would park a car-bomb at the car park near the Convent where the Royal Anglian Band routinely assembled. Third, because of the risk involved in repeatedly crossing the frontier, the ASU would *not* bring in a blocking car to reserve space for the car-bomb. If a car did appear at the assembly area, it would be a bomb and mean the attack was imminent. Finally, the car-bomb would be a "button job", set off by the simple act of pressing a button on a radio transmitter.

With this threat looming before them, the security forces on the Rock should have been – must have been – particularly vigilant. Yet by the British government's account, a little past noon on Sunday, March 6, Seán Savage somehow crossed into Gibraltar without being detected – past the Spanish police checking passports at the border, past MI5, past the SAS, past everyone. But according to the British, an incredible stroke of luck offset this monumental blunder. An MI5 officer spotted Savage's white Renault 5 easing into the second parking space on the left-hand side of the assembly area at 12:45 p.m.[8] That was the first in a sequence of events, over three house long, that the British authorities *said* happened in Gibraltar.

Why didn't the authorities immediately arrest Savage when they saw him there? Because there was serious doubt about his identity. "Officer N", the MI5 officer who watched the car arrive, was not sure that its driver, a young man wearing a black jacket, dark shirt, and denim jeans, was Savage. All he could report for certain was that the driver "had taken time and fiddled with something between the seats", before locking the car and walking south through the nearby Referendum Gate. From an observation post hidden in the Hambros Bank at the far end of the assembly area car park, Police Constable Albert Viagas was equally uncertain about the identity of the Renault's owner. Meanwhile, at the command post, the MI5 men who believed there might have been any danger relaxed after a watcher got up close to the man and reported back that he was *not* Savage.[9]

They must have relaxed – *must have* – because none of the MI5 officers at the headquarters told the police they were "helping" about Savage's arrival. Canepa was home eating lunch when Savage arrived. None of his special "advisors" thought to call him. And nobody told Deputy Commissioner

71

George Colombo, the Gibraltar police officer Canepa placed in charge, about Savage for over two hours.[10]

While Canepa enjoyed his siesta, Savage wandered about the town, walking first south and then north. On his heels were a number of MI5 watchers and plainclothes Gibraltar Police officers, all trying to determine who supposedly he was.

The first positive identification came around 2:00 p.m. "H", an MI5 operative, was standing near the Anglican Cathedral when the man from the white Renault passed on his way north toward the town centre. He confirmed that it was Savage and informed the operations centre that the IRA man had employed "anti-surveillance techniques" (i.e. he was using a newspaper to conceal the fact he was looking around him).[11]

Shortly after this, "Officer P" of the Gibraltar Police Special Branch independently identified the man as Savage. At one point, he even made eye-to-eye contact with him and noted that the suspect was using storefront windows to look behind him as well as other counter-surveillance measures.[12]

After those reports, the operations centre ordered N, the MI5 man who had first seen Savage arrive at the assembly area, to take a closer look at him. At 2:10 p.m., N informed his superiors that it was indeed Savage. Like the others, he noted that the IRA man was extremely alert and "trying to draw out stares".[13]

The next major event in the story took place twenty minutes later. Having parked their red Ford Fiesta a few hundred yards north of the border, McCann and Farrell crossed on foot into Gibraltar. The MI5 operatives on the frontier immediately saw the couple and began following them as they walked south toward the town. Like Savage, both wore casual clothes. McCann had on a white T-shirt, gray slacks, trainers, and a white cap, and Farrell wore a blue-gray jacket, white blouse, blue skirt, and shoes. She was also carrying a leather shoulder bag. It was the right way to be dressed that hot, clear afternoon.[14]

That weather was one of the things which would make

forthcoming events so memorable for both Gibraltar's residents and visitors. March 6 marked the beginning of spring that year in the Colony, the first day warm enough to enjoy the beaches. Besides the heat, there was the intensity of the light. The town of Gibraltar lies to the west of the Rock. In the afternoon, the sunshine beats down on it at double strength – directly from the sky and reflected off the waters in the bay it overlooks. This has a vivid effect. In the words of John D Stewart, the author of a social history of Gibraltar:

> The more light, the more colour. A grey stone in the sun [in Gibraltar] reminds you that gray is a mixture of colours. The light will find in it tints which we pay painters to find for us. Strong colours shriek in Gibraltar . . . [15]

Perhaps that was why the memories of the witnesses would be so vivid. Blood, after all, has a strong colour, and a great deal of it was about to stain the town's grey streets and footpaths.

In any case, just like Savage, McCann and Farrell appeared quite alert. "M", the watcher supervising the surveillance teams, noticed that Farrell was looking over her shoulder constantly. He also noted that when the couple was briefly held up at the airstrip because a plane was landing, McCann carefully studied everyone in his immediate area. [16]

Their appearance prompted Deputy Commissioner Colombo – still in the dark about Savage – to call Canepa at 2:30 p.m. to inform him about the Provisionals' appearance. The Commissioner remained at home.

By 2:50 p.m., McCann and Farrell had joined Savage down by the assembly area. From the Hambros Bank observation post, Officer Viagas heard on his radio that both suspects had been positively identified. With that, all of the indicators for an arrest were in place. There was a car at the assembly area, additional IRA operatives had entered the Colony, and now, they were walking north, looking like they were leaving.

Just before 3:00 p.m. at the operations centre, "Soldier F", the SAS commander, requested permission to take control of the situation. For that to take place, Colombo – finally briefed about Savage's presence in Gibraltar – would have to sign a document that read:

I have considered the terrorist situation in Gibraltar and have been fully briefed on the *military plan* [author's italics] with firearms. I request you proceed with the *military option* [author's italics] which may include the use of lethal force for the preservation of life.[17]

If Colombo signed it, the SAS could and would move against the IRA. But he hesitated and according to him, the SAS withdrew the request for operational control. The IRA trio were again walking south.[18] The crisis had passed. Colombo then rang up Canepa, updated him about the situation, and requested that he return to the command centre.

At this point in the official narrative, along with the police and MI5 officers, there were two teams of SAS men on the street, armed with Browning 9mm automatic pistols. Like the members of the ASU, all four soldiers wore casual clothing. Each had a small radio with a transmitter and receiver attached to his shirt collar. Using them, one man in the team listened to the operation's surveillance net while the other monitored the command net (where they received their orders).

Since noon, one SAS team – Soldiers A and B – had been standing by in a coffee shop not far from the Convent. Close to 3:00 p.m., they heard over the surveillance net that two suspected terrorists were walking south along Main Street toward the assembly area. A moment later, they received instructions to go to the Convent and meet up with their "Joe". They did so, and all three men went to a nearby shop where they were told again to wait.

The second pair of soldiers – C and D – had been waiting near Queen's Hotel and Trafalgar Cemetery, just south of the assembly area. Like everyone else, they heard over the radio that a car had been parked there and suspected members of the ASU were in Gibraltar. At 3:00 p.m., their commander notified them that the IRA members were walking in their direction and told them to see if they could identify them. Looking out from the cemetery, the SAS men had no trouble confirming that the three people were McCann, Savage, and Farrell. After reporting this, they received instructions to move away from the ASU and head north back to the airport.

Ten minutes later, the long-absent Canepa entered the operations room. After being updated by Colombo, the Commissioner told the SAS commander that he wanted a formal identification made of the suspects before he would allow the military to take control and make the arrest.

Months later, Colombo's and then Canepa's reluctance to authorize an arrest seemed particularly odd. For nearly forty minutes, the police, MI5, and the SAS had all been confirming that the trio were the Provos, but it still was not enough. Ian Jack, a Scottish journalist who followed the case closely, later wrote:

> What could have been troubling the commissioner? Wrongful arrest? Surely not; three badly scared tourists would have been the only result. Unless, of course, they were to be arrested in Lord Justice Gibson's sense of the word [i.e. shot to death].[19]

After returning to the assembly area at 3:25 p.m. and staring "hard" at the Renault, the suspects were walking north along Main Street. When they passed the candy store where Soldiers A and B were waiting with "their" policeman, Soldier A caught a fleeting glimpse of Farrell. Still under instructions to stay put, the SAS men heard over the surveillance net that Savage had split off from the other two and gone to the tourist office in the Piazza, the large square in the town centre. A few minutes later, he met up with McCann and Farrell, and all three resumed walking north along Line Wall Road.

# GIBRALTAR: MARCH 6, 1988

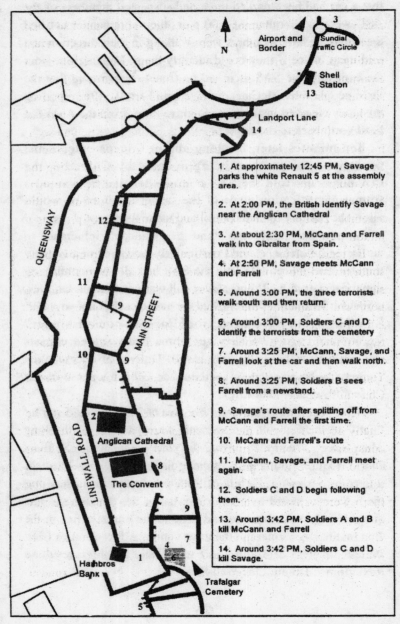

1. At approximately 12:45 PM, Savage parks the white Renault 5 at the assembly area.

2. At 2:00 PM, the British identify Savage near the Anglican Cathedral

3. At about 2:30 PM, McCann and Farrell walk into Gibraltar from Spain.

4. At 2:50 PM, Savage meets McCann and Farrell

5. Around 3:00 PM, the three terrorists walk south and then return.

6. Around 3:00 PM, Soldiers C and D identify the terrorists from the cemetery

7. Around 3:25 PM, McCann, Savage, and Farrell look at the car and then walk north.

8. Around 3:25 PM, Soldiers B sees Farrell from a newstand.

9. Savage's route after splitting off from McCann and Farrell the first time.

10. McCann and Farrell's route

11. McCann, Savage, and Farrell meet again.

12. Soldiers C and D begin following them.

13. Around 3:42 PM, Soldiers A and B kill McCann and Farrell

14. Around 3:42 PM, Soldiers C and D kill Savage.

The final act in the British account of events began at the command centre. There Commissioner Canepa had supposedly received a signed statement that the three individuals had been positively identified as McCann, Savage, and Farrell. After reading it, he ordered the operation's bomb disposal officer to examine the car parked in the assembly area. "Soldier G" returned just minutes later, out of breath, waving his arms over his head for silence. As instructed, he had performed a rapid technical inspection of the Renault. Based off what he had seen, he believed it should be treated as a suspect car-bomb. Somehow, when this was passed on to the SAS men stalking the IRA team, the word "suspect" dropped out of the report. Soldiers A, B, C, and D now *knew* there was a bomb at the assembly area just as they *knew* that the simple act of pressing a button would set it off.

By then, Soldiers C and D had received orders to move back south toward the Mobile Petrol station on Line Wall Road, the same street that McCann, Savage, and Farrell were walking north on. Meanwhile, the operations room gave Soldiers A and B instructions to leave the shop and go there as well. In just a few minutes, the two men passed through Casemate's Square and met with "Officer J", a female MI5 operative, by Landport Tunnel. Together, all three walked through it toward Winston Churchill Avenue.[20]

After receiving Soldier G's report about the Renault, he finally decided to have the Provisionals arrested on suspicion of conspiracy to commit murder. At 3:40 p.m., he signed over control to the SAS. A moment later, he turned to Colombo and told him to phone the Central Police Barracks to ensure that there were vehicles available to take the IRA members into custody. Colombo passed this order on to Officer John Goodman who was manning the switchboard there. The only available patrol car was the one being used by Inspector Luis Revagliatte. He and several others were in it out on routine patrol. Goodman radioed them with instructions to immediately return to headquarters.[21] It was 3:42 p.m.

A few minutes before, McCann, Savage, and Farrell had been walking north along Smith Dorrien Avenue with Soldiers C and D and "H", another watcher, trailing behind them. By the time the two SAS men learned they had permission to apprehend the suspects, the IRA members had reached Winston Churchill Avenue.

Soldiers A and B entered the street then as well. Fifty yards away on the right-hand side of the road, they could see the IRA members standing opposite its intersection with Smith Dorrien, talking and laughing. Some distance behind them, C and D were visible. After checking with the command centre to make sure that they still had control, Soldiers A and B moved toward the Provisionals to arrest them.

Then, their quarry gave a sign that they knew they were being watched. H saw all three IRA members take a hard look at the area around them. After this, Savage again split away from McCann and Farrell, walking south back toward town, brushing up against Soldier A as he passed him. He and his partner, Soldier B, thought about arresting Savage on the spot but decided to continue closing in on the targets in front of them. They would leave Savage to the other SAS team. Seconds later, with McCann on the right and Farrell on the left, the couple drew even with the Shell Petrol Station on the eastern side of Winston Churchill Avenue. The two SAS men (A and B) were only a few yards behind them. Meanwhile, from the corner of Smith Dorrien and Corral Road, Soldiers C and D saw Savage move south down Landport Lane. Walking quickly, they easily caught up with him.

At this point, fate decided to intervene in the situation. Held up by heavy traffic at the pedestrian crossing along Smith Dorrien not far from its intersection with Winston Churchill Avenue was Inspector Revagliatte's patrol car. Besides the

78

Inspector, there were three other uniformed police officers in the vehicle. According to Revagliatte all four had been on routine patrol duties since 1:50 p.m. and knew nothing about Operation Flavius. When Goodman's radio call to return to the police headquarters came in, they had no idea what it was about. After learning that it was "urgent", Revagliatte ordered his driver, Clive Borell, to drive up the wrong side of Smith Dorrien and onto Winston Churchill Avenue. From there, they would move to the roundabout by the sundial 150 yards to the north and come back into town. When he pulled the vehicle out of the traffic flow, to warn other drivers, Borell switched on the police siren. It rang out just as Soldiers A and B were about to shout out a command to McCann and Farrell to surrender.[22]

In this alleged sequence of events Revagliatte's siren spurred the killings. Startled by the sudden noise, McCann looked behind him and saw Soldier A. For the SAS man, it was a terrifying moment, something he tried to stress when questioned months later by Felix Pizzarello, the coroner at the inquest held into the Provisionals' deaths.

"So, McCann looks back?" Pizzarello asked.

"Over his shoulder," the soldier agreed.

"And what happened then?"

"He had a smile on his face and he looked over, and he looked straight at me, sir. We literally had what I would call eye-to-eye contact. We looked directly at each other, and the smile went off McCann's face, and – it's hard to describe – it's almost like McCann had a realization of . . . who I was, or [that] I was a threat to him. The look on his face was of alertness, and he was very aware. So this came over his face, and at that stage then I was going to shout a warning to stop."

"You were going to shout?"

Soldier A continued, "Yes, and at the same time I was drawing my pistol . . . I went to shout "Stop!" and *the events overtook the warning* [author's italics]. The look on McCann's face, the alertness, the awareness of him, he looked at me, then all of a sudden, his right arm, right elbow . . . moved aggressively across the front of his body, sir. At that stage there, I thought the man was definitely going to go for *the button* [author's italics]. Uppermost in my mind at that stage . . ."

"The button or a gun?" Pizzarello broke in.

It was the button. Soldier A was convinced that McCann was about commit an act that would kill hundreds of people.

So moving forward with Soldier B at a "brisk pace", he shot McCann once in the back and then saw, "Farrell had a bag under her left armpit at this stage. She had . . . moved to the right and was grabbing the bag."

"To the right? That means she was turning inwards towards McCann?" said Pizzarello.

"Correct, sir, just half a turn. I thought she was also going for *the button* . . ."

Soldier A's reaction to this was to shoot her once in the back as well. A split second later, he turned back to McCann.

"I then engaged [the man] with a further three rounds, sir, one to the body and two to the head. He was falling all the time."

Pizzarello was confused, "One to the back of the head?"

"Correct."

"In that order?"

"Yes, in that order. McCann then fell down. He was on the ground, and his hands were away from his body. At the same stage, Farrell was now on the ground. At no time . . . did I hear Soldier B firing. In fact, I thought at that time I was the only person who had in fact fired."[23]

Although Soldier A did not know it until he stopped shooting, Soldier B had reached the same conclusions he had and reacted much the same way or at least he would later testify to that effect. Directly behind Farrell, he shot her twice in the back, before snapping off one or two rounds at McCann. He then brought his pistol back to bear on his original target and put three more bullets into the young woman's body, stopping immediately after she fell to the ground.[24]

It was now Savage's turn. Soldiers C and D had been only a few feet behind him the moment gunfire erupted to their north at the Shell Station. Soldier C's testimony about those events painted an unbearably tense picture.

"There [were] a lot of people coming toward us. We had [permission] to effect the arrest. My intention at this stage was to effect the arrest, but as I was moving forward, there were shots to my left rear," he testified months later.[25]

The SAS men did not look back and see McCann and Farrell crumpling to the ground on Winston Churchill Avenue. For all they knew, the terrorists there had murdered Soldiers A and B. All of their attention was locked on Savage, the explosives expert, the man they "knew" had just parked a radio-detonated car-bomb at the assembly area.

According to Soldier C, Savage's reaction to the gunshots killed him.

"Savage spun round very fast. As he spun round, I shouted 'Stop.' At the same time, I was shouting 'Stop,' he went down with his right arm to the area of his jacket pocket."[26]

That did it. The Provo was going for a button. The SAS men opened fire. From close range, both shot Savage – C six times and D nine. While nearby pedestrians screamed and dived for cover, the soldiers' bullets ripped into Savage, spinning him around like a top. Seconds later, the young man from Belfast crashed to the street, dead.[27]

What had it been like for Daniel McCann, Seán Savage, and Mairéad Farrell those last few minutes before they died? For most of the time they were in Gibraltar, the town must have seemed as it should be, filled with locals and carefree tourists, certainly nothing to be alarmed about. As they wandered about the Rock, the IRA team might have even enjoyed the history and scenery that was all around them – recognizing, of course, that it was nothing more than a monument to British "imperialism".

Perhaps it was Savage, later described by his friends in the Republican Movement as quite security-conscious, who noticed it first – that there were simply too many fit young men dressed in casual summer clothing always wandering not too far away from them. Soldiers, even ones in plainclothes, tend to stand out in a crowd, particularly when they are non-Hispanics in a very Latin setting. Anyway, Savage's walking south away from McCann and Farrell was the surest sign that the Provisionals knew they were being watched. Splitting up after realizing something like that would make sense; it would divide the surveillance target.[28]

The Provisionals' realisation that they were under surveillance would also explain why Farrell kept glancing over her shoulder as she and McCann moved north along Winston Churchill Avenue. She might have been trying to decide if she had seen the two men strolling behind her – Soldiers A and B – before when she had been down by the Convent.

And then the police siren, a loud, shrill sound, must have cut through their thoughts like a knife. What did McCann, Savage, and Farrell feel then? Shock? Excitement? Did they even hear the strangled shouts that might have been commands to stop? Did Savage hear the screams from Gibraltarian children in the nearby playground as he was shot? Did McCann or Farrell realize at least two women were watching them die from the windows of apartment buildings that overlooked the petrol station?

As for the gunshots, McCann would have known what they were. He had used a pistol far too often not to. The bullets striking him and Farrell would have felt like great hammer blows as they ripped into their bodies. After the first hit, they probably were only dimly aware of the rest if they were aware of them at all.

As for Savage, almost three hundred feet to the south on

Landport Lane, he would not have had the time to realize was happening to him. He had heard the shots to his north and looked back – like anyone would – to see two men pointing guns at him. The last thing he possibly registered were the flash and sound of the first bullets they fired at him.

By their own testimony after the shooting stopped, the soldiers immediately donned berets to identify themselves as members of the security forces. Uniformed and plainclothes police converged at both crime scenes from almost every direction. Inspector Revagliatte was one of the first to arrive. He heard the gunfire when his car passed the Shell Station. Seeking to get out of line of fire, he had his driver speed north up to the roundabout and come back down again to park opposite where McCann and Farrell lay bleeding on the footpath. He and his men sprang out of the car and rushed across the street, jumping over the fence that divided the four-lane highway. After learning that the gunmen standing over the bodies were plainclothes soldiers, Revagliatte took charge and began directing his officers to block off traffic from the area. A few minutes later, a police car took Soldiers A and B away from the area while Soldiers C and D left on foot. Back at the operations centre, at 4:05 p.m., the SAS commander passed a document to Commissioner Canepa which stated:

A *military assault force* [author's italics] completed the *military option* [author's emphasis] in respect of the terrorist ASU in Gibraltar and returns control to the civil power.[29] It was over. Or was it?

## Notes

1. "Power behind the Scene", *Guardian*, September 5, 1988; Mary Holland, Simon de Bruxelles and Ian Mather, "IRA Hunts Top Level Mole," *Observer*, March 13, 1988. It is worth noting that in his own memoirs, Sir Geoffrey Howe states that he authorized the SAS presence in Gibraltar. This would have been at the direction of Mrs Thatcher.
2. James Adams, Robin Morgan and Anthony Bambridge, *Ambush: the War Between the SAS and the IRA*, Pan Books Ltd, London, 1988, p. 146. Many of

these individuals – particularly the MI5 watchers – had been on the Rock for weeks. According to various reports, the SAS team flew to Gibraltar on March 2, 1988 although it had been alerted to go at least once before.

3. Simon O'Dwyer-Russell, Donald Macintyre and Walter Ellis, "A Job for the SAS", *Sunday Telegraph*, March 13, 1988; "Rules Laid Down for SAS Action", *Independent*, January 10, 1989; copy of the Rules of Engagement distributed to the press at the Gibraltar Inquest.

4. This command centre was probably in Sir Peter Terry's offices.

5. Michael O'Higgins and John Waters, "The Anatomy of an Afternoon", *Magill*, October 1988, p. 25.

6. Jack, "Gibraltar", p. 26.

7. To protect themselves against possible retaliation from the IRA, the MI5, SAS and Special Branch operatives involved in the operation were identified by letters of the alphabet at the inquest.

8. Jack, p. 56.

9. O'Higgins and Waters, "Anatomy of an Afternoon", p. 28.

10. Jack, p. 58 and testimony of George Colombo, Day 9, the Gibraltar Inquest, September 16, 1988, p. 89, Channel Four Television.

11. Testimony of Witness H, the Gibraltar Inquest, Day 8, September 15, 1988, Channel Four Television, 1988, pp. 93-94.

12. O'Higgins and Waters, p. 28.

13. Testimony of Witness N, the Gibraltar Inquest, Day 9, September 16, 1988, Channel Four Television, 1988, p. 67.

14. O'Higgins and Waters, p. 29.

15. John D Stewart, *Gibraltar: The Keystone*, John Murray, London, 1967, p.13.

16. Testimony of Witness M, the Gibraltar Inquest, Day 8, September 15, 1988, Channel Four Television, 1988, pp. 80-82.

17. O'Higgins and Waters, p. 29; multiple citations from the inquest transcript.

18. Jack, "Gibraltar", pp. 58-60.

19. Ibid.

20. O'Higgins and Waters, p. 30.

21. Ibid, p. 31.

22. Jack, "Gibraltar", pp. 77-78.

23. Testimony of Soldier A, the Gibraltar Inquest, Day 6, September 13, 1988, Channel Four Television, 1988, pp. 82-85.

24. Jack, "Gibraltar", pp. 67-68.

25. Testimony of Soldier C, the Gibraltar Inquest, Day 7, September 14, 1988, Channel Four Television, 1988, p. 100.

26. Ibid.

27. Jack, "Gibraltar", pp. 67-70.

28. Interview with Ed Moloney, northern editor of the *Sunday Tribune*, Belfast, June 1996.

29. Jack, p. 59.

# CHAPTER SIX

## SHOCKWAVES

"When the IRA is down, you can always count on the British to give them a helping hand."
— Dr Joe Hendron, MP, Social Democratic Labor Party, March 1988

The Gibraltarians who didn't actually see McCann, Savage, and Farrell die did not have to look very hard to realize something extraordinary had just happened in their little town. They only had to glance out their windows to see the police barricades closing off Main Street and the ambulances parked by the Shell Petrol Station and on Landport Lane. It was a bit too much for them to grasp. In a place where murder was a crime usually only seen on American television shows, one person being shot dead would have been remarkable, but three was incredible.

Beginning at 4:05 p.m., Gibraltar's astonishment turned into fear when grim-faced police officers began ordering people living around the Convent to evacuate their homes. Hysteria spread among the locals when they saw soldiers clad in body armor and helmets on the streets searching for – a car-bomb? The tension only lessened four hours later. Word went out that a bomb had been dealt with, and the sight of an Army truck towing a white car from the assembly area car park appeared to bear this out. Gibraltar was safe.

With this chaotic scene, hardly anyone noticed a number

of young men checking out of the posh Rock Hotel that evening. Making their way quickly to the airport which divides the Colony, they boarded an RAF C130 "Hercules" transport plane that had been sitting idly on the airstrip all day. After the last of them embarked, the transport plane taxied down the darkened runway and took off, banking north. Without any running lights on, it was invisible in the night sky. Onboard, the passengers, members of the SAS Special Projects Team, settled down for the flight ahead of them.[1] The soldiers did not know it at the time, but some of them would be seeing the Rock again but under very different circumstances.

Even before the SAS men began their journey home, a series of "definitive" news flashes about what had happened on the Rock had filtered through to the outside world. What distinguished these reports was their total inaccuracy. At 4:45 p.m., the Ministry of Defense (MoD) issued a terse press release, stating, "A suspected bomb has been found in Gibraltar, and three suspects have been shot by civilian police." At 9:00 p.m., it gave out the first of several "corrections", now saying, "Security forces were involved in the shootings, and military personnel dealt with the suspect bomb." Also at 9:00 p.m., the venerable British Broadcasting Corporation (BBC) informed television viewers that "[the terrorists] were challenged by, it appears, plain-clothed policemen . . . Then [a] shootout happened." A quarter of an hour later, the Independent Television Network (ITN) reported that "A fierce gun battle broke out".

By then, an IRA casualty notification team had already performed its unpleasant duty. At 7:00 p.m., a knock had come at the door of the Farrell family's home, Mrs Farrell opened it thinking that it was Mairéad, back from Dublin. Instead, standing in the hallway were a man and woman. "What is it?" she had asked. "It's Mairéad," the man answered. Upon hearing those two words, Mrs Farrell began to sob uncontrollably. Her daughter would not be coming back to her.[2]

Meanwhile, the British media continued to spoon-feed the British public an increasingly inaccurate version of the killings. On March 7, speaking on the BBC radio news program Today, correspondent Joe Paley provided additional "details" about the incident for his listeners. The authorities had found a bomb in Gibraltar, one "packed with bits of metal [and] shrapnel". Later on in the same show, Ian Stewart, the government's Minister for the Armed Forces, stated unequivocally: "Military personnel were involved. There was a car-bomb found, which has been defused."[3] All eleven British daily newspapers reported that as a fact. Eight of them had the weight of the explosives discovered as 500 pounds. In each case, the reporters' sources had been MI5 and the MoD.[4]

Several hours later, the IRA weighed in with two public statements acknowledging that McCann, Savage, and Farrell had been on active service in Gibraltar and had "access and control over" 140 pounds of semtex high explosives. The Provisionals made the admission about the semtex because they believed that the car-bomb in Marbella had been found and the British were simply exaggerating its size for propaganda effect. As they would soon discover, the British and Spanish had not found the car-bomb and would not do so until March 8.

For people like Roger Bolton, the editor of Thames Television's investigative journalism programme *This Week*, what he was hearing on the news made it all appear fairly cut and dried. As he said in his memoirs, "It didn't seem to me that there was much in it for [my program] . . . Most people would think that the terrorists deserved what they got. I didn't disagree."[5]

Then, at 3:30 p.m. March 7, Sir Geoffrey Howe, the British

Foreign Secretary, entered the House of Commons in London and gave a short statement about what had happened to the ASU. It was a version of events that the Thatcher Administration would stubbornly cling to in the months ahead despite the avalanche of contradictions that would engulf it:[6]

> Shortly before 1:00 p.m. yesterday afternoon, [Savage] brought a white Renault car into Gibraltar and was seen to park it in the area where the band for the guard-mounting ceremony assembles. Before leaving the car, he was seen to spend some time making adjustments in the vehicle.
>
> An hour and a half later, [McCann and Farrell] were seen to enter Gibraltar on foot and shortly before 3:00 p.m. joined [Savage] in the town. Their presence and actions near the parked Renault car gave rise to strong suspicion that it contained a bomb, which appeared to be corroborated by a rapid technical examination of the car.
>
> About 3:30 p.m., all three left the scene and started to walk back towards the border. On their way towards the border, they were challenged by the Security forces. When challenged, they made movements which led the military personnel, operating in support of the Gibraltar Police, to conclude that their own lives and the lives of others were under threat. In the light of this response, they were shot. Those killed were subsequently found *not to have been carrying arms* [author's italics]."
>
> The parked Renault car was subsequently dealt with by a military bomb-disposal team. It has now been established that *it did not contain an explosive device*. [author's italics]

Sir Geoffrey must have lowered his voice when he said that last bit about there being no bomb. It was either that or the news stories provided by "official sources" about the "massive car-

88

bomb" had been so pervasive, so detailed that George Robertson, Howe's counterpart in the Labor Party, still believed that the IRA team had brought explosives into Gibraltar. Rising after his colleague sat down, he congratulated Mrs Thatcher's government for its victory, saying, "The very fact that this enormous potential car-bomb was placed opposite both an old folks' home and a school [underlines] the cynical hypocrisy of the IRA".[7]

Such was the emotion of the moment that no one in Parliament bothered to ask Howe or Robertson exactly what an "enormous potential car-bomb" was.

For Bolton, reading Howe's speech off a news prompter in his office, the assorted revelations "put a very different perspective on the whole matter."[8] What sort of suspicious movements could three unarmed members of the IRA have made to provoke their deaths? And why would they make them? At this stage, no one had said anything about the soldiers' supposed fears of a radio-triggered explosion. And if the authorities were so afraid of a bomb explosion, why did they fail to evacuate the Gibraltar town centre until nearly half an hour after the Provos were shot?

It wasn't just one thing about the killings. It was everything. Bolton felt there was a story lurking behind the question marks. By March 8, Julian Manyon and Chris Oxley, two of his best journalists, were on their way to Gibraltar.

In London, the jubilant mood lingered despite Howe's statement. Leading the cheers for the SAS were Fleet Street's tabloids celebrating the Provos' deaths in their headlines and with a *Daily Express* article about Farrell describing her as a "QUEEN OF TERROR, WEANED ON HATE".

Meanwhile in Belfast, the task of bringing the bodies home from Gibraltar for burial fell to Joe Austin, a senior member of Sinn Féin. He had been a close friend of all three of what the

Republican Movement was now calling "the Gibraltar Martyrs". Seán Savage had even dropped by his home to chat the day before he left Belfast on his mission.[9]

Austin remembered March 6, 1988 as the beginning of a three-week-long nightmare, one that got progressively worse after he and Terence Farrell, one of Mairéad's five brothers, flew to Malaga on March 9 and drove to Gibraltar.

Definitely unwelcome there, the two stayed just long enough to identify the bodies before returning to Linea de la Concepcion, the Spanish town adjacent to the Colony. From there, they began to make arrangements to have McCann, Savage, and Farrell brought home. Yet the two men quickly learned that Gibraltar's only commercial flight connection was to London. Shipping the coffins to Belfast by that route was unthinkable to Terence Farrell, not because (as some news stories claimed) his family objected to having Mairéad's body brought onto British soil. That, Terence angrily explained was "a total misrepresentation". He simply did not want to get "stuck there at [London] with three coffins, surrounded by Special Branch officers and the Press." Not a member of Sinn Féin or even interested in politics, all he wanted to do was take care of his sister's remains.[12]

That task proved harder than he and Austin could have ever thought possible. Each Irish airline and charter company they contacted refused to provide a special flight from Gibraltar to Dublin on such short notice. The reasons cited were always technical ones, but it was obvious that the companies wanted nothing to do with something so controversial. Finally, a British firm agreed to take the contract (receiving a payment of £25,000 from Sinn Féin). Landing in Gibraltar on the afternoon of March 14, its BAC-111 jet quickly taxied over to the military section of the airport where the bodies had been kept in a warehouse. Since none of the civilian airport workers would touch the caskets, the RAF used a forklift to load them into the plane. A few minutes later, driven to the scene by "Security Personnel", Joe Austin climbed into the jet, and it took off for Dublin.[13] Daniel McCann, Seán Savage, and Mairéad Farrell's protracted stay in Gibraltar had come to an end.[14]

A crowd over two thousand strong was on hand to greet the plane as it touched down in Dublin in the driving rain at 4:40 p.m. For the British television viewers who watched the scene on the evening news, it was an appalling sight, hundreds of people welcoming back the bodies of three would-be murderers.

Yet not all those standing on the tarmac were Republican sympathizers. Gibraltar had struck a very raw nerve for the Irish people in general. For centuries, the British had been dealing with Ireland whatever way they deemed expedient, regardless of Irish feelings and sensibilities.

That had been particularly evident during early 1988. On January 26, brushing aside Dublin's protests, the British government announced on "national security" grounds that it would not prosecute RUC officers who covered up the circumstances of the killing of five unarmed IRA and INLA men and one civilian in 1982. Two days later, despite strong evidence that they were innocent, the Court of Appeal in London upheld the convictions of six Irish men who received life sentences for taking part in the infamous 1974 Birmingham pub bombings. On February 21, a British soldier "accidentally" shot Aidan McAnespie in the back in broad daylight at a border checkpoint. McAnespie, a highly popular member of Sinn Féin, had been unarmed and on his way to a Gaelic football match. Just two days after that, Ireland learned that Private Ian Thain, the only British soldier to receive a life sentence for murdering a Northern Irish Catholic, had walked out of jail after serving just two years of his sentence. Throughout his imprisonment, the British Army had kept Thain on its active rolls and, on his release, sent him back to his regiment.[15]

Now had come Gibraltar, as a fresh irritant. One onlooker, Neil Blaney TD, said, "I have come here out of respect for the people who were killed, and to express sympathies for the relatives, and to protest at the brutality with which they were exterminated like vermin."[16]

While the crowd stood in respectful silence, the coffins were taken off the plane and into a nearby mortuary. There, with the friends and family of the slain watching, a priest said prayers for the dead. After this short ceremony, the pallbearers draped the caskets with Irish tricolours and placed them into three waiting hearses. At 5:45 p.m., followed by dozens of cars carrying mourners and the press, the black cars began the long drive to Belfast.

It would not be a peaceful evening. Several hours after the cortege set out from Dublin, there was a gruesome incident in Belfast near Savage's home in Downfine Gardens. The RUC and Army had flooded the neighbourhood with men to prevent the Provisionals from putting on any kind of display to honour their fallen comrade. The presence of so many police and soldiers proved irresistible to Kevin McCracken, a local IRA man, and he went out looking for a target. But soldiers on a nearby rooftop saw him first and shot him. An elderly woman passing by claimed that afterwards, the troops surrounded McCracken's body, kicking and beating him with their weapons. By the time an ambulance got McCracken to the hospital, he had bled to death.[17] The doctors examining his corpse noted it had bruises around the neck and body.

Meanwhile, as the cortege wended its way north through

town after town in the Republic, the scenes it encountered were always the same: black flags of mourning hanging from telephone poles and electricity pylons and onlookers lining the streets, many carrying flags as well. When the procession crossed the border into the North, it was no longer in such friendly territory. Waiting for it were hundreds of police and British soldiers, determined to prevent the IRA from using the funeral procession as a propaganda exercise. Up to fifty RUC Land Rovers cut into the long line of cars and at least ten security vehicles surrounded each hearse. When the police insisted on keeping a twenty-minute interval between them, the hostility between the mourners and the authorities grew. According to Sinn Féin funeral stewards, RUC vehicles rammed Savage's hearse twice.[18]

Moving through Newry, the cortege had to drive through a number of Protestant neighborhoods. For those living there, the procession was an obscenity – murdering rebels being feted by other murdering rebels. They did not greet the hearses with cheers, but pelted them with bottles, bricks, and anything else that came to hand, breaking a number of windows but mercifully not injuring anyone.[19]

Clearing Newry at 1:00 a.m., the procession proceeded up the M1 Coachway to Belfast. The bitter confrontations between the police and the mourners continued, and at one point, an RUC Land Rover forced a reporter's car off the road.

Despite the late hour, there were still over 4,000 Republicans waiting to claim their dead near the Andersonstown exit of the highway. The RUC had no intention of allowing them to do this. On the outskirts of the city, in an act that Sinn Féin would call a hijacking, the police closed the road to all vehicles except the hearses and the cars carrying relatives of the dead. Each coffin, still under heavy guard, went by separate routes to the McCann, Savage, and Farrell homes.

The marathon procession had been a new low in the so-called "Battle of the Funerals", a series of clashes between the police and mourners at IRA funerals. For years, the Republican Movement had used the occasions to put on shows of strength for the general population. These took the form of masked honour guards appearing at the grave sides and firing shots in the air as a salute. Then, as bystanders held up umbrellas to block the view of watching soldiers and police, the gunmen would melt into the crowd.

Such gestures of defiance were extremely embarrassing for the authorities. In recent months, RUC officers had taken to charging in to apprehend the gunmen the moment they appeared. Doing so led to ugly scuffles between the police and mourners. Sinn Féin found it easy to claim that the authorities had no respect for the dead and were little more than bigoted ghouls.

In time, the firing parties triggered a reaction from the Catholic Church. Never friends of the Republican Movement, the IRA's use of solemn religious ceremony deeply offended the hierarchy (particularly when one firing party hid its weapons in confession boxes). Some months before Gibraltar, the Church had persuaded the Provo leadership, many of them devout Catholics, to halt the practice of firing shots at burials. In response to guarantees that this policy would be upheld for the Gibraltar dead, the RUC agreed to maintain a minimal presence at their funerals. The bargain was more or less sealed on March 15, the eve of the funerals, when the police reassured the McCann, Savage, and Farrell families that they could bury their dead in peace.

Yet that was not to be. While well intentioned, the RUC's decision to step back was a recipe for disaster. The propaganda the IRA was making out of the Gibraltar incident had infuriated the hard-line Loyalist community. Whether they knew it or not, by failing to put a security cordon around the funerals, the authorities were gambling that members of the Ulster Defense Association (UDA) and Ulster Volunteer Force (UVF) would not take advantage of the situation and attack the mourners. On the afternoon of March 16, 1988, that was a gamble that the RUC lost.[20]

But even before the killing started in Milltown Cemetery, anyone could have seen what was taking place there was no ordinary funeral. The size of the cortege alone would have given that away. It stretched for almost a mile, with thousands of men, women, and children, many dressed in their Sunday best, streaming into the graveyard. From each side of the procession, dozens of reporters from news agencies around the world watched the scene. Television camera operators jostled each other for space, each trying to catch the most poignant shot of the mourners.

At the head of the cortege, flanked by two long lines of stewards was the funeral party. Leading it were three pipers, in sombre attire, playing "The Minstrel Boy," a martial tune that seemed to rise through the cold air toward the Army helicopter hovering high above.[21] Then came three hearses, each bearing a simple coffin, with an Irish tricolour on the lid. Behind them, walked the McCann, Savage, and Farrell families and friends, their faces masks of grief.[22]

Like a great snake, the procession slowly moved across Milltown's weedy fields. At length, the crowd halted and began to gather around the Provisionals' funeral ground, a small raised plot roped off that morning with yellow cord. Looking across it, the mourners could see two rows of small stone markers and a fresh grave, dug to accommodate three caskets.

With all eyes fixed on the ceremonies, no one noticed the man standing at the edge of the funeral plot who never stopped staring at the scene unfolding before him. Dressed in a heavy blue anorak, jeans, and wearing a gray knit cap, he was powerfully built with a thick, brutal face framed by unruly black hair. Right then, he had the look of a man entranced, caught half-way between awe and hatred. It almost seemed as if he envied those being put into the earth that cold day in Belfast.[23]

After the pallbearers lowered Mairéad Farrell's coffin into the ground, the man shifted his gaze to Martin McGuiness, Gerry Adams and the other Republican leaders waiting to speak by the grave. His face lost its previous dreaminess and took on a more grim expression, one that belonged on that of a soldier aiming a weapon at an enemy. Then, in a twinkling of an eye, he unbuttoned his anorak and shirt and reached into the crude pouch strapped across his chest. A moment later, he produced two hand grenades. Pulling their pins, he hurled both in the direction of the grave.

At first, the mourners had no idea what had just happened. Hardly anyone noticed the two small black objects arc over their heads. Yet the crowd's mood swiftly changed when those standing nearest to the man noticed that he now had an automatic pistol in his right hand and was advancing toward the funeral plot.

Screams split the air after the grenades exploded. The blasts from each tore into the packed assembly, driving shrapnel and fragments from nearby gravestones like tiny spears into the mourners. In the middle of all the panic, the man levelled his pistol at the solid mass of bodies that were desperately twisting away from him and convulsively squeezed its trigger.[24]

Interviewed about it later, he would claim he was trying to

kill Adams and the rest of the Republican leadership. But that was not the way one IRA man saw it:

He was firing into the crowd and wasn't looking for a specific target. He just wanted to kill Catholics – if they were Republicans, then it was a bonus. If he hit the leadership people, then it was ten free points. There was no sense of who he wanted. He just fired into the massive crowd and just wanted to kill people.[25]

In any event, the killer missed Adams, McGuiness, and the others. Ignoring the stones people began to hurl at him, he turned and trotted away toward the nearby highway.

At first, it seemed he would easily escape. There were no police to stop him. Yet urged on by those he tried to kill, a group of young men began following him, jumping from gravestone to gravestone for cover and shouting "Orange bastard!" at the man's back.[26]

Their taunts may have struck a nerve. Several times, the man turned on the crowd following him, screaming things like "Catch me if you can, you Fenian fuckers!" Sometimes, he added a grenade or burst of shots to the epithets. It was like a dance of death. Each time, the gunman spun around, the mob would scatter behind the nearest stone markers or throw themselves flat on the ground.[27] But that did not save two of them. John Murray died when the man shot him in the neck. Funeral steward Kevin Brady bled to death when a bullet tore through his body, lacerating his arteries.

Caught up in his bizarre game with the crowd, the killer did not notice the two young mourners running from the cemetery's gate until they were only yards away from him. Yet at the last moment, he saw the threat they posed. He fired his pistol at Thomas McErlean, the nearest of his new assailants. The bullet smashed through the young man's shoulder and into his chest cavity. He sank to the ground, blood streaming from his nose and mouth, his eyes already turning glassy with death.[28]

Finally, the killer reached the roadway, and waved his pistols at the cars whizzing by him, trying to force one to stop. None did.[29] So again he turned to face his pursuers. Screaming curses at them, he hurled his last grenade in their direction. As before, the shrapnel scattered the crowd, but there was no stopping its advance now. Realizing this, the man put his pistols on the ground. Almost nonchalantly, he turned and began strolling along the highway as if completely oblivious to the cries of rage of the mob behind him.

With an almost inhuman roar, the mob engulfed the man, beating him to the ground with fists, rocks, and clubs. He did not remain at its mercy for long. A small group of men seized him and threw him into a small car that had sped to the scene. He quickly found himself spread-eagled across its back seat with two IRA men keeping him pinned there. Only half-dazed by the beating he had received, he could hear his captors discuss his fate. One suggested that they "take a pliers to his balls" and find out who he worked for. Another, more direct in approach, simply said they should shoot him in the head, then and there.[30]

It was at this point that the police, long absent from the scene, began moving into Milltown in force. Seeing them approach, the men in the car hurled the murderer from their vehicle and roared off. Seething with hatred, the waiting crowd closed over his prostrate body.

When they finally entered the area around the cemetery, the police found what one officer later described as a "scene of chaos".[31] There was a crowd of almost three hundred people on the road and by the cemetery's entrance. Cars were speeding down the highway's median strip, their drivers frantically trying to avoid the stones some of the rioters were hurling at them.

It did not take the RUC long to discover the location of the man responsible for this mayhem. He was lying on the ground in front of the crowd. Six men were circling around his body, kicking and striking him with their fists. Drawing their guns, two officers ran to the scene. Slowly, unwillingly, the mob retreated, spitting and hurling stones and abuse at what it perceived as the assassin's friends. All the while, its members fiercely chanted over and over again, "I-R-A!! I-R-A!! I-R-A!!"

A few minutes later, more police converged on the site and formed a protective wall between the crowd and its prey. Anxiously looking around for signs of snipers, the officers placed their prisoner in the back of a Land Rover. Just before it began to move, the man blinked his eyes and asked, "How many of the bastards did I get?"[33]

The murderer in the custody of the RUC was Michael "Flint" Stone, a self-described "dedicated, free-lance, Loyalist paramilitary" on the fringes of the UDA and UVF. Miraculously, no one died after the grenades he threw at the funeral plot exploded. Instead, he only managed to wound dozens of ordinary civilians (including women and children) present at the ceremony. The three people Stone did kill had been among his pursuers and had died from gunshot wounds. Only Kevin Brady had belonged to the IRA.

Nevertheless, Stone's attack was unprecedented, and it terrified Catholics. Now, more than ever, they felt they were targets – by law and by gun. As Cardinal Cahal Daly, Archbishop of Armagh and Primate of All Ireland, recollected,

There was great fear, amounting to panic, in the community. It was seen as an indiscriminate attack on the whole community . . . [They were] . . . particularly atrocious murder[s]. The indiscriminate nature of [Stone's] attack and

99

the fact grenades were used with all their potential for widespread wounding and maiming and killing, that had a terrifying impact.[34]

Adding to the panic were the IRA's claims that it had been the police who had sent Stone into the cemetery.[35] The paranoia those allegations generated along with all the fear and anger welling up in the community would lead to an act three days later that many would say was the single most violent event of the Troubles and one with unimaginable consequences.

## Notes

1. "The Day Gibraltar Stood Still", *Panorama*, March 15, 1988, p. 3.
2. Taylor, p. 42.
3. Roger Bolton, pp. 189-190; Jack, pp. 19-20.
4. "Rock Bottom", *A Private Eye* Report, February 1989, p. 1.
5. Bolton, p. 190.
6. "Northern Ireland: IRA Terrorists, Gibraltar", British Information Services, March 8, 1988.
7. Jack, pp. 20-21.
8. Bolton, p. 191.
9. Interview with Joe Austin, Belfast, June, 1996.
10. Ibid.
11. Ibid.
12. "Three IRA Dead to be Flown Home on Monday", *Independent*, March 11, 1988.
13. Terence Farrell travelled home by a flight out of Malaga.
14. "IRA Bodies Flown to Dublin", *Panorama*, March 15, 1988.
15. Murray, pp. 396-397.
16. Tony Curry, Peter Makem, Patsy McArdle, Joyce Buggy and Fabian Boyle, "Confusion as IRA Trio are Brought Home",*Irish News*, March 15, 1988. Neil Blaney was dismissed from his government post during the Arms Crisis of 1970. He was involved in the formation of the Provisional IRA and during the cease-fire (1994-96) called on the Provisionals not to decommission their weapons.
17. Frank Connolly, "Death without End", *Magill*, April 1988, pp. 13-14.
18. "Confusion as IRA Trio is Brought Home", Irish News, March 15, 1988 by Tony Curry, Peter Makem, Patsy McArdle, Joyce Buggy and Fabian Boyle.
19. "Protestants Jeer March for IRA Dead", *Chicago Tribune*, March 15, 1988.
20. "IRA Pledge Silence," *Newsday*, March 13, 1988. The IRA had publicly

promised not to put on any paramilitary display at the funerals.

21. Francis X Clines, "Gunman Terrorises Belfast crowd at Rites for 3 Guerrillas", *New York Times*, March 17, 1988.

22. Tony Curry, "Thousands in Last Tribute to Gib Victims", the *Irish News*, March 17, 1988.

23. Martin Dillon, *Stone Cold: The True Story of Michael Stone and the Milltown Massacre*, Random House, London, 1993, pp. 150-157. When interviewed by Martin Dillon, Stone specifically said, "I saw the cortege and I was fascinated . . . I don't know what happened. I was so preoccupied I almost forgot why I was there. It was as if everything had stopped . . . I knew that if I was killed on active service I would like to know I would be given all the trappings they were receiving."

24. Ibid.

25. Peter Taylor, *Provos: the IRA and Sinn Féin*, Bloomsbury, London, 1997, p. 299.

26. Dillon, *Stone Cold* and other sources.

27. Ibid.

28. Ibid.

29. David McKittrick and Heather Mills, "Funeral Assassin Kills Three", *Independent*, March 17, 1988.

30. Dillon, *Stone Cold,* p. 158.

31. Ibid, p. 164.

32. Ibid.

33. Cran.

34. Clines.

# CHAPTER SEVEN

## SOMEBODY'S SON

"Great crimes come never singly;. they are linked to sins that went before."
— Racine, *Phaedra*

Between them, the SAS and Michael Stone triggered a boom season for Northern Ireland's undertakers. In the two weeks following McCann, Savage, and Farrell's deaths, five people there had lost their lives – all because of what happened in Gibraltar.

By the time Stone made his fateful appearance at Milltown Cemetery, one victim's funeral had already taken place. The deceased was Charles McGrillen, a Belfast Catholic with no connection to terrorism, just the bad luck to be within easy reach of Loyalist gunmen.[1] Then in quick succession, there were the funerals for John Murray and Thomas McErlean, the civilian mourners killed by Stone at Milltown. McErlean's death was particularly tragic. From the age of four, he had dreamed about becoming a hero by defending his fellow Catholics.[2] Now, dead at the age of twenty, he had finally got his wish. Although he had never been a member of the IRA, his name would be inscribed on a marble marker at the Republican Plot along with all the others who had died in the "armed struggle". But it was cold comfort to the family he left behind.

The next to be buried were the IRA men, Kevin McCracken and Kevin Brady. McCracken's burial on March 17 (St Patrick's Day) was a peaceful enough affair with the RUC and Army again conspicuous by their absence. Speaking at the graveside in Milltown Cemetery (which would soon have a sign over its gate advising that the owners were not responsible for damage to property or injury to those entering), Sinn Féin Councillor Jim McAllister struck a defiant note. He claimed that the people of West Belfast had "won" the Battle of the Funerals and that the RUC had retreated from their anger.

Kevin Brady's funeral, scheduled for March 19, promised to be a much larger event. A popular young man, Brady had been murdered while playing the IRA's most popular role, that of a defender of women and children from Protestant assassins. Thousands of people were likely to attend. For the movement, it would be an ideal time to translate the anger and fear welling up in the Catholic community into support for the armed struggle.

To the Provisionals, March 19 was a day to mourn a fallen comrade, but it was just part of the work week for Corporal Derek "Del" Wood. A twenty-four-year-old member of the Royal Signals unit stationed at British Army Headquarters at Lisburn, he had been on duty all the previous night, escorting civilian contractors to and from the military bases dotting West Belfast. Normally, after working the midnight shift, the young soldier would have had a few hours of sleep coming to him. However, Wood had only a week left to serve in his four-year tour in Northern Ireland and had to get a final performance evaluation from his commanding officer that morning.[3] After that, since his unit was so shorthanded, he would have to take the late morning escort shift.[4]

But Wood did not complain. Far from it, he saw the extra work as an opportunity to show twenty-three-year-old Corporal David Howes, the man replacing him, what his "patch" of West Belfast looked like. So after taking a quick shower, he changed and went to see his officer, enduring a little good natured-teasing from friends who were more used to seeing him in casual clothes than the suit he wore for the appointment.[5] On his

103

way over to the interview, Wood walked for a while with his girlfriend, Penny Lauder. At about 10:45 a.m., after changing into jeans, a T-shirt, and a pale green sweater, he met up with Howes (who was dressed the same way except for the jacket that he wore in place of a pullover).[6] Then, strolling over to the unit armory, both men signed out Browning 9mm Automatic pistols, the standard sidearms for British soldiers serving in Belfast. This took only a moment, and a little before 11:00 a.m., they drove out of Lisburn Barracks in a silver Volkswagen Passat to Kinnegar Army Ordnance Depot. The weather was crisp and cold, typical for Belfast in March.

Arriving at the depot a few minutes later, the two soldiers met Colin Kent, the telecommunications engineer they were supposed to escort to the North Howard Street Army base. After a short drive through Belfast's city centre, the corporals signed the contractor into that compound a little before noon.[7] Then, the silver Passat, with Wood at the wheel, rolled out of the base's front gate and turned right in the direction of the Falls Road into "Provoland", the working-class neighbourhoods where the IRA has its strongest support.

While Wood and Howes went about their chores, the funeral mass for Kevin Brady had been taking place at St Agnes's Church on Andersonstown Road in the middle of the district locals call "Andytown". Although the officiating priest spoke of a "desire for peace within a bewildered communit,," fear, both in and outside of the church, was a more tangible emotion.[8] It was a feeling fed by Stone's brutal attack, by the Army and RUC's complete absence from Andersonstown's streets, and accentuated by IRA claims that a terrorist attack on Brady's funeral was not only possible but likely. The fact that the area was swarming with Provisional security teams which stopped and frisked anyone entering St Agnes's reinforced the community's collective sense of relief that this was the last of the funerals.

As the congregation streamed out of the church and began the long, slow march up to Milltown Cemetery, the soldiers' Passat turned onto Andersonstown Road. Very quickly, it encountered two young men standing by that street's intersection with Stockman Lane. They were stewards with the task of directing cars out of the cortege's path.[9] It was just a few minutes after 12:00 p.m., and while Wood and Howes did not know it yet, their lives were about to end.

A priest witnessed what happened next. Instead of halting or turning onto the side street, the silver Passat sped through the checkpoint. After jumping out of its path, the Sinn Féin men kicked at the car and swore at what they thought at this stage were joyriders, members of Belfast's legion of youthful car thieves. In quick succession, the car roared past two more teams of stewards stationed further down Andersonstown Road.

By then, Kevin Brady's cortege had drawn parallel with Andersonstown's intersection with Slemish Way, a small side street angling north off the thoroughfare. Even for those used to Republican funerals, it was an impressive sight. Besides being a volunteer in the IRA, Kevin Brady had been a driver for the Falls Road Taxi Association. His friends from there had shown up in force. Acting both as an honour guard as well as a shield, more than twenty black taxis were at the procession's head, slowly moving forward. This day, again a steward, he was making sure his drivers kept their taxis in line.[10]

Behind this strange black cavalry was the funeral party: two more taxis followed by a piper playing a mournful tune, an empty hearse, and Kevin Brady's flag-draped coffin born by four pallbearers. Then came the mourners, over two thousand of them. Along the footpaths, hundreds of people quietly watched the cortege.[11]

# DEATH IN ANDYTOWN

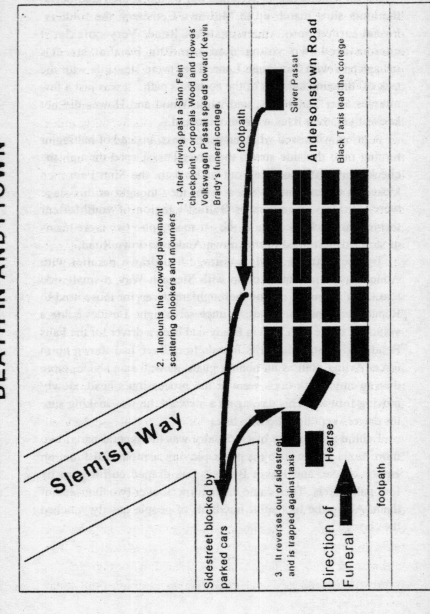

**Andersonstown Road**

Silver Passat

Black Taxis lead the cortege

footpath

1. After driving past a Sinn Fein checkpoint, Corporals Wood and Howes' Volkswagen Passat speeds toward Kevin Brady's funeral cortege.

2. It mounts the crowded pavement scattering onlookers and mourners

**Slemish Way**

Sidestreet blocked by parked cars

3. It reverses out of sidestreet and is trapped against taxis

Hearse

Direction of Funeral

footpath

When the corporals' Passat burst past the last check point by Dunmisk Park, it was just yards away from the funeral procession. Yet Wood, the silver car's driver, still could have braked and reversed away from the menace in front of him. But perhaps panicked by his encounter with the stewards, the young corporal did not stop.

Then, as a watching BBC reporter put it, "the unthinkable" happened.[12] The soldiers' car, still travelling at least thirty miles per hour, mounted the crowded footpath only yards away from the first rank of taxis, scattering onlookers and almost running down several children.

Even at that moment, with mourners and stewards chasing after them, the two corporals had a chance to escape. Wood could have spun the car's steering wheel hard right and turned up Slemish Way and away from the mob that was springing out of the crowd. But for some reason, he cut straight across the entrance to that street and into a small access lane that fronted the line of shops on the northern side of Andersonstown Road. Blocked by a taxi hired by a Canadian film crew, it was a dead end.[13]

Seeing this, Wood at last brought the car to a screeching halt, and then with the Passat's tires squealing and its engine revving crazily, he reversed back out onto Andersonstown Road. Hemmed in by taxis to the rear and the scores of men running toward his car from the direction of the hearse, he tried to turn into Slemish Way, but before the Passat could move more than a few feet, a black taxi blocked its path. Wood and Howes were trapped, like flies on flypaper.

Events during the next few minutes were recorded on film and video tape by the dozens of reporters and television cameramen present. The images they captured were flashed on television only minutes later to a shocked world audience. The commentary that came out along with that footage makes interesting reading. There is little real insight about what happened in any of it. The problem was that the video tape of those confused moments on Andersonstown Road could not capture was what was in people's hearts and minds at that particular time, a moment which resulted in so much horror and pain, not only for Wood and Howes but for many others as well. And what interviews with the residents of Andersonstown who were present there that day reveal is that two emotions drove the crowd – fear and rage. Fear caused by the belief that once again, Loyalist gunmen had invaded the Catholic heartland to kill and maim. Rage that after all the many deaths and mayhem of the last two weeks, it was still not over, that the people of West Belfast could not even bury their dead in peace. It was a feeling perfectly expressed by one funeral steward when asked years later to describe what he felt when the soldiers' car careered into the funeral: that he was not taking this any more![14] It was a reaction shared by scores of those present – Sinn Féiners, IRA men, and ordinary citizens. In effect, Wood and Howes had walked into a pool of psychological gasoline with a lighted match.

*"ORANGE BASTARDS!"*

*"THEY'RE SAS! THEY'RE SAS!"*

*"GET OUT OF THE FUCKING CAR!"*

These shouts and others rang out as the young men ringed the Passat, kicking its doors and beating on it with their fists. Mixed in among them were the Sinn Féin stewards who, after a moment, began to shout, "Pull back! Get back! Get back!"[15] For a brief moment, it appeared they had the crowd under their control. Reporters ran forward through the throng holding their cameras over their heads, trying to get a photograph of those inside the silver car.

But then, the crowd renewed its siege of Wood and Howe's vehicle. Weapons began to appear. A man began smashing at the Passat's rear window with a stick. Another seized a step ladder a television cameraman had been perched on a moment before and advanced on the car as well.

At this point, the two men who were the object of all this anger must have known that their deaths were a distinct possibility. Still, Wood had not given up. As hands began to thrust into the shattered driver's side window, he drew his pistol and pointed it at his attackers.[16]

The effect this had on the mob was electric. The men surrounding the car flung themselves away from it, many dropping to the ground to get out of the line of fire, shouting "Get down!" and "They've got guns! They've got guns!"

Wood had purchased himself only a moment's respite. Now, many convinced that they were facing Protestant terrorists, the mourners and Sinn Féin stewards sprang up from the ground and hurled themselves at the car. The man with the stick redoubled his efforts to break through its rear window. Another young man, bolder than the rest, approached the passenger side where Howes was sitting and smashed the window there with his fist. An instant later, two other men were at his side, all straining to pull the young soldier through it.

Only a few inches away from Howes, they could see the profound fear on the soldier's face. The corporal tried to draw his pistol, but his hand seemed to freeze. Meanwhile, Wood was beginning to stand up in the car, gun in hand.[17]

Wood may have recovered some of his self-confidence at this point. The crowd on his side of the vehicle still was partly cowed by the pistol he had produced a moment before. Yet he must have seen the men grappling with Howes and heard his friend crying for help. Perhaps the young corporal felt the situation was not yet beyond his control. If he could only get a clear line of fire at those attacking Howes, he might be able to hold the mob back until the RUC and Army could rescue them.

At first, the video tape did not show Wood. What it displayed was "Cleeky" Clarke, a prominent IRA man and chief steward of the funeral, rushing toward the driver's side of the vehicle and then backing away.[18] The reason why he did quickly became apparent. Identifiable because of his green sweater, Wood appeared, standing up through the window and twisting his body to the left, bringing the pistol around in his right hand.

Yet by doing so, he turned his back on Clarke who, along with another man with greying hair, wearing a brown cap, leaped forward and tackled the soldier, knocking him out of the car and onto the roadway. Then, at least a dozen other men piled into the melee, grappling with Wood.

The next few moments of the tape depict a scene of absolute confusion. Although Wood is out of the camera's field of view, some mourners can be seen kicking and flailing away at what must have been his body. Meanwhile, a man clad in a green jacket climbed onto the Passat's roof and began to swing blindly at the windshield with a wheel brace, spraying glass on Howes who was still in the car. A second later, a shot rang out, perhaps fired by Wood before his pistol was torn from his grasp. A woman began to scream, her shrieks rising above the din as the crowd again flung itself away from the car before returning – this time in a state of complete hysteria – to drag Howes from it.[19]

Then someone realized that there was still Kevin Brady to bury that day. For the cortege to be able to proceed to Milltown, the soldiers and their car would have to be moved out of the way. Two loose groups of about dozen men each surrounded the soldiers, raised them to their feet, and began to half-push, half-carry them across the street toward Casement Park, the local Gaelic games playing ground. The video shows first one and then the other dragged through the gate before a man runs up and puts his hand over the camera.

In retrospect, the most bewildering aspect of the affair was the total lack of reaction by the authorities. A British Army Lynx helicopter hovering a thousand feet above in the Belfast sky had been filming the funeral from the beginning of the incident to its grisly end. The colour feed from its camera had been transmitted to a ground barracks at Thiepval Army Barracks. There were hundreds of troops and police only minutes away from Casement Park. Yet no one moved to rescue the two soldiers, even when the helicopter pilot called for an ambulance to be escorted to the scene.[20] Nor did anyone act when a British Army patrol saw the smoke from the Passat (which the Provisionals had set on fire) rising in the air.[21] Requests by those soldiers and a heavily-armed RUC unit to enter the area were denied. The authorities would later argue that they were uncertain about what was happening because of the poor quality of the helicopter footage. Yet the police would use the same film to convict a number of men on charges ranging from assault to murder. In any case, despite its grainy quality, the "heli-tele" tape provides a haunting record of a brutal double murder.

Father Alec Reid, a priest from a local Redemptorist order, provides the best eyewitness account of what happened after the soldiers were pulled from the car. Present at the funeral as a mourner, he had run up to the Passat only moments after the crowd overpowered Wood and Howes. As he later told BBC reporters investigating the killings, the men holding the soldiers had stopped hitting them, but were still fearful that their captives might be armed:

[Standing near Wood] I heard a shout from the scrum: 'Watch he doesn't pull a gun.' . . . I heard someone [else] say 'Catch his hands.' I remember shouting 'Just do that. Catch his hands.' I then went back to the front of the [group holding Wood] which was by now on the footpath and nearly into Casement Park itself. Wood's hands were out now in front of him. It was as if he was holding them out. There was blood on one of his hands. There was blood on my coat. I held his hands, and he immediately gripped them. He squeezed them. I was trying to protect him. I knew that if he pulled a gun that would be the end of him. He would be torn apart by the crowd. When he kind of squeezed my hands that changed everything. It became more personal.[22]

Dragged into the park, both men were pinned up against its north-west corner wall and repeatedly kicked and punched. After a few moments of this punishment, the corporals crumpled to the ground, semiconscious. Meanwhile, on the street, several Provisionals were examining the Passat looking for weapons and clues to the soldiers' identities. One of the items they discovered was Wood's notebook which he always carried with him.[23]

Inside Casement Park, Father Reid managed to get the mourners to stop beating Wood and Howes by throwing himself over them. He began shouting for someone to call for an ambulance, and it seemed that the priest's presence was making some of the men in the park feel increasingly uncomfortable.[24] One of those was a balding, paunchy man wearing a green jacket with a hood, black pants, and white shoes. Apart from pressing on one of the soldier's feet for a moment, he had not taken part in assaulting them. Instead, he had been wandering around as if he was trying to find a way out.

By this time, Father Reid began to think that he had the situation well under control. As he later recalled, his main worry was not the IRA but simply people losing their heads again and inflicting even worse injuries on Wood and Howes.[25] Michael Timmons, who had entered the park and was, he said later, looking on out of "nosiness", was less optimistic. When he asked the priest if he thought the crowd would release the soldiers, Reid replied, "I hope so, son." To that, the young man said, "I doubt it very much, Father".[26]

Events proved Timmons right. An IRA man dressed in white who had been searching Wood found the soldier's military identity card. According to Father Reid, the man's face twisted with rage, and he shouted, "Look at that! He's a fucking Brit!"[27]

After the discovery that Wood was a soldier, the situation

inside the park took on an ugly tone. According to several witnesses, it became even worse when the Provisionals found phone numbers in the corporal's notebook for addresses in Herford. For someone unfamiliar with English town names, Herford, a British base where signals troops are stationed, looked a great deal like *Hereford*, the then headquarters of the SAS.[28] It was a lethal coincidence.

By this time, other IRA men had entered the park, and they, along with a few of the mourners, began stripping the soldiers of their clothing. Still holding onto the two men, Father Reid sensed the mood in the park had shifted. It was almost as if the police had arrived.[29]

Shortly after the stripping began, the Provisionals decided to get rid of the priest. Seizing him, one of them snarled, "Get up or I'll fucking well shoot you!"[30] Reid was lifted up and roughly passed over to the IRA man in white. After pinning the priest's arms back, he frog-marched him out of the park.

Timmons, still there, vividly remembered what happened next. An IRA man cried out, "Buck [the soldiers] over the wall!" Another yelled back, "Fuck them! Finish them here!"[31] But because they were hoping to question what had every appearance of being two members of the SAS, the IRA took the first option. Both soldiers were lifted up and dumped unceremoniously over the brick wall. They fell, like bags of garbage, to the footpath nine feet below. The wet thuds their bodies made on striking the ground was something that would haunt Timmons in the months to come. In fact, he would find himself praying for forgiveness simply for standing by and doing nothing while it happened.[32]

After bundling the soldiers over the wall, the IRA men in the park jumped down beside them. A black taxi pulled up, and they hurled Wood and Howes into the back. Then, after they leaped into it themselves, the car raced out onto Andersonstown Road past the taxi phalanx which had still not resumed moving.

News footage shot that day showed the man in white sitting in the taxi's front passenger seat, waving his fist in triumph to the crowd.

Judging by the path the taxi took, it appears that the IRA men had no real idea of where to go. They drove a sort of corkscrew route, turning right along Slievegallion Drive, right again onto Bingian Way, and then along South Link to a vacant lot not far from the northern side of Andersonstown Road. Just to the south of the waste ground was a narrow alley, that locals called Penny Lane, which ran back to the street.[33]

The events that followed just seconds after the black taxi's arrival by Penny Lane eerily paralleled the killings in Gibraltar two weeks earlier. Just as in that case, the murders did not take place under cover of night away from prying eyes. They unfolded in broad daylight in front of at least a dozen ordinary people who were walking by or watching the commotion down by Casement Park. Just like virtually all those who witnessed the shootings on the Rock, the passers-by in Penny Lane would remain silent about what they had seen.

Corporals Wood's and Howes's short ride had not been an easy one. The forensic evidence discovered by the police investigating their deaths would make that cruelly apparent. The back seat of the black taxi was literally soaked in blood. While some of it undoubtedly came from wounds inflicted on the soldiers on Andersonstown Road and in Casement Park, the spattering in the car clearly indicates that the two men were savagely assaulted while inside it. That the police found a piece of one soldier's scalp in the vehicle gives some idea of just how hard their captors were hitting them.[34]

The scene inside the taxi as it pulled into the waste ground is easy to imagine. The Provos must have been exhilarated. Given the close-knit nature of the IRA, they would have been friends of Daniel McCann, Seán Savage, and Mairéad Farrell. they must have been delighted that they had captured two apparent

114

SAS men. They now had an opportunity to get a little revenge for what they perceived as the murder of "colleagues".

Then, there would have come the sickening realization that their actions on Andersonstown Road had been witnessed by television cameramen, reporters, and an Army helicopter. The security forces were undoubtedly on the way to rescue the soldiers. Whatever plans the IRA men had to interrogate them would have to be abandoned. Time was running short.

Six men, including the driver, spilled out of the car. Then from the passenger door on the driver's side, a man dressed only in a T-shirt, socks, and underwear rushed out. Seen from a distance by someone with no knowledge about what had just happened and what was yet to come, Corporal Wood looked like the victim of a college prank. Only someone close to the taxi who could have seen the bruises and blood covering his face would have known that it was no game. Wood knew what was about to happen to him, and with fear and adrenalin overriding the agony he must have been in, he was running for his life.[35]

Perhaps had he escaped from the immediate area, the young soldier might have reached the British Army patrols that were close by, but he just did not move quickly enough. One of the IRA men and the taxi driver seized Wood and after a brief struggle, threw him to the ground, where he lay stunned, face down in the dirt, with his legs spread-eagled like those of a broken doll.

A moment after Wood tried to flee, Howes bolted from the car, naked except for his socks and underwear, his body streaked with blood. Yet dazed by the punching and clubbing he had been receiving for nearly a quarter of an hour, he paused to shut the taxi's door. That moment's hesitation, brought on by force of habit, cost him his life.[36] The knot of Provos around Howes easily caught him and after aiming a few more blows at his head, flung the young corporal across the hood of a small red car parked to the right of the taxi.

It was at about this time that two IRA men, one armed with

115

one of the Browning 9mm pistols taken from the soldiers on Andersonstown Road, ran up to where Wood lay bleeding on the ground. The man without the pistol stretched out his arm to the soldier, doing so to indicate that Wood was the one for killing. Then, with the same type of weapon the SAS used to dispatch the IRA volunteers in Gibraltar, the gunman shot him. He did so calmly, using a professional combat stance, taking his time to put two bullets into Wood's head, smashing his skull and ripping his brain apart.[37]

Then, it was Howes's turn. He might not have seen what had happened to his friend, but he certainly heard Wood's screams and then the shots. In any case, he made one last attempt to break free. Lurching off the red car's hood, he staggered a few steps toward the passenger side of the taxi and almost into the arms of his executioners, who beat him to the ground. The gunman, with the hood of his anorak turned up in what a journalist would later liken to a "cruel caricature of a monk's cowl," trotted over to Howe's prone figure and shot him in the chest repeatedly.[38]

Yet even that was not enough. Fully aware that with shots being fired, the RUC and British Army would soon be on the scene, the gunman began to run south down Penny Lane. There, under the watching eye of the helicopter, he met a second man who took the pistol and rushed up to Wood's body, being careful not to step in the blood that was pouring from it. Taking his time, just like his predecessor, he fired four carefully-aimed shots into the soldier's back. Then, moving over to Howes, he heeded the other IRA men's shouts to "Do him in the head!" and shot the young man in the face, just above the right eye.[39] Straightening up, the murderer turned and trotted back down Penny Lane where he caught up with his companions and disappeared from the heli-tele's field of view.

After the killings, the soldiers' battered and bloody bodies lay on the waste ground by Penny Lane. At first, it seemed that no one would go to their aid, but then in an action that Mary

Holland of the *Irish Times* would say "redeemed us all", Father Reid came onto the scene.[40] After leaving Casement Park, he had gone to get his car, but the sound of gunfire drew him to the killing ground. Seeing the two bodies lying there, the priest shouted at a nearby shopkeeper to call for an ambulance. One of corporals was still alive, gasping for breath, his eyes open and his head turning from side to side. Reid attempted to resuscitate the man. But it was far too late. Sadly, he began praying over what had been, only a few seconds before, a living, breathing human being while photographers snapped pictures of the scene. After a few minutes of this, a local woman came forward and covered one of the soldier's faces with her coat, murmuring, "He's somebody's son. God have mercy on him".[41] It was over for Wood and Howes, but for Timmons, the man in green, and scores of others, the storm was only just beginning.

## Notes

1. Sutton, p. 162. Another Catholic, Kevin Mulligan, was shot by Loyalists on March 16, and lingered for eight months before finally dying in November 1988.
2. Connolly, "Death Without End", p. 14.
3. Statement of Witness, Staff Sergeant Michael J Pound, Royal Signal Corps, British Corps, British Army, Taken by Royal Ulster Constabulary, Marc 26, 1988.
4. A number of people have alleged that Wood and Howes were specially trained surveillance personnel, members of a secretive British military intelligence group called the "FRU". I consider this extremely unlikely for two reasons. First, any undercover units operating in close proximity to Brady's funeral cortege would have had communications with a quick reaction unit that would extract them if trouble took place. Second, Wood and Howes behaved passively when attacked by the mob. A pair of trained SAS men or 14th Intelligence Company soldiers almost certainly would have killed a few IRA men before being overwhelmed (they would have also been more heavily armed).
5. Statement of Witness, Lance Corporal Michael Hugh James Kerr, Royal Signal Corps, British Army, taken by Royal Ulster Constabulary, March 23, 1988.
6. British soldiers routinely wear civilian clothing to maintain a low profile when performing duties like the ones Wood and Howes were performing.
7. Statement of Witness, Colin David Kent, Telecommunications Engineer, British Army, taken by Royal Ulster Constabulary, October 12, 1988.
8. Dillon, *Stone Cold*, p. 191.
9. Interview with a steward at Kevin Brady's funeral, June 1996.
10. Ibid.
11. Descriptions of the funeral procession come from a variety of sources

ranging from interviews conducted with those present, video tape shot of the incident by both the media and the British military, and still photography.

12. *The Casement Accused*, Casement Accused Relatives' Committee, Belfast, undated, p. 4.

13. Interview with a steward at Kevin Brady's funeral.

14. Ibid.

15. On the film taken of the incident, the stewards can clearly be heard ordering the crowd back. Despite the *Sunday Times*'s claims to the contrary, the people around the soldiers did not chant, "Kill the Brits!"

16. *The Queen versus Patrick Gerard Kane, Michael John Timmons, Seán Kelly, Joseph Patrick Coogan and Thomas Hawkins*, Judgment of Carswell J, Crown Court of Northern Ireland, 1991, pp. 4-6.

17. Interview with James Neeson.

18. Taylor, *Provos: the IRA and Sinn Féin*, pp. 103-105. Taylor provides a resume of Clarke's activities as a Provisional here.

19. Petition of Complaint on Behalf of Seán Kelly, Patrick Kane and Michael Timmons, submitted to the United Nations' Centre for Human Rights by the Lawyers' Alliance for Justice in Ireland, Inc, 1994, p.7.

20. "Pilot Tells of Seeking Aid for Attacked Corporals", the *Irish News*, April 20, 1989.

21. Fergus Pyle, "Army Unit was Close to the Killings", *Irish Times,* May 12, 1989.

22. Statement given by Father Alec Reid to *Rough Justice*, BBC One Television, 1993.

23. Statement of Witness, Corporal Ian Mark Robinson, Royal Signal Corps, British Army, taken by Royal Ulster Constabulary, March 23, 1988.

24. Statement given by Father Alec Reid.

25. Ibid.

26. *The Queen versus Patrick Gerard Kane*, p. 28.

27. Statement given by Father Alec Reid.

28. Variety of sources including individuals who handled the notebook and still believe that the soldiers would have been carrying documents directly linking them with the SAS on a covert mission.

29. Statement given by Father Alec Reid.

30. Ibid.

31. *The Queen versus Patrick Gerard Kane,* p. 28.

32. Ibid, p. 29.

33. Variety of sources including interviews and *Queen versus Patrick Gerard Kane*, pp. 5-6.

34. *The Queen versus Alex Murphy and Henry Maguire*, Judgment, Lord Chief Justice Hutton, Crown Court of Northern Ireland, 1989, pp. 21-24.

35. Ibid, pp. 50-52.

36. Variety of sources including articles written by Ed Moloney for the *Sunday Tribune* between March 1988 and July 1991.

37. Ibid.

38. Mallie and McKittrick, pp. 1-5.

39. Ibid.

40. Dillon, *Stone Cold*, p. 193.

41. Ibid, p. 195.

# CHAPTER EIGHT

## EVERY SECRET CRIME

"Whenever a man commits a crime, God finds a witness . . . Every secret crime has its reporter."
 – Ralph Waldo Emerson

After Corporals Wood's and Howes's truly brutal deaths, "It was not a time that encouraged the asking of difficult questions about the killings in Gibraltar."[1] Yet by March 19, Chris Oxley and Julian Manyon of *This Week* had been doing precisely that for over ten days. And after hearing what they had discovered in that time, their boss, Roger Bolton, quickly realized that his team was on to one of the biggest scandals in the history of the Thatcher Administration.

First, there was what Oxley had learned on the Rock. Arriving there on March 8, he found it odd that the police, who had been deeply involved in the shootings, were now investigating their legality. The conflict of interest in them doing so seemed obvious. Equally strange was what the locals told him, that the "investigators" had made no real effort to preserve the crime scenes or collect statements from civilian witnesses. Perhaps conscious of these problems, Gibraltar's coroner, Felix Pizzarello, told Oxley that he would welcome *This Week* looking into the killings and hoped that the journalists would identify witnesses for his own investigation.[2]

Meanwhile, Manyon had been in Spain seeing what he

119

could find out there. Arriving in Madrid on March 11, he quickly secured the services of Harry Debelius, an expatriate American journalist who covered Spanish affairs for *The Times*, as *This Week*'s consultant and interpreter. Together, the two wrote a letter to the Spanish police headquarters asking for help in "reconstructing the [surveillance operation against the terrorists] in exactitude." Debelius and Manyon also requested details about the "critical phase when the Spanish surveillance team followed the [IRA] commando to Gibraltar".[3]

Manyon and Oxley reported back to Bolton on March 15 in London. Encouraged by what they had to tell him, he added another reporter to the team, Alison Cahn.[4] A sympathetic young woman with tremendous energy, Cahn had a simple task – to visit every apartment overlooking the Shell Petrol Station where McCann and Farrell died and interview the occupants. On March 18, Manyon and Oxley, with Cahn in tow, returned to Gibraltar.

Cahn found her task a hard slog. She visited over 150 apartments, returning several times if the tenants were out. In her opinion, the Gibraltarians were frightened by what happened and at the consequences of speaking out. One asked her, "With the SAS on one side and the IRA on the other, what would you do?"[5] Sometimes during these interviews, the phone would ring at the subjects' apartments. When they answered it, the callers simply hung up. Like Oxley, Cahn was troubled by the behavior of the Gibraltar Police. They appeared to be spending more time following her than in investigating the case.

By now, *This Week* had made contact with two people who had already come forward as witnesses to the killings and were willing to be interviewed on film. The first was Stephen Bullock. A prominent local lawyer, he had been out for a walk with his wife Lucinda and young daughter. At that time, Lucinda had been nine months pregnant and overdue. Both she

120

and her husband had hoped that a little exercise in the March sunshine would finally set things in motion.

That afternoon, the Bullocks had been strolling north-west along Smith Dorrien Avenue when they passed a Gibraltar Police car that was stuck in traffic. Stephen and Lucinda noticed that the it was full of uniformed police. Then, as they neared the street's intersection with Winston Churchill Avenue, something remarkable happened. As Stephen remembered:

> I was pushing the push chair with [my daughter in it] . . . and Lucinda was walking alongside . . . As we went past the entrance to [the] playground . . . this guy in sort of T-shirt and jeans and running shoes came charging out of there . . . and he basically shoved us right up against [the barrier designed to keep children from running into the street], and he turned around and said, "Oh, excuse me, sir" and then went trotting on down the road . . . [6]

Now, all the lights at the intersection were on red, and traffic had backed up in every direction. Nothing was moving, including the police car the Bullocks had just walked by:

> As the guy . . . trotted down the road, he was looking over his shoulder back at the [police] car, and I saw at that point that he had a pistol . . . he had the butt of a pistol sticking out of the top of his waistband and jeans, and [he] was so close you could see [its magazine] . . . And I pointed this out to [Lucinda], [saying] 'Look this guy's got a gun!' [7]

The Bullocks were now wondering whether they were about to witness a crime. Neither had any idea that the man they had just seen belonged to the SAS. And the way the gunman kept looking back at the police car made them think he was waiting for it do something:

> He got to [the corner with Winston Churchill Avenue], and there was another guy, he must have been sitting on the wall, and they sort of went into a huddle, and I could see the other guy had a pistol as well . . . [A moment later] they were

121

peering through the bushes up towards [the tunnel where Savage was walking] . . . While we were watching that, suddenly this . . . police car pulls out and goes down the wrong side of [Smith Dorrien] . . . Anyway, it pulled out, turned its siren on and [sped down toward the intersection with Winston Churchill] and as it did so, there suddenly [was a] bang, bang, bang . . . and we look[ed] over [at the Shell Station to the north] and we see this guy in a white shirt [McCann] falling back [with his hands in the air] with this other guy standing in the road [firing a pistol at him] going bang, bang, bang, bang, bang, bang!"[8]

And I look back and I see [the first two gunmen standing at the corner] . . . and they're watching what's going on outside the petrol station, and after [the shooting stopped there], these two suddenly get into another huddle up and go [running] around the corner out of sight [where Savage had been walking], and very shortly after they disappear . . . there was this continuous volley of shots.[9]

The other eyewitness was Josie Celecia, a housewife living on the second floor of the George Jeger House, an apartment building just across the street from the Shell Station. Josie had been standing by her bedroom window which overlooked the road, waiting for her husband Douglas to take her for a walk. Glancing out at the scene below, she could see a couple strolling along the footpath not too far away the Shell Station. It was McCann and Farrell. Interviewed by *This Week* in Gibraltar on March 19, she described what happened next:

I was staring at the man because he had spiky, blond, short hair . . . then all of a sudden I took my sight off them and looked [north] Suddenly, I heard two shots . . . I was just looking [for] where that came from, and . . . I saw . . . [McCann and Farrell] on the floor [by the Shell Station].[10]

Josie was terrified. But she could not take her eyes away from the spectacle that was unfolding just forty feet away. From her vantage point, she could see a man standing over the two IRA members' bodies with his back to her, his hands outstretched and pointing down toward them. Another man was standing on the footpath a few feet further north. To the south, she could see a Gibraltar Police car, its siren wailing, racing up Winston Churchill Avenue:

"As you saw the two lying on the ground and another man standing above them, what happened?" Manyon asked her.

"I heard shots . . . about four or five shots" Josie replied.

"More shots?"

"Si."

"What were they like?"

"Continuously."

"Like automatic fire?"

"Like that. One after the other."[11]

Early on, Bolton felt that his team needed technical advice about the shootings. But the best source of that, the British government, was remaining silent. So *This Week* retained Lieutenant Colonel George Styles as a consultant. A highly decorated officer who had retired from the British Army in 1975, Styles had been one of the original "felixes," the bomb disposal officers who operate in Northern Ireland. The author of *Bombs Have No Pity*, the colonel was an acknowledged expert about IRA explosive devices and had pursued a life-long interest in firearms and ballistics. Furthermore, he was experienced at interviewing the survivors of bombings and other traumatic incidents.

Arriving in Gibraltar on March 23, Styles immediately went to work. Along with the journalists, he visited the assembly-area car park where Savage parked his car, walked through a route which the ASU might have taken through the town, and personally spoke to a number of witnesses the reporters had identified.

Asked about the credibility of the government's claim that the SAS men shot the IRA team because they thought there was a car-bomb in Gibraltar, his response was devastating:

"Well, I'm sure that the army bomb-disposal man was somewhere near and observing the scene . . . and when [Savage's] car came in . . . I'm sure that he would have quickly seen that it carried no significant weight of explosive," he told Manyon.

"How would he have seen that?" the reporter asked.

"Well, the posture of the car on its springs is dictated by the weight it's carrying, and if you put a hundred [pounds] of cement in the boot of a car, it shows."[12]

*This Week* later obtained a photograph of the Renault 5 while it was still parked at the assembly area. It was riding high on its springs.

Styles also cast serious doubt on the "button job", the argument that the SAS men had shot to kill because they believed McCann, Savage, and Farrell had radio devices that could trigger the car-bomb simply by flicking a switch or pushing a button. In his view, that was "very unlikely indeed" because of the building work standing between where the Provisionals had died and the assembly area. Another obstacle to detonation would have been the sheer number of ordinary radio signals bouncing around Gibraltar. Styles felt they would have drowned out any detonation signal emanating from the Shell Station.[13]

Besides this, Manyon had the Colonel examine the shooting scene by the petrol station. And it was while he was inspecting the ricochet marks left on the petrol pumps by the SAS men's bullets that one of the most controversial witnesses to the shootings emerged.

Alison Cahn had been looking on when an elderly

woman came up and spoke to her. The reporter's Spanish was not good enough to understand what the lady was saying. Nevertheless, her curiosity aroused, she allowed herself to be led over to Rodney House, an apartment building a couple of hundred feet south of the petrol station. Once there, Cahn's guide called up to a window and Carmen Proetta put her head out to see what the old woman – her mother – wanted.[14]

Proetta, a red-haired, strikingly attractive woman in her mid-forties, worked as a legal secretary on the Costa del Sol. She spent most of her time in Spain but routinely stayed at the family apartment in Gibraltar on the weekends. Proetta had witnessed the action by the Shell Station, and after some pleading by Cahn, proved willing to talk about it. In a sworn affidavit, she gave a dramatic account of what she had seen:[15]

The windows on the west of the [Rodney House, my apartment building] overlook Winston Churchill Avenue, and I have a very clear and almost uninterrupted view of the Shell Petrol Station . . .

On Sunday, the sixth day of March 1988, I was in the kitchen of my flat washing up after lunch when my attention was drawn by the sound of a police siren . . . I instinctively looked out of the window, and I saw a Gibraltar Police car, travelling from north to south on the opposite side of Winston Churchill Avenue, screech to a halt. The noise made by the [tyres] when the car stopped was very audible.

As soon as the car came to a halt, all four doors opened, and four persons got out. Three [of them] wore civilian clothes, and I could clearly see that they were armed with [pistols]. The fourth [man] to get out of the car was a Gibraltar police constable who was the driver of the vehicle . . .

The three men [in civilian clothes] jumped . . . over the

125

central barrier separating the east side of the [highway] from the west of Winston Churchill Avenue, and as they did so, I heard a shot.

At the same time as this was happening, I was aware of a young couple walking down from Winston Churchill Avenue on the east side footpath from south [to] north. The man had spiky blond hair and was carrying something, possibly a jacket. The woman was dark-haired and was carrying a bag . . .

As the gunmen leaped over the central barrier, and the shot was fired, I saw this couple *immediately stop and put up their hands* [author's italics]. Because the scene was so unusual and alarming, my attention was riveted to what was happening.

The three gunmen separated slightly and I remember at least two in front. The third gunman moved to the left and to the rear. This took a couple of seconds or so.

I can describe the gunmen as follows: The man who I think moved to the side and rear was a large man with curly, fair hair. He was the most striking of the three . . . I remember that one of the other[s] wore a dark jacket, and he was much shorter and darker with a receding hair line . . .

As soon as the gunmen were in position, a fast fusillade of shots were fired by I believe all three men . . . *There is absolutely no doubt in my mind that* [McCann and Farrell's] *hands were in the air when this occurred and they made no movements either towards the bag or inside their clothing. I was very shocked by what I was seeing* [author's italics].[16]

Carmen estimated that the gunmen fired at least six shots at the Provisionals before they collapsed to the ground. Then:

the tall, blonde man went into a crouch position and took deliberate aim at them. He . . . fired . . . three or four shots into the couple as they lay there. He appeared to be aiming at their heads, and the blood squirted out like water from a broken pipe.[17]

The shooting was over. A moment later, the police car the SAS men arrived in drove down the road, turned at the gap in the barrier near Proetta's apartment building and sped up to the Shell Station. A second police car drove up from the same direction and stopped there as well, disgorging a number of uniformed and plainclothes Gibraltar Police. From what Carmen could see, two of the SAS men appeared to be arguing with the big, blond gunman who had shot McCann and Farrell on the ground. After a moment or two, they shoved him into the police car which brought them, and it roared away with all three men in it.[18]

Proetta impressed not just Finch and Bolton's reporters but Colonel Styles as well. In his opinion, only someone who had actually seen high-velocity bullets strike a human being would have talked about the blood gushing from McCann and Farrell's bodies. Her account of gunmen firing from the road also squared with the bullet strike-marks on the petrol pumps.[19] Besides this, several of the very first newspaper articles about the killings corroborated her story. On March 7, *The Times* reported that, "Witnesses say that police in plain clothes jumped out of a car and shot a man and a woman dead." The *Daily Telegraph*, *Independent* and *Irish Times* carried similar pieces.

Proetta's statement was of enormous help in understanding what had actually happened on the Rock. So was the information that the Spanish government provided to Manyon and Debelius. On March 21, the two had an evening interview with Augustin Valladolid, the spokesman of the Spanish Interior Ministry. During this meeting, Valladolid confirmed that the bombers had been under constant surveillance on March 6. Notes taken by Harry Debelius gave a good idea of just how thorough that effort was:[20]

a. Four or five [unmarked] police cars "leap-frogged" each

other on the road while trailing the terrorists so as not to arouse suspicion.

b. A helicopter spotted [the] car during part of the route.

c. The police agents [involved] were in constant contact with their headquarters by radio.

d. [There was] observation by agents at fixed . . . points along the road . . . Valladolid further said that the Spanish police sent minute-by-minute details of the car's movements to the British in Gibraltar. *He confirmed that the British were aware of the car's arrival at the border and permitted it to enter Gibraltar* [author's italics].

The Spanish were so proud of their surveillance effort that two Malaga police officers involved in the operation participated in a filmed reconstruction of how they watched the Renault 5 travel down the costal road to the Colony.[21] Sparing no expense, the British reporters rented a helicopter and filmed the view from the air as well as from the ground.

Meanwhile, near the end of March, Alison Cahn traced two witnesses to Savage's death. The first was Diana Treacy, a Gibraltar bank employee who had been just a few feet away from the large oak tree Seán Savage was near when the SAS shot him. Like Josie Celecia and Carmen Proetta, Treacy, the daughter of a former Gibraltar Police officer, had been badly frightened by what she had seen, and the *This Week* crew had to talk to her through the door for fifteen minutes before being admitted to her home. After some negotiation, she agreed to be filmed but on the condition that her identity remained secret. Speaking in a hushed voice with her back to the camera, Treacy told Manyon that she first saw Savage when he rushed toward her pursued by a man with a gun in his left hand.

"[The gunman] just lifted his left arm, and I heard the first shot. It was then when I looked back and saw the other man [Savage] who was running fall back as the other man continued shooting at him," she said.

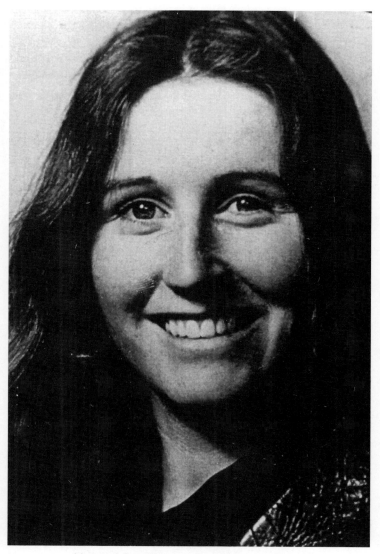

*Mairéad Farrell* © *Pacemaker Press International*

*Seán Savage* © *Pacemaker Press International*

*Daniel McCann* © *Pacemaker Press International*

*Seconds after killing McCann and Farrell.*

*The Milltown Massacre: with over one hundred mourners
chasing him, Michael Stone turns on his pursuers* © *Pacemaker
Press International*

*Michael Timmons and family at the Maze prison*

*Pat Kane*

"Did you hear any warning of any kind given by the man with the gun?" Manyon asked.

"No, no."

"Did you hear him say 'Stop, police'?"

"No, no, [it] just happened so sudden[ly]."

"He just opened fire, just like that?"

"Yes."[22]

Looking over her shoulder, Treacy saw what happened next. Savage was falling as an SAS man shot him repeatedly in the back. It was a grisly scene. According to her, " . . . [the man] was bouncing on the floor when the other man continued shooting at him about three or four shots more . . ."[23]

Treacy's story was gruesome, but the statement that the second witness, Kenneth Asquez, gave about the shootings made the SAS look more like gangsters than soldiers "assisting the civil power". Like Proetta, he had come to *This Week*'s attention through an intermediary, Bob Randall, a resident of the housing estate near the Shell Station. Randall had had the presence of mind to grab his video camera when he heard about the shootings and film their aftermath. On March 22, Cahn visited him at his home to get a copy of the tape he made. While talking with Randall, she asked as a matter of routine whether he knew anyone who had seen the three IRA members die.[24]

The retired military officer said he did: a young man who had been in a car that had passed the site where Seán Savage was killed. Randall would not give Cahn the witness's name because he thought that he "did not want to get involved". (a response the *This Week* reporter heard with monotonous regularity from the Gibraltarians).

Randall did agree to contact the reluctant witness and ask him for a detailed account of events on Landport Lane. And on March 25, Kenneth Asquez, who worked as a clerk at the Algemene Bank, gave Randall, his former football coach, an unsigned, handwritten statement about what he had seen. Reading it, Manyon and Oxley felt it was potentially useful, but that they had to have proof Asquez that had written it.

So on March 30, Cahn turned to Christopher Finch for help. Without giving any details about what Asquez's purported statement contained, she asked him to contact the young man on *This Week*'s behalf. Finch, who knew the Asquez family, obliged, and the next day interviewed him in his office around noontime. Since Finch felt his subject would not talk if any reporters were present, Cahn stayed away. Visiting the *This Week* crew at their hotel later in the day, the lawyer confirmed what Randall had said. Asquez desperately wanted to avoid being named as a witness. He was happy for the reporters to use his statements but only if he was kept out of the picture.[25]

In Christopher Finch's opinion, one he maintains to this day, Asquez told the truth when he described what he had seen on March 6.[26] When the reporters compared the handwritten "Randall" statement with the draft affidavit that Finch had typed up after talking to Asquez, they found they were nearly identical. So after Cahn made a last ditch effort to get Asquez to sign the affidavit (he refused), *This Week* incorporated it into the program. In it, Asquez described how he had been a passenger in a car with three of his friends, driving on Corral Road toward the border. They were passing the intersection with Landport Lane when the SAS shot Savage. Asquez said he looked out the car window and could see a:

> . . . man on the ground . . . lying on his back [it was Savage]. The man standing over this man had his foot on the [other] man's chest. I could see that he also had a gun in his hand . . . I then saw the gunman point his gun deliberately at the man [who] was lying on the floor and fire two or three times at him at point-blank range. I was horrified by what I saw.[27]

Between Colonel Styles's comments, the information the

130

Spanish had provided about the surveillance, and particularly the statements of the eyewitnesses, Roger Bolton had the elements of a disturbing and thought-provoking documentary. But he did not have an ending for it. Normally, such a program would conclude with a reporter presenting a summary of its information to a high-ranking government official with a request for comment. Yet the Thatcher Administration had been maintaining an eerie silence about the shootings. *This Week*'s requests to the government for information and assistance in developing the programme, now titled *Death on the Rock* – on or off-the-record – met with blanket refusals.

So Bolton turned to George Carman, a highly respected lawyer who had a practice in London, for his views about the case. One question that came up when *This Week* interviewed him was how the incident should be investigated. By now, Margaret Thatcher had already contemptuously rejected a request by Amnesty International for a high-level probe into the killings, saying that an inquest held by the Gibraltar coroner was all that was necessary. Carman disagreed. He felt that a more powerful commission of inquiry should be set up, perhaps one presided over by a High Court judge.

"Do you believe this case is so important that the government should actually consider such extraordinary steps in order to clarify the facts?" Manyon asked him.

"It's not for me to advise Her Majesty's Government as to what steps they should take. But clearly, from everything you say, the programme indicates that there are serious important public issues involved, and speaking as a lawyer, one is always anxious that where there is [disagreement] on the facts in such important areas, they should be properly and efficiently investigated."[28]

That was it. The last piece of *Death on the Rock* was in place. The only question was what would happen if and when it were broadcast.

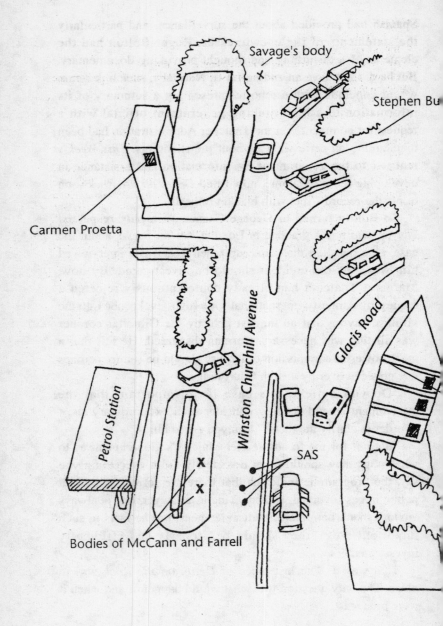

Savage's body

Stephen Bu

Carmen Proetta

Glacis Road

Winston Churchill Avenue

Petrol Station

SAS

Bodies of McCann and Farrell

# Notes

1. Jack, "Gibraltar", p. 37.
2. Bolton, pp. 195-196.
3. Affidavit by Harry Debelius, dated September 21, 1988.
4. Bolton, pp. ix. An additional journalist, Eamon Hardy, also worked on the *Death on the Rock* project.
5. Ibid, p. 206.
6. Interview with Stephen and Lucinda Bullock, June 1996, Spain.
7. Ibid.
8. Ibid.
9. Ibid.
10. Lord Windlesham and Richard Rampton, *Windlesham/Rampton Report on Death on the Rock*, Faber and Faber, London, 1989, pp. 51-52. In 1989, the Windlesham-Rampton Inquiry, an independent commission established by Thames Television, to investigate the making of *Death on the Rock* found with several minor exceptions that it had been a "trenchant" piece of journalism and had been made in good faith.
11. Ibid, pp. 55-56. During this interview, Celecia's husband (off-camera) made several comments to his wife. For clarity's sake, I omitted them.
12. Ibid, pp. 49-50, 60-61.
13. Ibid.
14. Bolton, pp. 212-213.
15. Affidavit by Carmen Proetta, dated April 1988.
16. Ibid.
17. Ibid.
18. Ibid.
19. For some time after the shootings, the Gibraltarians referred to them as "the leaded pumps".
20. Debelius Affidavit.
21. The Spanish government later vehemently denied that this took place.
22. Windlesham and Rampton, p. 58.
23. Ibid.
24. Bolton, pp. 208-211.
25. Ibid.
26. Mr Finch did not make himself available to me. However, during our very short conversation on the phone in 1996, he emphatically stated that Asquez was telling the truth in his original statements.
27. Testimony of Kenneth Asquez, the Gibraltar Inquest, Day 12, 23 September 1988, Channel Four Television, 1988, p. 10.
28. Bolton, p. 226.

# CHAPTER NINE

## "THE NATURE OF THE BUSINESS"

"What is at the heart of the matter is British hypocrisy. They don't mind murdering. They just don't like to be called murderers."
   – Danny Morrison, Sinn Féin National Director of Publicity, April 1988

As Roger Bolton quickly learned, Margaret Thatcher was not about to stand idly by and let *This Week*, Amnesty International, or any other busybodies publicly question what "her boys" had been up to in Gibraltar. The cabinet sub-committee that she had established to contain the propaganda fall-out from the killings had been receiving regular reports about *This Week*'s inquiries. This committee, which had been set up *prior* to the shootings, had, in their immediate aftermath, coordinated the dissemination of the stories about fierce gun battles taking place and car-bombs being found on the Rock.[1] As a result, by mid-April 1988, a large segment of the British public still believed McCann, Savage, and Farrell had been armed and dangerous when they died. There were some who knew this was not true. But most of those better-informed souls had read a *Sunday Times'* article which offered an easy-to-hear explanation for the killing of three unarmed people. It seemed that the SAS men had been afraid Savage's "car-bomb" might have a radio trigger.[2] That story would justify the killings. After all, if the SAS had believed that the lives of hundreds of civilians might depend on preventing a button from being pushed, who could blame the soldiers for shooting first and asking questions later?

Yet now a fly by the name of *Death on the Rock* was in the ointment. On April 21, the Thatcher Administration discovered just how large and pesky that insect was going to be. That day, in a final bid to get at least something on record from the government, Julian Manyon had met with Brigadier General Sam Cowan, the Army's public relations officer and Hugh Colver, a MoD spokesman, to discuss the shootings.[3] During their basically one-way conversation, Manyon gave the general and his associate a broad outline of what Bolton's program would contain. Learning that *This Week* had lined up five eyewitnesses to the shootings who would contradict the official version of events could have hardly been a pleasant discovery for Cowan, Colver, or their superiors.

So, on April 26, just two days before its scheduled broadcast, the government tried to prevent the transmission of *Death on the Rock*. Telephoning the Independent Broadcasting Authority (IBA), which had oversight on television companies like Thames, Sir Geoffrey Howe, personally asked Lord Thomson, the IBA Chairman, to delay the programme until after the inquest into the killings was held in Gibraltar. Otherwise, Howe argued, *Death on the Rock* might prejudice that hearing.[4]

That was an interesting argument for the Foreign Secretary to make since on March 7 in Parliament, he had already stated "the facts" about what had happened in the Colony. It was even more interesting given that the Thatcher Administration had made no attempt to stop the British tabloids from indulging in wild – but pro-government – speculation about the shootings.

Whatever the Foreign Secretary's expectations may have been, Lord Thomson was not about to play censor for Mrs

Thatcher. After personally viewing *Death on the Rock,* he cleared it for transmission, writing later that his decision:

> was not a difficult one. My colleagues and I saw no reason why the IBA should [have prevented *This Week*'s] journalists interviewing those who claimed to be eyewitnesses and investigating the affair exactly as numerous other journalists had done since the shootings.[5]

That did not end the matter. On April 28, with just hours to go before *Death on the Rock* went out, Sir Howe rang up the IBA again with a new argument. By broadcasting statements of eyewitnesses to the shootings, the programme might "contaminate" their evidence. In simple terms, this meant that someone who had lied while appearing on the programme might be very reluctant to tell the truth at the inquest. Conversely, witnesses who spoke the truth might fall under pressure to change their evidence at the hearing. It was an argument that at least some members of the British government must have snickered about given what was about to happen to Carmen Proetta.

Unfortunately for Howe, the contamination argument cut no ice with the IBA. As Lord Thomson himself pointed out, the government's sudden concern about this problem rang rather hollow. Far from keeping witnesses from the press, the Gibraltar Police had cast a spotlight on Stephen Bullock by encouraging reporters to talk with him about what he had seen.[6] And no one had told Josie Celecia to stop giving interviews about what she had witnessed either.

With *Death on the Rock*'s broadcast imminent, the Thatcher Administration began attacking the motivations of those behind it. Speaking in Parliament, Jerry Hayes, one of the Prime Minister's stalwarts, characterized *This Week*'s actions in the Colony as "raking through the gutters of Gibraltar finding people to rubbish [our] security forces".[7] Hayes did not let the fact that he had not seen *Death on the Rock* prevent him from

136

expressing his opinion.[8] And Thatcher, who had also not seen the program condemned it as trial by television, giving the public a lofty warning that, "trial by television or guilt by association is the day freedom dies".[9] It was a beautiful performance, a neat attempt to shift the focus of the controversy to the "irresponsibility" of the press and away from the actions of the SAS.

In the end, *Death on the Rock* went out as scheduled at 9:00 p.m. on April 28. It had been a close call. The technicians at *This Week* had finished the final transmission tape just ten minutes before the programme was due to air. Watching the credits roll forty-four minutes later from his seat in the Thames Television Company hospitality room, Bolton felt satisfied. His reporters had uncovered important new evidence about the shootings. The serious press would have to intensify their investigations into the case.[10] Or would they? Writing in his memoirs, he would admit how naive he had been that night. He had forgotten the prescription of Colin Wallace, a former member of a British Army psychological warfare team who had worked in Belfast in the 1970s:

> The important thing is to get saturation coverage for your story as soon after the controversial event as possible. Even when the facts come out, the original image is the one that sticks.[11]

Bolton, his reporters, and a number of other people were about to get "saturated". But he could have been forgiven for being optimistic at first. Reaction to the program in the "serious" papers the next morning was generally favourable or at least open-minded. In *The Times*, William Holmes wrote that:

> the report seemed a significant, thoroughly responsible and serious examination of a most disturbing case . . . [the] . . . script jumped to no conclusions and argued no extreme case with "partial witnesses", nor could it remotely be described

137

as "trial by television" . . . It simply raised serious questions and suggested they required deep examination.[12]

But Mrs Thatcher's committee wasn't working on the readers of *The Times*, *Independent*, *Guardian*, and *Daily Telegraph* just yet. The first priority was reaching the over twelve million British tabloids readers. Longtime fans of the SAS, those papers routinely celebrated less-than-savory killings in Northern Ireland by the security forces with banner headlines like "String em up!" Encouraging them to attack a programme like *Death on the Rock* was easy.

The *Sun*, part of Rupert Murdoch's media empire, led the charge against Thames Television and *This Week*. Like Mrs Thatcher, the tabloid had no doubt about what *Death on the Rock* had been. The title of its editorial about the program, "BLOOD ON THE SCREEN – *Thames' cheap telly scoop is just IRA propaganda,"* was quite succinct. In the *Sun*'s opinion, it had been wrong for Bolton's people to broadcast interviews with eyewitnesses to the shootings until after the inquest. Like Sir Geoffrey Howe's sudden worries about "contamination" and "prejudice", it was an interesting view for the paper to express since it had been breathlessly reporting accounts of the incident from almost the start (along with its more standard fare of racy pictures of semi-nude starlets and exposes of the love lives of various members of the government).

There was equally bad news for *This Week* on the pages of the *Daily Mail*, one of the *Sun*'s cohorts. Its headline – "FURY OVER SAS '*Trial by TV*'" revealed its owners' bias just as much as the *Sun*'s commentary did. In an inside story, the *Mail* described Roger Bolton as a man who had collaborated with the IRA in the past just so his reporters could get sensational film. As it turned out, that statement was a lie, not the first that was to be told about *Death on the Rock*, and one the *Mail* – much to its embarrassment – had to retract, but only later after the "damage" was done.[13]

138

*Death on the Rock*'s assailants did not count on just the tabloids to blunt the impact the programme had on the British public's perception of the killings. Bolton discovered this when he appeared on April 29 on Channel Four's *Right of Reply*. A feedback show, *Right of Reply*'s format was to have the producers of controversial programmes listen and respond to viewer criticism of their projects. Walking into the Channel Four studio, Bolton met the two "ordinary" citizens who would question him. As he recalled:

> One was a retired naval commander, and the other a young man called Christopher Monckton . . . I seemed to have heard [his] name before, but couldn't place it, yet it troubled me. The recording began, and the former naval officer politely put a number of questions and criticisms to me that I felt I answered adequately . . . Monckton was different altogether. He avoided the facts and attacked my motives. He sounded like a *Daily Mail* editorial, and I half-waited to be called a Communist.[14]

As was *Right of Reply*'s custom, the ordinary viewers got the last word, and Monckton made the most of it. Listening to his comments, the Thames editor felt that he had been ambushed:

> With the seconds ticking away, [Monckton] seemed to look down at a piece of paper and proceeded to slander me, accusing me of being associated with terrorists . . . I tried to come back [with a reply], but the recording was over.[15]

Bolton believed he had been the victim of a bit of "straightforward character assassination". He emphatically told Monckton and *Right of Reply*'s producers that if the programme went out unedited, he would sue them for slander. Then he suddenly realized where he had seen his critic before – at a Conservative Party Central Office cocktail party. Not long before that Monckton had been a member of Mrs Thatcher's personal staff at Number 10 Downing Street. Yet he had not bothered to tell Channel Four about that part of his background. To its credit, *Right of Reply* put that information into the program, and ended the broadcast before Monckton's little speech at the end.

Because of that, Bolton avoided being defamed twice in one day. Carmen Proetta was not so lucky. The first time *This Week*'s star witness had any idea that something might be wrong was the day after *Death on the Rock* aired. A man claiming to be a policeman rang up the Proetta household and told Maxie, her husband, that the family's life "would be made a misery" because of what his wife had said on television.[16]

Later the same day, a story appeared in the *Evening Standard* that gave Carmen a preview of what the anonymous caller had meant by "misery". According to the paper, Gibraltar Police press officer Glen Viagas had put out the following details about Maxie:

Mrs Proetta's husband . . . is well known to us. He has served two terms in Spanish prisons for smuggling drugs.[17]

Yet that was tame compared to what the tabloids were printing. In a story titled "The Truth About SAS Ambush Witness," the *Daily Mail* claimed that Carmen Proetta was the director of a "Spanish escort agency" and that "her fellow directors are wanted in Britain for alleged conspiracy and credit-card fraud." The *Mail* also reported that "police say [the escort agency] is just a cover for vice." The *Daily Express* and *Mirror* ran similar lurid stories with the *Express* informing its readers, "Trial by TV Carmen is Escort Girl Boss." Even the *Daily Telegraph*, a well known "serious" paper, joined the feeding frenzy with the claim that Proetta was one of the forty-four people who had voted to end British rule in Gibraltar during the 1967 referendum. The paper's source of that particular piece of information was "several residents of the Colony who will not be named". Just how these individuals would have known the details of a secret ballot, the *Telegraph* did not say.[18]

But it was the *Sun* that would emerge as the undisputed champion of the Proetta-bashing tournament that had erupted. On April 30, it published a picture of Carmen below the banner headline "TART OF GIB". Underneath, the paper's lead story pulled no punches:

> *The Sun* discovers the Shock Truth about IRA deaths witness Carmen. She's an ex-prostitute, runs an escort agency and is married to a sleazy drug peddler.[19]

Almost as an afterthought, the paper added that "police say both Carmen and her husband have criminal records in Gibraltar," and that her call girl business "catered to rich Arabs."[20]

It made compelling reading, but the story was false. Carmen had been smeared with what British media analyst David Miller would later describe as a "strange concoction of . . . misinformation, innuendo, gossip, and speculation."[21] But where had it come from?

According to Heather Miller, a journalist working for the *Independent*, a large part of the libel appeared to emanate from the Gibraltar Police. Supposedly, a "friendly" police officer had given a number of reporters quite an earful about the Proettas.[22]

When later asked if he was the policeman in question, Inspector Viagas denied it. After all, such a thing would be grossly improper and illegal. Speaking to a correspondent from *Magill*, an Irish magazine, he said:

> I speak to many journalists. I am the police press officer. I do not remember what I say to each of them, but you can take it [from me] that the [*Sun*'s] story is inaccurate.[23]

When pressed about the part of the *Sun*'s article where he was quoted as saying that Carmen Proetta was "somebody we have had dealings with in the past," Viagas admitted that he might have said that, but he had meant only as a fellow citizen. As far as he was concerned about the matter, it was a case of "the less said the better".[24]

Indeed. Given that "citizen" Viagas made that statement only weeks after the original stories about Carmen ran, his denial must have come as cold comfort to the so-called "Tart of Gib". By then, she had grown quite used to seeing the *Sun*'s little exercise in creative investigative journalism plastered on walls near her home by some of the Rock's more "loyal" residents. It was, after all, a *British* newspaper.[25]

Like any good lie, the smear contained a few grains of truth. At the time of the shootings, Maxie had been facing a charge in Spain for allowing his boat to be used by drug smugglers.[26] At the inquest, he would admit under questioning that he had a conviction "for receiving".[27] Yet Bolton's journalists had interviewed Carmen, not him. And it had been Carmen who had told *This Week* about her husband's legal difficulties, expressing her concern that they might prejudice the programme.

It is also worth noting that none of Proetta's many detractors have been able to explain what possible advantage she would have gained for Maxie by appearing on *Death on the Rock*. Even Michael Fielder, the author of the *Sun*'s "Tart of Gib" story, could not answer that question, contenting himself to say only, "She appears to be the architect of her own annihilation in print."[28] As for the *Sunday Times*, which surpassed the *Sun* as Proetta's fiercest critic, it has never squared the contradiction within its argument that Proetta was not worthy of belief because various criminals allegedly told the paper that she was a "crook". Nor has it chosen to elaborate on its apparent belief that someone with a criminal background cannot be a reliable witness, a viewpoint that would certainly disturb Scotland Yard's drug and organized crime squads.[29]

As for the allegation that Carmen Proetta was the ringleader of a call-girl service, there was even less substance there. She had been on the board of a company called Eve International. That company had started as a *tourist* agency, not an escort agency, and Carmen's appointment as one of its director had been purely technical. Eve International had been chartered at the Costa del Sol law firm where she worked. Spanish law at the time required all Spanish companies to be at least fifty per cent owned by a Spanish citizen. As such, Proetta was a natural candidate to fill this requirement for the company's real owners. A year after the company was established, she surrendered her interest in it – something the *Sun* overlooked – and was able to provide written proof of that to *Magill*. When asked about this and other errors in his story, Michael Fielder could only say that it wasn't always possible to check and recheck the facts and that journalism could be "a bit hit and miss . . . but that is the nature of the business".[30]

That was not the complete story. There had been more contributors to the attack on Carmen's character besides careless journalists and possibly loose-lipped Gibraltar policemen. Some of the worst accusations against the Proettas came from their neighbours on the Rock. Something the tabloid and serious journalists agreed on was that there was no shortage of Gibraltarians – from taxi drivers to a government minister – willing to damn her as an unpatriotic whore, provided of course that their names were kept out of print. As to their motives, speculation has its limits. Yet a large number of people appeared to believe an attack on the SAS was in effect an attack on Britain and by extension, Gibraltar's Britishness. The fact that Proetta held Spanish citizenship did not help her. Most Gibraltarians, while hardly elated over the triple killing in their quiet little town, felt Proetta would have been wiser to keep quiet and like the apes on the Rock, see, hear, and speak nothing.

That was a sentiment that someone in London appears to have shared. According to Michael Cockerell's book, *Live from Number 10*, shortly after *Death on the Rock* was transmitted, a member of Thatcher's cabinet called up three newspapers and provided them with defamatory "information" about Proetta.[31]

Yet the most disturbing thing about the smear is that no one in the government said a word in protest about it. Sir Geoffrey Howe and all the other Conservative Party MPs who had been so vocal in their condemnations of Thames Television remained silent throughout the entire attack on a potentially vital eyewitness to an event that had serious national security implications for Britain. As Roger Bolton would later write, "[The tabloids] harassed a witness; the government spoke not a word.[32]

Meanwhile, interviewed at her home by John Waters, the *Magill* correspondent who would later write a major article for his magazine about what he felt had been her vilification, Carmen Proetta was a trifle more philosophical, telling the reporter:

I merely had the misfortune to see something which I shouldn't have seen. If it had been the other way around, [the press and government] would have liked it a lot more.[33]

While the *Sun* and the other tabloids acted as the club in the assault on *Death on the Rock*'s credibility, the *Sunday Times* elected to play the role of finely-honed scalpel. It was well-suited for this task, because it had a reputation of a "serious paper" with a long tradition of investigative journalism.

Yet from the early 1980s onward, some felt that the paper had taken to covering events in Northern Ireland less than objectively. Its journalists still had scoops for its readers – provided by its extensive sources in the British intelligence community. But the collective tone of the stories the paper published was black and white. In the world of the *Sunday Times,* the IRA was a gang of murderous criminals, ruthless, often clumsy, and *always* on the brink of defeat. As for the soldiers and intelligence men fighting the IRA, they were the bravest and best in the land, with none nobler than the SAS. By the end of the Gibraltar affair, some members of its staff proved they had two traits in common with those writing for the *An*

*Phoblacht/Republican News*, the Provisionals' newspaper: one-sidedness and an incredible carelessness with the facts.

This was evident in the *Sunday Times's* very first story on the shootings: "Ambush on the Rock." In it, the paper informed its readers that Gibraltar had a total of 4,000 residents, when it actually has closer to 30,000.[34] It was a harmless mistake, but it was one that could have been easily avoided. More significant was the paper's incorrect statement of basic facts of the shootings. According to the *Sunday Times*, Daniel McCann died on Landport Lane. In reality, it had been Seán Savage who died there. And according to the paper, the SAS men had fired a "dozen or so" shots at the Provisionals. In reality, they discharged their pistols at least twenty-five times.[35]

This paled in comparison with the story the *Sunday Times* printed on May 1, 1988, three days after *Death on the Rock* was shown. Titled "Inadmissable Evidence". it purported to be a detailed analysis of the allegations made by the documentary, the product of research by the paper's journalists in Britain, Gibraltar, and Ireland. According to the article, *Death on the Rock* was "crucially flawed", but a great deal of that contention seemed to rest on statements like "Official sources told the *Sunday Times* that the . . . version of the shootings broadcast last week bore no resemblance to what happened".[36]

Yet neither the government nor the *Sunday Times* had elaborated on what *had* happened in Gibraltar. The article seemed to imply that because the government had said *Death on the Rock* was nonsense, it must be nonsense. Coming to that conclusion without any hard evidence reflected a touching degree of trust in authority on the *Sunday Times's* part.

Some of the other claims the paper made, though, were far more damaging to *Death on the Rock's* credibility. Specifically, the *Sunday Times* announced that Josie and Douglas Celecia had told its reporters that Proetta's version of the shootings was "ridiculous". It also stated that Stephen Bullock felt that

McCann could have had his hands up in self-defense and not surrender. Furthermore, the paper attacked Proetta's credibility using an interview Bullock had given it just four days after the killings, saying that:

Bulloch [sic] told us categorically that the police car [involved in the shootings] had "five uniformed officers in it," not plainclothes SAS men. It had pulled up alongside him, perhaps 100 yards away from the [Shell Station], as two SAS men travelling on foot had raced along the footpath [toward McCann and Farrell].[37]

In the *Sunday Times*'s opinion, this account "destroyed" Proetta's story about the SAS men who shot McCann and Farrell arriving by car. She had not witnessed this but had been confused by the police car Bullock had seen.

The paper also claimed that Colonel Styles, *Death on the Rock*'s technical advisor, was an "angry man" because *This Week* had left out two "key" opinions of his about what had happened in Gibraltar. The first of these was his belief that Proetta had not seen McCann and Farrell raise their hands in surrender but had witnessed an involuntary reaction on their part to the bullets striking their bodies. The second was his opinion that while the IRA team could not have detonated a bomb at the assembly area from where they died, they could have set off one in the red Fiesta parked at the border.

When he read the *Sunday Times*'s piece at his home in London, Roger Bolton felt a momentary stab of panic. As he later recalled:

what was really damaging were the quotes attributed to two of our witnesses, Stephen Bullock and Josie Celecia and to Lt-Col. George Styles . . . it was very worrying. I had not been to Gibraltar myself during the filming and therefore did not have all the detail needed to refute the allegations. Sitting at home with none of my team with me, I momentarily despaired.[38]

He need not have worried. A media organization had distorted the truth, but it had not been *This Week*. That became evident when some of the *Sunday Times*'s "sources" made vocal complaints about "Inadmissable Evidence" in the *Sunday Tribune*. As it turned out, the Celecias had not dismissed all of Proetta's evidence as "ridiculous", just one small detail.[39] And Stephen Bullock denied being certain that McCann had raised his hands in self-defense, pointing out that he had not seen the beginning of the incident when he could have had his hands up in surrender. Bullock's only complaint with *Death on the Rock* had been its statement that he had not heard any warning given before the SAS men killed McCann and Farrell. The British lawyer could not have heard anything like this because of the sound from the cars on the street he was walking along.

The *Sunday Times*'s most serious distortion also concerned Bullock. Its argument, that the lawyer's memory of seeing a police car near him "destroyed" Proetta's story about seeing a Gibraltar police car with gunmen in civilian clothes arrive at the Shell Station, was based on a faulty premise. Bullock and Proetta had not been talking about the same police car but two different ones, a fact that the paper either failed to understand or neglected to share with its readers.

Regarding the comments that the *Sunday Times* had made about Colonel Styles's evidence, there was more smoke than fire to them. Contrary to the paper's claims, *Death on the Rock* had incorporated Styles's suggestion that Proetta had simply seen the Provisionals' hands fly up in reaction to the bullets hitting their bodies. This possibility had been put to Proetta and emphatically rejected by her. As for Style's theory about a bomb being in the car parked along the Spanish border, it was true that *Death on the Rock* omitted it, but only because Bolton and the rest of his staff could not see any sense in the IRA setting a bomb off in a Spanish car park. Furthermore, nothing the authorities had done in Gibraltar after the shootings suggested they had seriously thought the Fiesta contained a car-bomb.

The *Sunday Times'* story also failed to mention Styles's view that the killings were the result of a pre-emptive strike. He made that particular belief of his quite clear when interviewed for the documentary:

> I look at the whole piece as being two active service units waging war, and thank goodness our side won . . . I think it would have been reckless for the security forces to have tangled with these people, who may well have been armed; so taking them out quickly, cleanly, and without other people being hurt – that seems to be the only way.[40]

Speaking to Chris Oxley, after "Inadmissable Evidence" appeared, Styles told the reporter that he didn't have anything to apologize for, saying, "the thing that makes me most cross is the way the press has gone for Carmen Proetta, because you know what she said was true".[41]

## Notes

1. Letter from David Miller, Media Studies Centre, Stirling University, Scotland to me, April 8, 1997.
2. "Ambush on the Rock", *Sunday Times,* March 13, 1988. After the documentary was shown the paper, in another story, stated categorically that a button job had been feared.
3. Bolton, pp. 222-223; David Miller, "The Damage Was Done", *Magill,* April 1989, p. 18.
4. Windlesham and Rampton, pp. 111-130.
5. Bolton, pp. 230-231.
6. Interview with Stephen and Lucinda Bullock.
7. Bolton, p. 234.
8. Ibid.
9. Ibid.
10. Ibid, p. 235.
11. Ibid.
12. William Holmes, "Question of Truth", *The Times,* April 29, 1989.
13. Bolton, p. 237.
14. Ibid, p. 238.
15. Ibid.
16. John Waters, "The Vilification of Carmen Protetta", *Magill,* June 1988, p. 20.

17. Miller, "The Damage Was Done", p. 22.

18. Ibid.

19. "Tart of Gib", The *Sun*, April 30, 1988.

20. Ibid.

21. Miller, "The Damage Was Done", p. 22.

22. BBC Two Television *Newsnight*, January 25, 1989.

23. Waters, "The Vilification of Carmen Proetta", p. 20.

24. Ibid.

25. Proetta ultimately won her libel cases and several hundred thousand pounds in damages from the *Sun* and other newspapers.

26. Waters, "The Vilification of Carmen Proetta",and other soiurces.

27. Testimony of Maxie Proetta, Day 13, September 22, 1988, Channel Four Television, p. 32.

28. Waters, "The Vilification of Carmen Proetta,"and other soiurces.

29. "Truth on the Rock", *Sunday Times*, May 17, 1992.

30. Waters, "The Vilification of Carmen Proetta", p. 20.

31. Michael Cockerell, *Live from Number 10: The Inside Story of Prime Ministers and Television*, Faber and Faber, London, 1989, p. 315.

32. Bolton, p. 241.

33. Waters, "The Vilification of Carmen Proetta", p. 21.

34. "Ambush on the Rock", *Sunday Times*, March 13, 1988.

35. Ibid.

36. "Inadmissable Evidence", *Sunday Times*, April 1, 1988.

37. Ibid.

38. Bolton, pp. 242-244.

39. This had to do with the actions of one of the men who emerged from the police car.

40. Windlesham and Rampton, p. 64. Colonel Styles was apparently unaware that a bystander, Victor Adams, had been grazed by one of the SAS men's bullets presumably ricocheting off the petrol pumps at the Shell Station.

41. Bolton, p. 245.

# CHAPTER TEN

## CAUGHT ON THE CONVEYOR BELT

"The only point I would make about [the claim that the British do not coerce confessions] is that it has as much relevance to what actually goes on at RUC and Army interrogation centres as the proceedings at Disneyland."
— Tim Pat Coogan, *On the Blanket*

Well before the broadcast of *Death on the Rock*, Republican West Belfast had been experiencing the consequences of what had happened at Kevin Brady's funeral. Events at Casement Park triggered revulsion throughout the world. Northern Ireland had always been the scene of brutal crimes.[1] But few took place in front of television cameras.

At first, Andersonstown's residents felt sorrow over the soldiers' murders. One local woman told an RUC officer, "Son, I thought we couldn't sink any lower until I saw what they did to those two wee boys . . . It's terrible. Simply terrible."[2] At City Hall, thousands of Catholics and Protestants, many weeping, signed letters of condolence to the Wood and Howes families. At Mass the day after the killings, Father Tom Toner, the parish priest at St Agnes's, told his congregation, "Our parish is seen as dripping in the blood of the murdered, and one thinks of the mob baying for the blood of Jesus."[3] In anguish, the priest asked, "My dear people, what has happened to us?"[4]

In Britain, the killings struck a nerve that Michael Stone's rampage in Milltown Cemetery three days before did not. The victims then, after all, were Irish. Wood and Howes had been *British soldiers*. At Casement Park, courtesy of BBC and the other networks, British television viewers got to see – over and over again– the two young men falling victim to what looked like a lynch mob. The words of Hilda Butler, Wood's grandmother, who raised him as a child, give some sense of the bitter anger that those television images generated:

The IRA monsters who murdered my boy should be strung up. [Derek] was a wonderful grandson. The Army has had its hands tied for too long. They should be allowed to go sort out those evil men, once and for all.[5]

Margaret Thatcher was beyond rage. To her, the killings were "the single most horrifying event in Northern Ireland" during her term of office. In her memoirs, she set out her feelings precisely:

No one who saw the film of the lynching of the two young soldiers trapped by that frenzied Republican mob, pulled from their car, stripped and murdered, will believe that reason or goodwill can ever be a substitute for *force* [author's italics] when dealing with Irish Republican terrorism.[6]

West Belfast's grief over the corporals' deaths did not last for long. Mrs Thatcher made sure of that with her comment that "there seems to be no depths to which these people will not sink".[7] Those in Belfast's Republican community, not among the Prime Minister's admirers, naturally assumed the phrase "these people" referred to them.

A statement by Tom King, then Secretary of State for Northern Ireland, who had already said that the people of West Belfast had proved capable of "unknown depths of evil", made "those people" even angrier. Attempting to explain why the RUC did not act to save Wood and Howes' lives, he told the assembled House of Commons:

It is no secret that the first impression was of a further

attempted bomb attack on a funeral. *As soon as it became clear that the matter was indeed serious* [author's italics], the police acted with considerable determination.[8]

To Andersonstown's inhabitants, King's meaning was clear. Their lives were not important; those of British soldiers were.

Yet what came after the politicians stopped making speeches and the reporters went home did the most damage. For the next four years, it was as if Corporals Wood's and Howes's ghosts were haunting Belfast. In the largest murder investigation in the history of Northern Ireland, hundreds of police spent thousands of man-hours searching for those who played a role in the soldiers' deaths. All told, the RUC arrested over two hundred people and put forty-one on trial on charges ranging from conspiracy to pervert the course of justice to murder.

Many Northern Ireland Catholics, and not all of them Republicans, bitterly noted that this was a far greater effort than any the police had made to arrest the killers of Catholic civilians. Over time, they began to see the prosecutions as persecution, not an effort to bring murderers to justice.

That assumption was debatable. Most RUC officers, prosecutors, and judges sincerely believed that the crowd's actions at Casement Park had been unforgivably criminal behaviour. Yet the overwhelming majority of those men and women also had little sympathy for Kevin Brady's mourners, people they saw as IRA supporters. Whatever the case, in Northern Ireland, intentions count for little. Results are everything, and those of the Casement Trials were quite disturbing.

That was not evident at the first trial. There, the accused were Alex Murphy and Henry Maguire, veteran IRA men.[9] The police caught them together just minutes after the corporals died. When arrested, Murphy was literally covered in Wood's blood. Fibres from the soldier's green sweater were on his clothing.[10] Murphy claimed the blood and threads came from a brief scuffle he had with the man before the crowd dragged him into Casement Park. Yet the quantity and nature of the blood stains were consistent with him being in the back of the taxi that took the corporals to Penny Lane. Fibres from the taxi's seat covers were on the IRA man as well. This forensic evidence made his prosecutors' interpretation of the blurry heli-tele film quite credible. They argued that that footage showed Murphy forcing both soldiers into the black taxi. At the execution ground on Penny Lane, he pointed Howes out to the first gunman who shot him.

The case against Maguire was stronger. Howes's blood stained his clothes, and fibres from Wood's sweater were on him as well. Maguire testified that this was because he searched the soldiers' car for a bomb. But his shoes matched tracks left on the ground where the IRA men put the corporals into the black taxi. After enhancement, a news video clip showed Maguire sitting in the car's front seat as it sped away from the funeral.[11] Those facts supported the prosecution's argument that Maguire was the "man in white" in the heli-tele film who ejected Father Reid from Casement Park and later beat the soldiers on Penny Lane.

In January 1989, Lord Chief Justice Hutton, presiding over a juryless Diplock court, convicted the two men of murder, false imprisonment, possession of firearms, grievous bodily harm, and assault. He sentenced both Murphy and Maguire to life sentences with a recommendation that they serve a minimum of twenty-five years in prison.

In time, the IRA men's convictions became a show piece for the RUC. It underpinned the image the police wanted the British public to have of the Casement Trials, textbook prosecutions of obviously guilty men. Yet that image is false. The guilt of many of the remaining thirty-eight men who were tried was far from clear. And what three of the defendants, Pat

Kane, Michael Timmons, and Seán Kelly, experienced at the hands of Northern Ireland's judicial system was Kafkaesque.

Pat Kane was the first of the three to be caught in the criminal justice "conveyor belt". Thirty years old, he had been born partially deaf and, as a child, he had been unwilling to wear a hearing aid because of the taunts the device drew from other children. Because of that, Kane got nothing out of school, leaving it at fifteen almost completely illiterate. He could write his name, something his mother taught him, and a few other words but that was all. The only work Kane could find was general labour. Painfully shy, deeply ashamed of his handicaps, his biggest ambition was to get a steady job, find a girl, and settle down.[12]

The day of Kevin Brady's funeral, Kane, along with several thousand others, turned out to watch it. That was something many from outside his community would not understand. Even in West Belfast, an IRA funeral was a spectacle, something that drew the attention of the curious along with the true believers. Kane definitely fell into the former category. The child of devoutly religious and pacifistic parents, he had steered clear of any involvement with the IRA.

After the funeral and the murders, Kane quickly learned that people thought he was the man news footage showed smashing the passenger side window of Wood and Howes' car. Afraid he would be arrested because of this, he went into hiding at his aunt's house. After several weeks, Kane then resumed his normal routine. It was not until over eight months later that the police came for him. At 6:30 a.m. on December 12, 1988, as his parents looked on with disbelief, the RUC arrested him.

Michael Timmons was next. A resident of the Poleglass district of Belfast, he was twenty-nine years old in 1988. He had steady work as a house painter and decorator and was not a member of the IRA. He did not have time for politics. For him, his wife, children, and parents were the only things that mattered. Describing her son, his mother said, "All Michael ever [did] was work for his family. As long as his family was alright, as long as his mum and daddy were alright, that was everything."[13]

Timmons had not known Kevin Brady very well. But though badly hungover from drinking the night before, he decided to attend the funeral and say a few prayers for the man's soul. Those prosecuting and judging him interpreted this – a decision hundreds of other people made – as "proof" that he supported the IRA. They might not have reached that conclusion had they heard Cardinal Daly explain:

In Ireland as a whole, there is an attitude [toward funerals] quite different from that which prevails over in other countries. It's not a private occasion. It's not a family occasion. [Attendance] is not an act of approval of the lay person's life style. It's an act of intercession for a dead sinner.[14]

By the time Timmons reached St Agnes's Church on March 19, the funeral Mass had already started. He entered the church, prayed for a time, and left. Thirsty, he had an hour to kill before the pubs opened and decided to walk along with the cortege. It was then that Corporals Wood and Howes made their fateful appearance in Andersonstown.

For eleven months after their deaths, Timmons' life was normal. He worked, took care of his family, and tried to forget the terrible things he had seen inside Casement Park. Then on February 5, 1989, something strange happened. A policeman came by and asked him his name. Upon being told "Michael Timmons", the officer told him that his car had been stolen and was burning down at Divis Flats, a West Belfast flats complex. Timmons said he did not own a car. The policeman smiled and replied, "Well, congratulations then. We must have made a mistake."[15]

But it was no mistake. The RUC man had been there to

155

confirm Timmons' location. The story about the car had been a ruse to get close to him. The next day, at 6:00 a.m., the police returned to his house and took him into custody.

It was also Seán Kelly's turn. A happy-go-lucky nineteen year-old, Kelly, like other two, was not in the IRA. He had no real interest in politics. Sports were much more fun. An active member of the Gaelic Athletic Association, Kelly was fanatical about football. At one match, he broke an arm, at another an ankle. It did not matter. In each case, after a few weeks, the young man took off the casts and started playing again. [16]

Throughout 1987, Kelly was in England, working as a barman. He liked it there and had a number of English friends. But near the end of the year, he got disturbing news. His grandfather, William Stevenson, was very ill. Kelly had always been close to him. The two men shared the same passion for sports, particularly football. Just before Christmas 1987, Kelly returned to Belfast. In between matches and visiting his "granda," he earned money as a painter and decorator. He was hoping to save enough so he could return to England or start a new life in the United States. [17]

On March 19, 1988, Kelly had been in Poleglass, baby-sitting for his Aunt Roisín. After she returned, he set off for home. The taxi he was riding in travelled on Andersonstown Road. When it reached St Agnes, Kevin Brady's funeral cortege blocked its path. Getting out of the car, Kelly walked along the footpath toward his parents' house on Rockville Street. A few minutes later, he found himself in the centre of a panic-stricken crowd. After the cortege resumed moving, Kelly followed it for a time. He had heard Wood's pistol go off and was worried that his father, Jim, who had attended the funeral, might be hurt. He caught up with the older man at the Kennedy Way roundabout. From that location, the Kellys suddenly heard a burst of shots from Penny Lane, over a quarter of a mile away. [18]

After that traumatic event, life went back to normal for

young Seán. It was not until 5:00 a.m., February 6, 1989 that a hammering came at the Kellys' door. When Briege, his mother, opened it, there were four Land Rovers filled with police and soldiers outside the house. Pushing past Mrs Kelly, the RUC men pulled Seán out of his bed and arrested him.

At first, the police did not have a substantive case against the trio. What they did have were press photos and video showing Timmons, Kelly, and Kane outside the park; the heli-tele film (so unclear that the facial features of people in it could not be made out); and suspicions. There was no hard forensic evidence to tie the trio to the killings: no fingerprints, no hair, no fibers, nothing. Yet in just a few hours, the RUC's interrogators produced much of the evidence needed to convict the three men.

This was particularly the case with Pat Kane. He fell victim to a peculiarity of Northern Ireland's criminal justice system: the police's right to interrogate a man outside the presence of his lawyer. Between December 12 and December 13, 1988, he underwent a total of seven hours of questioning at Woodburne RUC barracks.

According to his interrogators, at his first interview, Kane denied being inside Casement Park, let alone committing crimes there. But during his second, after the detectives told him he was lying to them, he became visibly nervous and began to change his story. He admitted that the crowd had "swept him" into the park. Kane maintained that once inside, he did not touch the soldiers. He just stood there and a few minutes later, was thrown out along with Father Reid.[19]

At the third session, when the police said that they believed he was still not telling the truth, Kane expanded his story. He informed them that on March 19, he had been wearing a hooded green anorak, black pants, and white shoes. He admitted to following the group of men that took the first soldier into Casement Park. When he saw them beat and strip the man, he realized "something bad was going to happen". Wanting to leave, he walked over to the park's north wall and looked down it. But the nine foot drop was too far for him to jump. Going over to where Father Reid was, Kane took him by the shoulder. A second later, a man pushed them both out of the park.[20]

During the fourth interview, the detectives told Kane that the heli-tele film showed a man wearing clothes like his kicking or stamping on one of the soldiers. Kane allegedly responded by saying, "Aye, I was afraid of that".[21] Asked why he did it, he replied, "Just to be a big fella like all the rest". Kane then gave further details of his activities. He said that he had closed the gates after the first soldier had been brought in, opened them to admit the second, and closed them again after someone told him to do it. It had been after he came back from looking down the wall that Kane kicked the soldier. Following that, he used Father Reid to get out of the park.

The written statement Kane signed contained this version of events with a few differences. In it, he claimed that he had kicked the soldier in "the heat of the moment". He also said the sight of Father Reid praying over the corporals made him realize that he did not want to be a party to events in Casement Park. He had taken hold of Reid after a man shouted, "Get that priest out!"[22]

At his trial, though, Kane would return to his original story. He had not been inside the park. Counting that testimony, he had given six different accounts of his actions, the surest sign that he was a liar and a criminal.

Or was it? Testifying in his own defense, Kane said he had been afraid of the detectives questioning him, particularly after they began to shout and threaten to send him off to Castlereagh interrogation centre. Several times, he thought the policemen were going to hit him. So he began "agreeing with everything they said, so they would let [him] out". That was how his written statement took shape. The police would write down a sentence and ask if it was correct. In his emotional state, Kane agreed with everything they suggested to him. Later, he told his parents that he had been so frightened that if the RUC had accused *them* of killing the corporals, he would have agreed with it – anything to get out of the interrogation room.[23]

There was no proof this abuse took place. That was because, despite having the technology and the means to do so, the RUC made no audio or video-tape of any of the Casement interrogation sessions. Yet by the police's own testimony, they used psychological pressure on Kane. Twice, they deliberately and falsely accused him of smashing the passenger side window of the soldiers' car. The impact this would have had on a desperately frightened man can be imagined.[24]

Michael Timmons had somewhat different experience at the RUC's hands. Taken directly to Castlereagh, he underwent multiple interrogations the day of his arrest. During the first, Timmons told the police that he had been walking about a hundred yards behind Kevin Brady's coffin when Wood's and Howes's car drove into the cortege. Like scores of other people, he ran toward their car after the black taxis trapped it. As he approached the vehicle, he thought its occupants might be joyriders or loyalist gunmen. That latter possibility scared him so he turned and tried to hold people back from the car. But the crowd just overwhelmed him.[25]

A second after that, a gunshot rang out, and Timmons threw himself to the ground. He got up, and the next thing he knew, he was in Casement Park. Once there, he stood near the soldiers and watched the other men beat them. He saw Henry Maguire there, but did not talk to him.[26] He denied helping to strip the corporals or put them over the wall.

Timmons' version of events began to change as the day wore on. Shown a photograph by the police, he admitted that he had been at the rear of the group of men who took Corporal Wood into the park. He denied making physical contact with him. Once people started stripping the two soldiers, he tried to leave, but a line of men were standing in front of the gate, refusing to let anyone in or out. After several minutes though, they finally let him leave Casement Park, and he walked over to where the IRA men were putting the corporals into the black taxi. When it drove off, he ran after it but did not know why.[27]

The painter from Poleglass also gave the RUC officers questioning him a written statement that contained that version of events. In it, he said that he remembered an English accented voice shouting "Signals", as the crowd forced Corporal Wood into Casement Park. After hearing that, he decided that Wood and Howes probably were soldiers. It made no difference, though; he continued to help push Wood into the park.[28]

Timmons allegedly made additional damaging verbal admissions. At his fourth interview of the day, he told the detectives that inside Casement Park he had looked at a card that one of the soldiers had which said, "I am a member of Her Majesty's Forces. Please treat me as a civilian." After examining it, he kicked one of the corporals in the foot. Asked why, he told the detectives, "I don't know. It was just for the sake of kicking him". Asked if he helped strip the soldiers, he said that he thought he had taken the boots off the man he had kicked. Finally, when questioned about what, at that point, he thought was going to happen to Wood and Howes, Timmons replied, "I thought they would be taken away from [Casement Park] or shot there."[29]

When he testified on his own behalf, Timmons did not deny being inside Casement Park. Yet the story he told in court had some subtle differences to the final version of events the RUC claimed he gave. In the dock, Timmons would say that he joined the group pushing Corporal Wood into Casement Park out of sheer "nosiness". He had heard Wood shout out "Signals" in an English accent, but had not known what that meant. Even after that, he still believed the soldier might have been a Loyalist gunman. He thought the crowd around the soldiers' car might kill the two men and that by bringing them into the park, he was helping to take them out of harm's way.[30]

Timmons would not challenge the police's testimony about his admissions with two major exceptions. The detectives had repeatedly told him that no court in the land would believe that he had been there and done nothing to the soldiers. If he did not tell them the whole truth, there was no chance he would get bail. Desperate to get back to his family, Timmons made up the story about kicking one of the soldiers and taking off his boots. It got him bail, but it also got him charged with murder.

Finally, there was Seán Kelly. The last thing that his parents told him before the police took him to Castlereagh was to say nothing until he talked to a solicitor. Kelly heeded their advice. Once at the interrogation centre, he refused to discuss his actions on March 19 with the police. It was not until 12:10 p.m., after consulting with the lawyer his family had retained, Kelly gave the police the following unsigned statement:

On the 19th of March 1988, I was at the funeral of Kevin Brady, while going along the Andersonstown Road, a car sped towards the funeral cortege. It then stopped and reversed. At this, a crowd ran towards the car. I ran towards the car but heard a loud bang which sounded like gunfire. I scattered back from the car towards the crowd. I then seen what seemed to be a scuffle round the vicinity of the car. I could not make it out because I was too far away from the car at the time. I then observed a crowd going towards the gates of Casement Park and noticed a man being brought into Casement Park . . . When the crowd entered Casement Park, I felt reluctant to be part of anything that was going to happen so I decided to avoid the incident and rejoin the funeral . . . That is all I can recall of that day . . . [31]

After that, Kelly kept his mouth shut. Using the heli-tele film and the press footage as a justification, the police charged him, like Kane, with falsely imprisoning and inflicting grievous bodily harm on Corporals Wood and Howes. After six weeks on remand in the Crumlin Road Jail, he was released on bail. He did not know it at the time, but remaining silent would be as costly to him as Kane and Timmons' willingness to talk with the police had been to them.

## Notes

1. The murders of Wood and Howes eclipsed a crime that was equally savage. The victims were Gillian Johnston, a young Protestant from Belleek, and Stanley Leggett, her fiancé. The day before Kevin Brady's funeral, Provo gunmen ambushed the couple's car, riddling it with bullets. They thought Johnston's brother was inside. Leggett survived, but his intended bride did not.
2. McCallion, *The Killing Zone*, p. 247.
3. "Horrified Priests in N Ireland Assail 'Foul, Bloody Murders'", *Courier Journal*, March 21, 1988.
4. Ibid.
5. Godson, "The Real Face of the IRA".
6. Thatcher, *The Downing Street Years*, HarperCollins Publishers, 1993, p. 407.
7. *The Casement Trials: A Case Study on the Right to a Fair Trial in Northern Ireland*, The Committee for the Administration of Justice, Belfast, 1992, p. 5.
8. Ibid.
9. O'Brien, p. 151.
10. *The Queen Versus Alex Murphy and Henry Maguire*, The Crown Court of Northern Ireland, Lord Chief Justice Hutton presiding, January 1989, pp. 21-32. Murphy also had threads from the taxi's seat covers on his clothes.
11. Interview with Bernard and Maureen Kane, Belfast, November 1996.
12. Ibid.
13. Interview with Trudy Timmons, Belfast, November, 1996.
14. *Murder in Mind*, Rough Justice, BBC Television 1993.
15. Interview with Trudy Timmons.
16. Interview with James and Briege Kelly, Belfast, November 1996.
17. Sworn Statement of Seán Kelly, January 17, 1995, p. 1.
18. Interview with Seán Kelly, Maze Prison, Belfast, November 1996.
19. *The Queen V Patrick Gerard Kane . . .* pp. 13-20.
20. Ibid.
21. Ibid.
22. Ibid.
23. Interview with Bernard and Maureen Kane.
24. *The Queen V Patrick Gerard Kane . . .* pp. 13-20.
25. Ibid, pp. 26-35.
26. Asked by the prosecution if Maguire had the reputation of being an IRA man, Timmons declined to answer.
27. Ibid.
28. Ibid.
29. Ibid.
30. Ibid.
31. Ibid, pp. 41-42.

# CHAPTER ELEVEN

## BRITANNIA WAIVES THE RULES

"To no one we will sell, to no one will we refuse or delay right or justice."
— Magna Carta, 1215

The arrests of Kane, Timmons, and Kelly were quiet events, overshadowed by the controversy over *Death on the Rock*. The documentary had goaded Mrs Thatcher into one of her famous set-piece rages against the "irresponsibility" of the press.[1] Yet the uproar the program sparked did not change her mind that a special inquiry into the killings was unnecessary. An inquest would be an adequate enough investigation and would be entirely in the hands of Mr Felix Pizzarello, Gibralter's Coroner.

There was a long delay in setting a date for the inquest. That was not unusual for Northern Ireland where inquests take place as long as eight years after a disputed death, but it was decidedly strange for Gibraltar. Finally, almost eight weeks after the killings, Pizzarello announced that the inquest would begin on June 27.

That date was changed after two weeks. On May 23, at 11:00 a.m., in London, Bernard Ingram, the Prime Minister's press secretary, announced that the hearing would be indefinitely postponed.

Meanwhile, in Gibraltar, Pizzarello did not appear to know that he had changed his mind. The same time Downing Street announced the postponement, the Coroner had been chatting with Dominic Searles, a reporter for the *Gibraltar Chronicle*. Pizzarello told Searles that he was considering, but only *considering,* a change in date. Upon hearing the news from London, Searles returned to the Coroner's office where he was again informed there had been no formal decision to reschedule the event. At last, at 4:00 p.m., Pizzarello announced that the inquest had indeed been postponed. Back in Britain, Kevin McNamara, the Labour Party's spokesman on Northern Ireland, drily commented, "I'm surprised the government did not announce the verdict as well".[2]

Meanwhile, the IRA campaign continued. Throughout the summer of 1988, ASUs operating in Northern Ireland, England, Germany, Holland, and Belgium killed fifteen British servicemen, three reservists, and a policeman, injuring many others.

The security forces were also busy. On July 1, an SAS mistake claimed the life of another innocent civilian. This time the victim was Ken Stronge, a Protestant taxi driver. He had been unlucky enough to drive his car past the RUC's North Queen Street Barracks in Belfast just seconds after an IRA man sprayed the building with automatic rifle fire while another launched an RPG7 anti-tank rocket at it. Stronge did not know – nor did the IRA – that a team of six SAS men and two police officers were inside the barracks waiting for just such an attack to occur.

The moment the IRA opened fire, the soldiers intended to rush through the barracks' gate and engage them. It was a simple plan which might have worked but for the foolishness of the SAS officer controlling the operation. Demanding complete control of the facility, he replaced the police reservist who normally operated its gate with one of his own men. When the IRA attacked, the soldier pulled the wrong lever and shut the gate instead of opening it.[3] By the time he got it open, Stronge's taxi was in the kill zone. Three of the eighty high-velocity bullets the SAS team fired at the Volvo the IRA men used passed through it and struck the taxi driver in the neck and arm. Taken to the hospital, Stronge died of a heart attack brought on by his wounds on July 4, 1988. He was forty-six. Curiously enough, when the inquest into his death took place, all of the soldiers involved were "overseas" and unable to appear.[4]

Then, on August 20, the IRA staged a "spectacular". The Provisionals' target was a coach moving south on Northern Ireland's A5 Highway. Inside were thirty-five British soldiers returning to their barracks in Omagh after taking leave in England. As the vehicle passed a hay wagon parked on the roadside, an IRA man hiding nearby triggered the two hundred pound charge of semtex concealed within it. The blast tore into the unarmoured coach, hurling it through the air. It landed in a hedgerow a hundred feet down the road, a mass of twisted, smoking metal. Inside, the bus resembled a slaughterhouse with the mangled bodies of the dead mixed in with those screaming in agony from blast burns and cuts from flying glass. Mortally wounded, one soldier – his training taking over – began crawling from the wreckage to find cover in an abandoned cowshed. As a local woman recalled, "He crawled through the mud and into the shed. Then he leaned back on a bale of hay and died. He was just a boy, no older than my son [who was eighteen]."[5]

Eight soldiers were killed in the coach bombing, and the survivors suffered serious injuries. Compounding the tragedy was that it had resulted from appalling security lapses on part of the British Army. There had been no effort to disguise the bus, and it had been on the A5 route despite it being off-limits.[6] The fact that the Army tried to conceal these facts from Downing Street only magnified the embarrassment.

The IRA and British tabloids perceived what happened next

as the SAS's revenge. For weeks, British intelligence had known that an IRA unit had been shadowing a part-time member of the Ulster Defense Regiment (UDR) who worked as a truck driver in Drumnakilly. On August 30, just nine days after the coach bombing, the SAS set a trap for the Provisionals, complete with a suitable bait. One soldier posed as the driver and stood for hours on a roadside, pretending to change one of his truck's tyres. This drew the attention of three IRA men who drove up to the scene in a white Ford Sierra. What they did not know was at least three SAS men were watching them from a roadside dugout.[7]

There are two versions of what happened next. According to the government, the Provisionals took the decoy driver by surprise, opening fire and chasing him back to where the other soldiers were waiting. It was only then that the SAS men began shooting, killing all three gunmen. But according to witnesses interviewed by Father Raymond Murray, the former prison chaplain and friend of Mairéad Farrell, it was the other way around. The soldiers were the only ones who fired their weapons. The ASU never got the chance. One local resident's account suggested at least the possibility this was true – that the SAS had raked the car with machine-gun fire and continued pumping bullets into it long after the IRA men were helpless or dead. Nevertheless, the British tabloids treated the event as a case of good conquering evil. The *Star* headline – SAS RUB OUT IRA RATS – said it all.[8]

On September 6, eight days after that round in this murderous game of "tit for tat", the inquest finally opened on the Rock. For the Gibraltarians, the six months leading up to it had been bewildering. Until March 6, 1988, their home had been an obscure little corner of the United Kingdom, a place written about in history books but hardly a centre of events in the modern world. Then, without warning, three people had been gunned down in broad daylight on their city's streets.

Before the Colony's inhabitants could catch their collective breath, the terrifying news had come that those killed had been terrorists, hell-bent on detonating a massive car-bomb in the heart of their town. Very few of the Gibraltarians could understand why Catholic Irishmen would travel hundreds of miles to kill their co-religionists in Gibraltar. It made no sense.[9]

The Gibraltarians also had to deal with the media circus that descended on their town. Before the killings, Gibraltar was lucky if a London correspondent dropped by every now and then to file a story about negotiations with Spain over the Colony's status. But for months, dozens of reporters had been in Gibraltar and southern Spain, all searching for the big story. With the inquest taking place, there were even more press on the scene – from *The Times, Guardian, Sunday Tribune* – all the major papers.

Along with the "serious" press came the "hacks", tabloid reporters, the same worthies who libelled Carmen Proetta and Roger Bolton. Although reporters, their behavior was similar to sailors on leave after a long cruise at sea. Each night after the inquest closed and after filing their stories, the hard-drinking employees of the *Star, Daily Mail, Express*, and others would close Gibraltar's pubs down. When the night's festivities came to an end, they would stagger down the city's narrow streets, shouting out Protestant songs that belonged more in Belfast than they did in on the southern tip of Spain. Growing bored with that, a number of reporters purchased water pistols and took to creeping up behind their more respectable brethren and shouting, "Stop! Police! Hands up!" It was the challenge the SAS supposedly issued to the ASU. Anyone who turned around received a squirt of water across the chest.[10] Times were strange in Gibraltar.

The Gibraltar Supreme Court chamber, the scene of the event the reporters had come to cover, had a simple layout. The

167

coroner's raised bench dominated the room. Behind it on the wall was the coat-of-arms of the British Empire, "splendidly done up in red, white, and blue, picked out in gold, and complete with its legends in courtly French which say the English monarchs have God and right on their side and that evil will come to those who think it".[11]

The jury box where eleven Gibraltarian men would sit was to the right of the coroner's bench. In the well of the court, the lawyers representing the "interested parties" (John Laws for the British government, Michael Hucker for the SAS, and Paddy McGrory for the McCann, Savage, and Farrell families) shared a common table with Eric Thistlewaite, the Gibraltar Attorney General.

Felix Pizzarello, the man who presided over the proceedings, was something of an enigma for those watching the proceedings. Fifty-seven years old, the descendant of a Genoese merchant, he had been Gibraltar's Coroner for seven years. Before that, he had been the Colony's stipendiary magistrate, a position held by his father. Now, he worked at both posts. One of the Rock's very few Protestants, he was a devout church-goer and the former opening batsman for the local cricket team.[12] The reporters present at the inquest considered him quite camera-shy, something that prompted the satirical magazine *Private Eye* to dub him "Coroner Paparazzi".

Pizzarello enjoyed a reputation for integrity and fairness, but he was also known as a cautious man. This may have been the reason why he did not publicly question Downing Street's decision to change the inquest date without bothering to inform him of that fact. Yet sometimes, Pizzarello appeared quite determined to uphold the standards of justice in Gibraltar for the world to see. At one point in the inquest, the Coroner appeared to indicate his own opinion of what had happened on March 6, when he referred to the places where

168

McCann, Savage, and Farrell died as "the scene of the crime".[13]

Paddy McGrory was a less ambiguous figure. He would prove to be the only one really interested in challenging what the British government had to say about what took place on March 6 on the Rock. A small man with snowy white hair, he was a Belfast native – the Falls Road to be precise – who had been practicing law for decades. Ever since he had been a small boy, the courts had held a special appeal for him. During the 1950s, when he was first establishing his practice, there was no lucrative civil work for a Catholic lawyer. McGrory had to find a niche working criminal defense cases, something he grew to love.[14]

McGrory was a Republican but did not believe in the use of force to unite Ireland. When the Troubles returned to Northern Ireland, the people of the Falls Road naturally turned to McGrory for help when they became caught up in the violence and its inevitable legal consequences. He represented many Republicans in court, including Gerry Adams.[15] Yet while other Catholic lawyers who did the same quickly became hate figures for the police and the Protestant community (one being assassinated in 1989), McGrory managed to avoid this fate. Perhaps it was because he made a point of taking the cases of members of Protestant paramilitary organizations as well as Republicans. Above all else, he was a man who believed that the end does *not* justify the means and that there always has to be someone willing to ask the hard questions and stand up to "authority".[16]

As a skilled lawyer, McGrory knew well that inquests are heavily weighted toward giving authority its say without being forced to answer any impertinent questions from those with different views. Inquests must take place if a death occurs in "circumstances . . . prejudicial to the health or safety of the public." Such proceedings have a limited scope. They only consider the "how, when, and where" of a death. When examining a case where someone dies because of the actions of another human being, an inquest jury cannot fix individual guilt, it can only bring in a ruling of lawful killing, unlawful killing, or an open verdict.[17] If death is determined "unlawful," the local Director of Public Prosecutions – in Gibraltar's case, its Attorney General, Mr Thistlewaite – would decide whether someone should be prosecuted. As early as July, he had announced that there would not be any prosecutions resulting from the killings. But the Attorney General did allow that if the inquest found that the deaths were unlawful, that decision might change.

Inquests are not adversarial. There is no prosecution or defense with a judge acting as a legal referee. Instead, the coroner is the investigator. After receiving evidence and statements of witnesses, he decides what should be heard by the jury and when. When a witness testifies, the coroner conducts the initial examination.[18]

Under this system, lawyers retained by individuals or groups with an interest in the case can cross-examine witnesses and attempt to shape the coroner's conduct of the hearing. But they have no right to police investigatory reports and statements of witnesses who will testify. They are allowed only a copy of the autopsy report. The interested parties do not receive any legal aid for expenses they might incur.[19]

With the Crown being one of the parties to the inquest, these rules put McGrory at a marked disadvantage. With every official giving testimony – from the lowliest Gibraltar Police officer to the MI5 and SAS men – a British government employee, his opponents, John Laws and Michael Hucker could see their statements in advance (as well as the ones the police collected from civilian witnesses). Both lawyers had unlimited budgets. In contrast, McGrory was working for free, paying his own expenses. When the Gibraltar authorities abruptly decided to raise the price of the inquest transcript from fifty pence to five pounds per page the day before the proceedings started, the Belfast solicitor could not afford to buy a copy. Instead, he had to rely on longhand notes taken by one of his assistants. "Equality of Arms", the idea that no one side should enjoy a legal advantage over the other, simply did not exist in Gibraltar.[20]

Another serious handicap placed on McGrory was the way Pizzarello called the witnesses. There was no correlation between the order of their appearance and the sequence of events at the time of the shootings. All the SAS and MI5 operatives gave evidence before the ordinary civilian witnesses.[21] As a result, McGrory could not compare their different testimony for contradictions and inconsistencies. He could not really cross-examine individuals who might – in that memorable British phrase – be "economical with the truth".[22]

At first, though, it seemed that would not matter because he would have very few people to cross-examine. Under British law, there is no obligation for witnesses to a death to appear before a Coroner's Court if they are outside its jurisdiction. Citing this rule, the Thatcher Administration frequently hinted that the SAS men who killed the Provisionals would appear at the proceedings only if they chose to do so. The decision would be theirs and theirs alone.

But then Pizzarello publicly stated at the inquest's preliminary hearing, which took place between 4 and 5 July, that the inquiry would be meaningless without the soldiers' presence. After that, the world quickly learned that the SAS men had "volunteered to appear". Ultimately, the jury would get to hear from seven soldiers and eight MI5 officers. Identified only by letters of the alphabet, they would testify behind a curtain, invisible to the press and the IRA supporters present in the courtroom.[23]

Their presence completed the stacked deck of witnesses. Counting Soldiers "A" to "G" and MI5 officers "H" to "O", seventy-nine people would give evidence at the inquest. Twenty-seven of them were Gibraltar police officers (including three anonymous Special Branch men "P", "Q", and "R"). Another twelve were forensics experts, nine of them British government employees. One more was a Gibraltar Public Works Department map-maker.

Then, there were the twenty-five people who happened to accidentally witness McCann's, Savage's, and Farrell's deaths. Of that number, five worked as Gibraltar Services police officers (guarding military installations on the Rock); one was a former Gibraltar policeman; one witness's father worked for the Gibraltar Police; one worked for the MoD; and three were Gibraltar government employees. In total, just sixteen individuals completely independent of the British government appeared as witnesses in Pizzarello's court.[24]

The inquest jury's composition also promised to be a problem for the McCann, Savage, and Farrell family attorneys. Despite McGrory and Christopher Finch's pleas for him to do so, Coroner Pizzarello decided not to exclude British government employees from the panel.[25] At least two civil servants of Higher Executive grade were on it, one of whom acted as its foreman.[26]

As if this was not enough, the day the inquest began, government attorney Laws submitted three "public interest immunity" (PII) certificates to the court. Signed by the Minister of Defense, the Home Secretary, and the Deputy Governor of Gibraltar respectively, under British law, these documents make specific types of evidence inadmissable. Laws's certificates dealt with the means by which the British collected intelligence on the IRA and the methods they used against them. The government's position was that the disclosure of information

172

about these topics would give the IRA critical insights about MI5 and the SAS.[27]

This might have been true, but Pizzarello's accepting the PII certificates would also close off any attempt by McGrory to explore two fundamental questions of the Gibraltar Killings. Had the British government conspired to kill McCann, Savage, and Farrell? And just when and where were the Provisionals under surveillance in Spain? Pizzarello, of course, could have refused to honour the PII certificates. McGrory urged him to do that. But defying London would have been brave behavior for a minor colonial legal official like him. In the end, he chose to accept the documents. That meant any time that McGrory put a question to a witness that touched on an area Laws or Hucker felt was "sensitive", they could have the coroner prevent the witness from answering. It was something that would repeatedly happen throughout the hearing.

Pizzarello did throw one small bone to the Belfast lawyer. If McGrory felt that an objection was unreasonable, the coroner was willing to hear arguments from him about why he should not sustain it. If McGrory's argument had merit, Pizzarello would compel the witness to answer the question posed.

In effect, what was about to take place in Gibraltar would be "a controlled explosion of the truth".[28] Certain aspects of the killings would be publicly discussed but others would remain dark areas forever. For nineteen days, McGrory would wage a frustrating, lonely campaign to convince a jury of eleven Gibraltarians – brimming with patriotic sentiment – that representatives of *their* government had unlawfully killed three terrorists, who had been planning to set off a massive car-bomb in *their* city.

That was the way the game would be played. Under normal circumstances, persuading the jury that murder had taken place would be extremely difficult. But with the IRA's campaign on the Continent and the PII certificates constricting the inquiry, McGrory had an almost impossible task to perform.

# Notes

1. BBC Television Northern Ireland, *Spotlight*, May 5, 1988. The Thatcher Administration was nearly as irate over a shorter documentary compiled by BBC Northern Ireland. As with *Death on the Rock*, Geoffrey Howe tried to have the programme stopped but failed. For the most part, it echoed the concerns raised by *This Week*.

2. Bolton, p. 249.

3. David Hearst, "Inner City Doubling as War Zone", *Guardian*, August 14, 1989. The IRA men escaped uninjured.

4. Murray, pp. 437-438.

5. "'Just a Boy' Among 8 Soldiers Killed in IRA Bus Bomb Blast," *Houston Chronicle News Services*, August 22, 1988.

6. Thatcher, *The Downing Street Years*, p. 407.

7. Murray, pp. 439-448.

8. Ibid.

9. Interview with Dominic Searles, editor *Gibraltar Chronicle*, Gibraltar, June 1996.

10. Jack, "Gibraltar", p. 15.

11. Ibid, p. 42.

12. "Coroner with a passion for Cricket", *Guardian*, September 5, 1988.

13. Michael O'Higgins and John Waters, "A Controlled Explosion of the Truth", *Magill*, October 1989, p. 38.

14. Tony Parker, *May the Lord in His Mercy Be Kind to Belfast*, Jonathan Cape, London, 1993, pp. 236-240.

15. On February 18, in the wake of the La Mon House Hotel bombing, the RUC arrested Gerry Adams in Beechmont, off the Falls Road in West Belfast, and charged him with IRA membership. Paddy McGrory represented him before the court and successfully argued for the charge to be dismissed on the grounds that Adams had no case to answer. Sharrock and Devenport, *Man of War, Man of Peace*, pp. 154-161.

16. Ibid.

17. *The Deaths on Gibraltar 1988*, British Irish Rights Watch, September 1996, p. 14.

18. Ibid.

19. Ibid, pp. 17-18.

20. Ibid.

21. Another critical limitation was that McGrory was not allowed to see the original statements the soldiers gave to the Gibraltar police about the shootings.

22. "The Deaths on Gibraltar, 1988", Submission to the United Nations Special Rapporteur on Extra-Judicial, Summary, or Arbitrary, British Irish Rights Watch, September 1996, p. 18.

23. Ibid, pp. 16-17.

24. Jack, "Gibraltar," p. 44.

25. Finch was assisting McGrory as local counsel.

26. "The Deaths on Gibraltar 1988," p. 17.

27. Ibid.

28. Hence the title of the O'Higgins and Waters' article cited above.

# CHAPTER TWELVE

## COPS, SPOOKS, AND SHOOTERS

"You use a gun to kill."
– Soldier C

From the very beginning, McGrory took a basically passive approach when examining witnesses. Whenever Laws or Hucker objected to a question he posed as straying into the grounds set off limits by the PII certificates, he quickly conceded the point. And, very early on, McGrory exonerated the entire Gibraltar Police Force of any wrong-doing, before or after the killings.

He had good reason to do this. Despite Pizzarello's pledge that he might allow questions dealing with "national security" topics on a case-by-case basis, the Belfast lawyer knew full well that the government witnesses would never provide any answers damaging to their employers. But if McGrory allowed Hucker and Laws to obsessively invoke the PII certificates, the jury might decide they were gagging the witnesses for other than "national security" reasons. But the PII certificates effectively put any serious discussion of the surveillance of the ASU in Spain off-limits. Because of that, McGrory could never attack a central premise of the British version of the incident: that McCann, Savage, and Farrell's appearance in Gibraltar had been unexpected and had set off a panic.

Given the peculiar behavior of the Gibraltar Police,

McGrory's decision to treat them with kid gloves was more difficult to understand. Seen in retrospect, it was a realistic approach to take. Certainly, he could demonstrate the police's actions on and after March 6 were suspicious. Yet McGrory had no hard evidence that any members of the Gibraltar Police had acted in a "conspiracy to pervert the course of justice." Attacking them on the witness stand would only alienate the Gibraltar jury he faced.

Unfortunately, like the decision not to fight the PII certificates, that particular tactic tied his hands. It allowed Hucker and Laws to ridicule the notion that MI5 and the SAS could have conspired to murder or covered up the murder of McCann, Savage, and Farrell. How could such a thing happen with the Gibraltar Police acting in good faith? The whole idea was absurd – or at least appeared to be with McGrory's concession.

In effect, the Belfast lawyer could only search for and point out the various inconsistencies and contradictions within the Crown's case. One reporter cynically titled the proceedings "The Bomb That Threatened The Gibraltarian People".[1] The story was simple enough. The IRA had planned to set off a car-bomb in Gibraltar. The SAS and MI5 had stopped them. Mistakes had been made, but thanks to the security forces, Gibraltar was safe, and the terrorists "mercifully . . . dead".[2]

The anonymous witnesses were the principal tellers of the tale. In a supporting role was the Gibraltar Police. At times, the story they collectively related became so vivid that even skeptical listeners had to pinch themselves to remember the critical fact – McCann, Savage, and Farrell *did not* have a bomb with them when they died. Yet despite its careful rehearsal, cracks existed in the framework of the government's presentation, some of which McGrory readily seized on while others became apparent only years later.

"Mr O", the senior MI5 executive whose information had

set Operation Flavius in motion, was story-teller-in-chief. Speaking in a polished voice that indicated his upper-class origins, O provided the first official explanation for why the SAS had been so certain that McCann, Savage, and Farrell were going to use a radio device to detonate their car-bomb. According to him, it had been the Belgian police's discovery of an apparent IRA arms cache in Brussels that provided the vital clue.

"On the twenty-first of January [1988], a car was discovered in Brussels and inside it was a large amount of semtex military explosive, together with four detonators and the equipment for a radio detonation system. Taken altogether, this equipment found in the vehicle constituted very much the sort of device with which we are very familiar with in Northern Ireland" the figure in the veiled witness stand told Pizzarello.

"You believed that [the] semtex explosive [found there] would be used in Gibraltar?" the Coroner asked.

"We assessed that that would be the case."[3]

But why would the Provisionals use a radio signal to trigger the bomb? Wouldn't it have been safer to set a timer (something they apparently planned to do), drive the car into position and walk away? Perhaps, but O believed the IRA team would not have done this because of the operational requirement to avoid unnecessary civilian casualties.

Pizzarello then asked how O believed the IRA attack in Gibraltar would have unfolded. The MI5 man replied by saying he had expected the ASU to drive the car-bomb into Gibraltar on Monday night or early Tuesday morning. He had not felt that they would park an empty "blocking" car to reserve space for the car-bomb on Saturday or Sunday because that would have been an "over-complicated and unnecessarily risky procedure" (entailing repeated trips across the border).[4]

"How did subsequent events confirm your original suspicions?" the Coroner asked.

O said, "In essence, they were confirmed in all but three respects. The IRA did intend to carry out a massive car-bomb, and we were right as to the target and the target area. The three areas where we were not correct were: first of all, that on the sixth of March when the incident took place, the three were *not* armed; the second respect, the car [which Savage parked] was a blocking car; and the third respect, when the car-bomb was eventually discovered in Marbella, it did not contain a radio-controlled device, it contained a timer device . . ."[5]

The MI5 executive's testimony had several contradictions in it. The first was obvious. Somehow, O had correctly anticipated every move the Provisionals made except for the ones that the SAS used to justify killing them.

The second would be apparent to anyone who has ever been unlucky enough to drive a car in Gibraltar. It is one of the worst places in the world in terms of available parking space. The British military's presence on the Rock is to blame for that. The MoD owns most of the land in Gibraltar. So, "money can't chase property so it chases after cars instead". In 1988, there were 15,000 cars in the Colony, 555 for every mile of road there.[6]

Thanks to "Mary Parkin", the ASU's scout, the IRA team had seen this as a problem and had planned to use a blocking car. With the Gibraltar Police advising him, it is difficult to see how O could have assumed the Provisionals would not use one, unless he thought they would have enjoyed driving a car-bomb into Gibraltar and discovering there was no place to put it.

Finally, O's reasoning about why the IRA unit would use a radio device to trigger the explosives was logically absurd. According to him, using one would be safer for McCann, Savage, and Farrell because they would not have to be on the scene as required when using a command wire. But in all their previous operations, the IRA had never used a radio detonator to set off a bomb without having a clear line of vision to the target. Employing a radio device in Gibraltar would have forced someone to stay behind after putting the car-bomb in place to detonate it at the right moment. That same person would have had to escape from Gibraltar when the authorities' first reaction in the wake of a massive explosion would be to seal the border.

O also never explained the contradiction between his supposed belief that the Provisionals would use a radio-detonator to minimize the risk of civilian casualties, but would blindly detonate the bomb if confronted by the security forces. This last bit of Orwellian logic was brought to its logical conclusion when Soldier F, the overall commander of the SAS mission in Gibraltar, took the stand. His testimony about why the IRA would behave the way O said they would reflected a degree of contempt for the jury's intelligence.

"Isn't [the assumption the IRA would set off the bomb if challenged] quite contrary to the other assumption or deduction, that . . . their anxiety after Enniskillen and all that would be to avoid civilian casualties?" McGrory asked the British Army colonel.

Soldier F brightly replied, "Yes but that's two different deductions. There's one deduction . . . that in [the IRA's] terms, the perfect operation is where they can use radio-controlled device to minimize the number of casualties. But the other supposition is that when they are cornered, a different set of factors pertain [that] they will have no qualms about either resorting to weapons or pressing a button, knowing full well the bomb was there . . . they'd achieve some degree of propaganda success [by] exploding a bomb in the centre of Gibraltar."

McGrory was bewildered. "I'm sorry. I can't follow that, because, if . . . Enniskillen caused a propaganda disaster of great magnitude for them, why should they cause another propaganda loss like that, not a propaganda gain that you are talking about?"

"In my opinion, they are adept at turning disaster into

179

triumph in their own propaganda terms, and therefore, if they could claim that they got a bomb into Gibraltar, that they had . . . successfully exploded it in Gibraltar, I believe they would claim that to be a propaganda success and would try to derive credit and publicity from it."

"Propaganda success that had emulated Enniskillen which was the greatest propaganda disaster? Surely that can't be right?"

"I believe it is."[7]

Another witness for the Crown, Commissioner Joseph Canepa, displayed a similar ability to reconcile contradictory facts. Under examination by Pizzarello and Laws, he explained in reassuring tones that there had been no conspiracy hatched in London to insert the SAS into Gibraltar. Instead, after being briefed by MI5 about the IRA's plans, Canepa formed an advisory committee consisting of himself and a number of military officers and intelligence officials. It was only after due consideration of the threat that this group decided the police needed help. Once Operation Flavius began, the police commissioner had been in complete command, except for the twenty-five minutes when the SAS "arrested" McCann, Savage, and Farrell. Everything had been done strictly by the book.

But after McGrory began to question the witness, who became increasingly evasive and edgy as the day wore on, a few inconvenient details began to emerge. For instance, it turned out that high ranking military officials in Gibraltar, including Sir Peter Terry, the colony's governor and Canepa's boss, "assisted" the Commissioner in making the decision to establish an advisory committee. Under McGrory's prodding, Canepa grudgingly told the jury that he had not specifically asked for the SAS's help, and he agreed that there had been many soldiers in the local garrison with experience of arresting terrorist suspects. He also admitted that he had been utterly dependent on what "outside sources" told him about the IRA's intentions and that his own men had not been capable of confronting the ASU or even conducting surveillance of it. Even more tellingly, during his time in the operations room, Canepa had been unable to hear the radio instructions his "advisors" gave to the MI5 officers, the soldiers on the ground, and his own men (because the radio operators in the control centre used headsets and not speakers).[8]

Curiously enough, although the SAS men testified that the military had twice briefly taken control of the operation at 3:00 p.m. and 3:25 p.m., Canepa and his deputy, George Colombo, seemed unaware of either event.[9] Given that and the fact that the SAS and MI5 did not bother to tell Colombo about Savage's presence in the Colony until two hours after the young man's arrival, the Gibraltar Police appear to have been in somewhat less than complete control of events on March 6.

McGrory also questioned Canepa about why the authorities had let Savage wander the streets of Gibraltar for over an hour after he parked what would eventually become "the suspect car-bomb" at the assembly area.

"At this stage, you have a position where one of your surveillance team has a man, probably Savage, in a car, and there are fears that a car-bomb would be brought into Gibraltar. That is the position when [your officer] reports back?" McGrory asked.

"Yes."

The next question was for the jury's benefit, "Was there not the possibility of immediate and terrible danger to anybody in that car park?"

"We didn't consider it at that stage."

"You didn't?"

Waving his arms for emphasis, something he often did, Canepa explained, "First of all [we were] not positive it was Savage. So . . . we would not know whether that car contained anything which would hurt anybody. Those are the main

181

reasons. It was later, as time progresse[d], that it became more positive."

"In a matter of this kind, having regard to the stakes in human life, was mere suspicion not enough to act at once?"

"No."

"Why?"

"If we are expecting other people [meaning McCann and Farrell], it is our job to find them all, not just the one."

The small man from Belfast pounced, "Are you saying that the people of Gibraltar were *deliberately put at risk* because you wanted to get three in the bag instead of one?"

The question struck a nerve, "That is the way you are putting it!" Canepa snapped.

"You think that is an unfair interpretation, do you?"

"Yes."

"So the decision was taken that there could be a bomb in there, and the IRA have been known to make mistakes about these bombs which can go off," McGrory said, letting that point sink home with the jury, "Maybe [Savage] is the only one [in Gibraltar] but it was [his car that was left to] lie there?"

"You are right, yes," the Commissioner conceded.[10]

Two conclusions can be drawn from this section of Canepa's testimony. Either the authorities had been willing to take a terrible risk with the lives of everyone in Gibraltar on March 6, or they never believed there had been a bomb by the Convent, until just minutes before McCann, Savage, and Farrell were shot.

At first, Canepa appeared to have a firm grasp of the facts of Operation Flavius. This began to change when McGrory pressed him on how the authorities could have allowed Savage to enter Gibraltar and drive a possible car-bomb into the assembly area. Under examination by Pizzarello, Canepa had already blamed that on the sheer volume of people moving across the border. In an effort to cope with the traffic, the police and MI5 teams had only looked for cars with two men and a woman in them.

Given the knowledge and skill MI5 had displayed in uncovering the IRA plot, that seemed like a curious mistake. Why were there no allowances made for the possibility that one of the IRA team might cross the border alone? Didn't the authorities have the details of McCann's, Savage's, and Farrell's false passports so they would know who to look for?

"No, I don't think so, at that stage. I am not quite certain, but I don't think so." The man in charge told McGrory.

"The question is did you know that [McCann, Savage, and Farrell] would have been travelling on passports in certain names, and you are saying, I understand, that you are not too sure about that."

"I am not sure at this moment."[11]

"And then I added that I was asking you to agree that it would have been – since you did not know what vehicle they might be travelling in – it would have been one way of checking whether they entered the territory if you knew their passport was in a certain name?"

Canepa nodded. "Yes, of course."

"But you are telling his Honour and the jury at the moment you don't know if you had that information or not?"

"Yes, I am not certain of that."

Another uncertain witness was Detective Constable Charles Huart.[12] He testified a week after Canepa took the stand. The day of the shootings, Huart had been on the Spanish side of the border in a windowless "computer room" with several Spanish police officers.[13] By prior arrangement, the Spanish had agreed to display to him the passports of any individuals matching the physical descriptions of McCann, Savage, and Farrell on a visual aid unit. Huart, who was familiar with their photographs, would then be responsible for alerting the Gibraltar Police and MI5 if anyone suspicious was entering the Colony. Like

Canepa, Huart implied that Savage had been missed because he was travelling by himself.

When it was McGrory's turn with the Detective Constable, he focused on the passport issue.

"Did you have any aliases that any of these three people might be travelling under?" he asked Huart.

"No."

"None?"

"No."

The lawyer found that a little hard to accept. "You didn't know of any name at all that they might be using?"

"Names had been mentioned previously to me, but the names I had at the time [were] the three names, the proper names."

"Yes, but names had also been mentioned to you at the [March 5] briefing under which they might travel?"

"They were," the witness conceded.

"And was the name Coyne mentioned to you?"

"I think I came across Coyne."

"As a possible alias for Savage?"

Huart's memory began to fail him. "I can't remember."

"I beg your pardon?" McGrory politely asked.

"I can't remember if it was an alias for Savage or [McCann]."

"Having regard to your role in this operation, why don't you remember that vital piece of information?"

"I don't know. At the time – I can't remember now."

"I'm sorry. I don't understand."

"I can't remember," said the policeman.

"You can't remember?"

Huart shook his head, but McGrory was not finished just yet. "But when you were keeping this vigil at the Spanish frontier, you must have remembered it then?"

"I had a note of it then."

"You had a note of it. So you were looking for a passport not just in the name of Savage but one in the name of Coyne?"

"That's it."

It wasn't often that a witness contradicted himself in the space of five minutes. McGrory was surprised. "Sorry?"

"That's it," repeated Huart.

"In fact, you would have had a note at that time of aliases under which all three of them were, in fact, found to be travelling?"

"I must have, but I can't recall now. I can't recall that name."

McGrory allowed a touch of sarcasm to creep into his next question. "You do surprise me, Detective Constable. Why should you forget a vital matter like that within six months? There was not a lot of point in you looking for these people if you didn't even know what names they were travelling under, was there?"

"At the time, I knew."

"Did you?"[14]

By this point, Pizzarello's curiosity had been roused. Turning to Huart, he asked, "Are you aware whether the Spanish knew these names?"

"I would say so, yes."[15]

In effect, Huart was telling the jury that despite the fact the Spanish knew the physical descriptions of the IRA team's members and knew what false passports they were using, Savage had somehow managed to slip across the border. Now, while getting past a bunch of "incompetent" Spanish policemen must have been easy, how could Savage had evaded the fully alerted Gibraltar authorities? Did they really make that elementary mistake of looking for members of the IRA team only in cars which had two men and one woman in them?

Not according to Detective Chief Inspector Ullger. He appeared the day after Huart, and contradicted both his subordinate and Canepa, informing the jury that the authorities had no preconceived notions about how the ASU would cross

185

the border. They might cross on foot, by car, or by a combination of both. He had never told the Spanish police to concentrate on cars with three people in them. In his opinion, the Spanish had missed Savage at the border because they had been careless. As for the British side of the frontier, Savage had got through it because of the obsessive secrecy surrounding the operation. None of the regular police, customs, or immigrations officials had been told to look out for the ASU.[16]

Ullger also appeared to have ideas about counter-terrorism radically different from those held by most experts, who believed that it is imperative to keep possible car-bombs out of populated areas. In answer to a question by McGrory about the surveillance lapse at the border, the Special Branch man said, "The only way [Operation Flavius] could succeed was to allow the terrorists to come in and be dealt with the way they were." Then realizing what he seemed to be saying, Ullger added, "as far as surveillance was concerned".[17]

Ullger, like Canepa and Huart, was expecting the jury to believe:

1. The authorities knew the IRA members were armed with a massive car-bomb that would devastate Gibraltar if it detonated there.

2. They did not have any idea where McCann, Savage, and Farrell were in Spain and when they might appear in the Colony.

3. The Spanish police on the border were familiar with the Provisionals' false passports, but their Gibraltarian counterparts were not.

4. The SAS, MI5, and Gibraltar Police sincerely believed the best way to prevent an IRA outrage in Gibraltar was to allow Savage to enter the Colony with a possible car-bomb.

Unlike the police, when it was their turn to testify, the SAS witnesses' testimony was much better choreographed. Soldier E, the tactical commander of the men who had actually done the killing, gave very little away during McGrory's examination of him. There was one glaring exception to this. It came in response to a question about why the SAS did not arrest the Provisionals before 3:40 p.m. despite having several opportunities to do so. The SAS officer said that "at any stage before [then] there was a chance that . . . [the terrorists] could be in a position to detonate [the bomb]."[18] In other words, Soldier E was saying that it would have been unsafe to try to arrest McCann, Savage, and Farrell until they moved away from the "car-bomb" parked in the assembly area. A few minutes later, Soldier E contradicted himself, saying, "the transmitter, the button job device, would have been capable of detonating the car-bomb itself up to the border and possibly beyond into Spain".[19]

The testimony of E's subordinates, Soldiers A, B, C, and D, was all cut from the same cloth. They had come to Gibraltar to "assist the civil power" (the police). They had never intended to murder the Provisionals; they had not fired at them while they lay on the ground. Such things were unthinkable. The fact that all three members of the ASU had made furtive moves for nonexistent weapons or radio detonation devices was only a remarkable coincidence.

At times, the soldiers' accounts of the shootings were so identical, it prompted McGrory to pointedly inquire whether they had rehearsed their testimony or been briefed about what to emphasize. Although the SAS men vehemently denied this, his suggestion became more and more plausible as the witnesses repeatedly used expressions like "uppermost in my mind" that belonged more in law schools than in working-class soldiers' vocabularies.[20]

Yet it was the SAS men's insistence that they had believed beyond a shadow of doubt that there had "definitely" been a bomb at the assembly area and it was "definitely a button job" that was the oddest part of their testimony. Their absolute certainty about Savage's car being dangerous contrasted sharply with Soldier G's testimony that he felt there was only a possibility it was. And unlike the SAS men, both the police and MI5 witnesses testified that no one had explicitly ruled out the possibility of a timer as the detonation device.

But somehow, the SAS men left the midnight meeting on March 5 "certain" that the car-bomb would be detonated by a radio device. In fact, one of the SAS men, Soldier C, *still* seemed to believe it.

That came out during a discussion between him and McGrory about whether Farrell had known she was being watched.

" . . . you and your surveillance teams were so good at your jobs that she doesn't appear to have twigged, so to speak, that she was being watched closely?" McGrory asked.

Soldier C replied, "No, sir. Well, they had just laid a bomb."

"Had just *what*?"

"Had just laid a bomb in the [assembly area]."

"No, they had not," the lawyer informed the witness.

"I was told by [Soldier] E!" the SAS man snapped.

"You are . . . saying they had just laid a bomb. You know perfectly well they had not laid a bomb."

Soldier C was insistent. "I was briefed on that day and categorically told there was a definite bomb in [the assembly area]. I can only operate from that information at that moment in time."

"And at all times, you were acting with the information that had been fed into you by [Soldier] E?"

"Fed into me by [Soldier] E, yes."

"Can we get it clear that you are not saying now that there was a bomb?"

"I don't understand what you are saying."

"It can't be the fault of my accent this time. I am saying to you, you are not telling his Honour and the jury now that you still believe there was a bomb?"

Soldier C's answer had a touch of *Alice in Wonderland* to it. "I am not talking about that. I am talking about information I had; on the day there was a bomb at [the assembly area]."

McGrory was annoyed. "I am talking about *now* . . . would you tell me whether you now believe that now, as you stand there, that there was a bomb?"

"I still believe that there is a bomb in Gibraltar."

It was after some prompting from Pizzarello that Soldier C finally agreed that there had been no bomb in Gibraltar, saying, "At this point in time, I'd be a fool not to know".[21]

Like their officers, Soldiers E and F, the four SAS soldiers were unlikely to admit any criminal behavior. Despite this, McGrory kept after them, hoping to get a damaging inconsistency on the record. This strategy was apparent when he examined Soldier D. That SAS man had shot Savage nine times, supposedly firing all his rounds before his target hit the ground. McGrory clearly felt that he might be able to goad the young soldier, who had only three years of experience in the SAS, into making an incriminating statement. After running him through the same series of questions he had given the others, the lawyer took a new tack. Speaking in his soft, almost squeaky Belfast accent, he began by reminding Soldier D that the forensic evidence indicated that Savage *had* been shot while he was lying on the ground.

"I put it to you that you fired at [Savage] on the ground repeatedly," McGrory said.

"That is not true," replied Soldier D, his voice clearly audible from the screened-off witness stand.

McGrory turned to Kenneth Asquez's allegations. "Did somebody place his foot on the man's chest or thereabouts and hold him down with that foot and shoot him repeatedly in the upper body and head?"

"That is definitely not true."

"Quite sure?"

The soldier did not hesitate. "I am positive that is not the truth."

"At the same time, showing some sort of identification to keep people back and shouting, 'Stop! Police!'"

"That was shouted, 'Stop, police,' yes, but not when somebody stood there with his foot on [Savage's] chest. That is not true."

McGrory did not let up. "It would be a dreadful thing if it were true?"

"It is not true."

"It would be sheer murder, if it were true?"

"By standing on someone's chest?"

"And shooting them in the head?"

Soldier D snapped back, "That is not true. That is not the facts that happened on that day."

"I merely said to you is it your view that, if someone did that, it was sheer murder." McGrory patiently explained.

The SAS man seemed to feel he was being drawn into a legal version of an ambush, "You are implying that if I did that it was sheer murder?"

"If anyone did it."

"It is not a nice thing to do and it wasn't done that day."

With sarcasm and disbelief creeping into his voice, McGrory continued, "Is that the best that you can do? It isn't a nice thing to do?"

"It's not, is it?"

The Belfast lawyer then brought up the fact Soldier D had fired nine times into Savage's body.

"Did you totally lose your head that day?" he quietly asked.

"No, I certainly didn't."

"Were you in a frenzy?" McGrory asked, deliberately using the word that the pathologist had used in describing the attack on Savage.

Soldier D refused to be provoked. "I definitely was not in a frenzy. No."[22]

A moment later, McGrory asked him again, "You were not in a frenzy?"

"I definitely was not in a frenzy. I take the word 'frenzy' to mean that I had lost control. That is totally not true."

But the small man with snowy white hair and a red face clearly did not believe him. "When you fired nine shots at this man, you knew exactly what you were doing?"

"I fired nine rounds in this man; I knew exactly what I was doing. I fired at him. If I had been in a frenzy, if I did not control my actions – there was a lot of people in that area – there would have been far more people hit than Savage. Everything I did was controlled."

"How did you miss him from the distance you were firing from?"

A little uncertainly, Soldier D replied, "I don't believe I did miss him."

By his next question, McGrory emphasized the point-blank nature of the killing. "I know you didn't miss him, so what are you talking about the people in the [immediate] vicinity for? Your *victim* [author's italics] was right in front of you, a few feet away."

"Yes."

"You have told his Honour and the jury that certainly once you had started fire you intended to go on firing until you had killed him?"

It was an easy question for Soldier D to answer. "That is correct. Yes."

"Supposing, in the midst of the firing, he had shouted, 'Stop! I surrender'. Would you have carried on killing him?"

The soldier's response was the same. "I would have carried on firing until I no longer believed he was a threat."

"Even if words of surrender like that had been uttered like that?"

"He may well have said that and pressed the button at the same time."

"It would not have mattered to you when the challenge was shouted, if he had said, 'I surrender' you would have gone on shooting him anyway?"

"No, we gave him the opportunity to stop and he didn't."

McGrory's next question was again more for the jury's benefit. With disbelief, sarcasm, and perhaps a little anger tinging his voice, he asked, "The startled man was wheeling, and the shout and the shot had come on top of each other. What chance had he to surrender?"

"He had been given the chance. He was told to stop and he didn't," insisted Soldier D.

"You didn't even finish the warning!"

"Because we didn't have the time to finish the warning."

"I am suggesting to you, Soldier, that you appointed yourself Lord High Executioner of Mr Savage that day."

"That is definitely not true."[23]

That was it for the SAS. After a few minutes of examination from Hucker and Laws, the witness left the courtroom, climbed into a government van with blacked-out windows, and departed from the scene. Like his comrades, Soldier D had acquitted himself well. McGrory had got nothing overtly incriminating from him.

The British public loved it. There was the SAS in public for the first time since the Iranian Embassy siege. Just reading the press's reconstruction of their testimony was a thrill. But the reporters in Gibraltar missed an even more dramatic story. The IRA had been in the courtroom with the SAS. Not in the form of masked men brandishing rifles and grenades but in the person of Seamus Finucane, Mairéad Farrell's fiancé.[24]

By 1988, Finucane had been a member of the IRA for sixteen years. He had been interned in 1972, the same year his brother John, also an IRA man, died in a car crash while on active service. Released in 1973, Finucane immediately resumed IRA activities. By 1977, he was in prison again, serving ten years of a fourteen-year sentence for possession of a pistol. On his release from prison in 1986, he met Mairéad Farrell. As he later recounted:

I was in love with her. We had been involved for eighteen months . . . We set up together the first home for either of us

192

. . . It was a very, very precious time. Mairéad was very independent, very determined, a strong woman. She wanted children; she was like any other girl . . . She was murdered without a shadow of a doubt, irrespective of what she was [in Gibraltar] to do.[25]

Finucane, Mary Savage (Seán's sister), and Niall Farrell (Mairéad's brother) went to the Rock to watch McGrory press their case that their loved ones had been unlawfully killed. Not unreasonably, the authorities kept them under tight watch. Yet the behaviour of the gentlemen of the tabloid press − some of whom were sporting SAS regimental ties − was less understandable. Fleet Street's finest followed the trio around constantly and filed a number of stories suggesting that they had only come to Gibraltar on vacation. Once, Finucane almost came to blows with a photographer who would not stop taking his picture.

Sitting in the courtroom listening to the SAS soldiers testify about how they shot his friends and lover was a chilling experience for the IRA man:

It was as if [the soldiers] were describing having a cup of tea . . . We inadvertently saw the photographs of the death they gave Mairéad and Dan; they just peppered their bodies. If they were close enough to be able to shoot them like that, then they were close enough to arrest them . . .[26]

Asked years later if he had any qualms over the morality of setting of a massive car-bomb in a densely populated city, his reply was as chilling as the demeanor of the SAS men he had been listening to:

Everything that happen[s] abroad put[s] the IRA on the agenda . . . You do not bear arms not to take life.[27]

**Notes**

1. O'Higgins and Waters, "A Controlled Explosion of the Truth", *Magill*, October 1988, p. 39.
2. Jack, "Gibraltar", p. 37. The quote is from Ian Gow MP. See also p.
3. Testimony of Mr O, the Gibraltar Inquest, Day 2, 7 September 1988, Channel Four Television, 1988, p. 7.

4. Ibid, p. 8.

5. Ibid, p. 9.

6. Jack, "Gibraltar", p. 32.

7. Testimony of Soldier F, the Gibraltar Inquest, Day 5, 12 September, 1988, Channel Four Television, 1988, pp. 57-58.

8. Ibid, pp. 26-27, Soldier F, who testified after Canepa "corrected" the Commissioner's testimony. According to him the radio operators had worn headsets but repeated out loud incoming and outgoing transmissions. In the SAS officer's opinion, the Commissioner had been too preoccupied to pay attention to what was going on.

9. Testimony of Deputy Commissioner George Colombo, The Gibraltar Inquest, Day 10, Channel four Television, 1988, p. 4. Colombo told McGrory that he "never" passed control to the SAS.

10. Testimony of Commissioner Joseph Canepa, the Gibraltar Inquest, Day 4, 9 September 1988, Channel Four Television, pp. 29-30.

11. Ibid, p. 26.

12. John Hooper and Peter Murtagh, "Writer Frightened Into Silence", *Guardian*, April 7, 1989. Someone was very unhappy about Huart's presence in the immigrations building becoming public knowledge. The car belonging to the Spanish reporter who unearthed that fact had its tyres slashed and the words "You Bastard" etched on the driver's side door.

14. Geraghty, *Who Dares Wins*, p. 321. In his book, Tony Geraghty suggested that while the Spanish surveillance operation *was* effective, "sovereignty" issues forced the Spanish to report to the British authorities in London. Supposedly, communications broke down and this allowed the Provisionals to take the British by surprise. Huart's presence in the customs hut makes that hypothesis laughable.

14. Murray, p. 397. According to Murray, Farrell may have been a last minute addition to the IRA team. The fact that the Gibraltar Police had McCann and Savage's aliases but not hers would tend to confirm this. However, Farrell was probably involved in the support aspect of the operation from its inception.

15. Testimony of Detective Constable Charles Huart, the Gibraltar Inquest, Day 11, 20 September 1988, Channel Four Television, 1988, pp. 54-55.

16. Testimony of Detective Chief Inspector Joseph Ullger, the Gibraltar Inquest, Day 12, 21 September 1988, Channel Four Television, 1988, pp. 76-81.

17. Ibid, p. 91.

18. Testimony of Soldier E, the Gibraltar Inquest Day 6, 13 September 1988, Channel Four Television, 1988, p. 59.

19. Ibid, p. 60.

20. Or like Soldier E's use of the expression "compos mentis".

21. Testimony of Soldier C, the Gibraltar Inquest, Day 8, 15 September 1988, Channel Four Television, 1988, pp. 8-9.

22. Testimony of Soldier D, the Gibraltar Inquest, Day 8, 15 September 1988, Channel Four Television, 1988, pp. 75-77.

23. Ibid.

24. Toolis, pp. 84-190. Seamus Finucane gave Toolis a detailed overview of his career in the IRA and is described as an IRA man in his book.

25. Ibid, pp. 176-180.

26. Ibid.

27. Ibid

# CHAPTER THIRTEEN

## PUZZLEMENTS

"Maybe what happened in Gibraltar was perfectly lawful and defensible . . . Maybe; but there is another possibility. The possibility that it was deliberate, cold blooded, premeditated murder."
  – Enoch Powell, former MP, April 1988

Once during the inquest, Paddy McGrory described the killings as having a puzzlement to them. He might have better used the word "puzzlements".

Most of these riddles had to with the way the Gibraltar Police behaved in the wake of McCann, Savage, and Farrell's deaths. For decades, police forces throughout the world have followed "the golden rule of homicide investigation". While the words may vary, basically that rule is:

Never touch, move, or alter a death scene until it is first visually observed in detail, fully recorded by photographs with all items of potential evidence in the pictures, recorded in the investigator's notes, and measured in place and identified on a rough death scene sketch.[1]

There are corollaries to this. The first is obvious. The pathologist investigating the deaths must have adequate facilities to conduct the autopsies. Without proper equipment, particularly an x-ray machine to track the path bullets take through a body, a simple death can become an unsolvable mystery.

Equally important is to leave the clothing on a corpse so an examiner can observe it in relation to wounds on the body. This is critical in cases where death resulted from close range shootings because clothing filters gunshot residue expelled from a pistol or rifle when it fires. Tears in fabric can help distinguish entry and exit wounds and the way blood seeps through clothing can enable a pathologist to determine whether a murder victim was standing or prone when shot.[2] Items like a tight belt or bra can make a gunshot exit wound look like an entry wound. All these reasons make stripping a corpse the last thing a responsible police officer would do before a pathologist performs an autopsy.

Those are simple principles, things British police officers and military personnel with law enforcement training would know. They must have been on the minds of the SAS and the Gibraltar Police officers. Long before the killings, Commissioner Canepa had repeatedly stressed to Operation Flavius's participants that evidence against McCann, Savage, and Farrell was to be diligently collected and preserved. Without it, the authorities could not convict the Provisionals of anything. Yet on March 6, 1988, and afterwards, the Gibraltar Police and SAS did not simply break these rules. They shattered them.

Destruction of evidence began immediately after the trio died. Both on Winston Churchill Avenue and Landport Lane, most of the shell casings ejected by the soldiers' pistols disappeared before anyone could record by photograph or sketch where they were lying. When they vanished, so did any chance of determining exactly where the soldiers had been when they fired the killing shots.

Who picked up the shells? In Savage's case, it had been Sergeant Acris and Constable Kassam, uniformed Gibraltar Police officers. The two men had felt that if they had not collected them, the shells might have vanished. At the inquest, Acris told the Coroner:

My concern at the time was to preserve the evidence. Like I said before, there were a lot of people in the area . . . and my fear was that some children or people could have taken the cartridges . . . I didn't want any of them to go missing . . .[3]

It seemed a well-intentioned thought. Yet the Sergeant never explained, and Coroner Pizzarello never asked why he and Kassam did not shout for people to keep back from Savage's body. Nor did the Coroner inquire why preserving a handful of shells was more important than preserving the crime scene they defined.[4]

As for the cartridges around the other corpses, they had gone into the pocket of Q, one of the plainclothes Gibraltar Police officers who assisted the SAS men that day. Q, along with officers P and R, had been among the first policemen to converge on the Shell Petrol Station after McCann and Farrell died there. Under direct examination at the inquest, Officer Q explained that he had just been following orders when he collected the casings:

"Did you know how many cartridges there were?" Pizzarello asked him.

"Yes, your Worship, after speaking to a superior officer, I retrieved eleven cartridges."

"Did you find any more?"

"No, your worship."

"Were there many people around?"

Q hesitated, "There were quite a number of people . . . police officers."

"What superior officer did you speak to, to pick up the cartridges?" the Coroner inquired.

"A chief inspector," came the response.

"A chief inspector?"

"Yes, your Worship."

"Who?"

"Chief Inspector Ullger."[5]

Ullger, head of the Gibraltar Police Special Branch, was Q's boss. Presumably, he had been Canepa's liaison with MI5. He was a veteran police officer who had probably attended a death scene or two in his day. Yet the Chief Inspector had ordered one of his men to pick up the shell casings around McCann and Farrell's bodies, destroying another vital piece of evidence.

Or had he? When he testified, Ullger denied telling anyone to pick up evidence. Perhaps Q was mistaken or Ullger's memory failed him (a problem a number of Gibraltar Police witnesses seemed to have). Or perhaps, just perhaps, someone was lying.

As a conscientious policeman with five years experience as a "scene of the crimes" technician, Sergeant Comely must have been particularly unhappy with another error made by his superiors. All three of the IRA members' bodies had been loaded up on ambulances and whisked away to the Royal Navy Hospital before Comely or any other officers could photograph them *in situ*. During his testimony, Canepa placed responsibility for that action on Superintendent Maginnis, one of his many subordinates. But over a week later, Inspector Ullger would tell the jury that he had ordered the bodies moved – after getting Canepa's permission. This conflict in the two men's testimony went unnoticed by the press, as did the Gibraltar police's eliminated another piece of critical evidence.[6]

Given these blunders, Sergeant Comely and his supervisors no doubt felt particularly fortunate when Douglas Celecia, Josie Celecia's husband, stepped forward and told them that he had taken a series of photographs of the immediate aftermath of McCann's and Farrell's deaths.

It had been one of the few "coincidences" that worked against the British government in Gibraltar and blind luck for Mr Celecia, who worked as an engineer at a power plant not far from his apartment in George Jeger House. He had bought a camera several days before the shootings from a local photo shop and had been eager for a chance to try it out, using the roll of black and white film that came with his purchase. Taking a walk with his wife on Sunday afternoon after work offered just such an opportunity.[7] As he told the coroner:

I finish[ed] work possibly about 3:30 [p.m.] because my relief came early. That would mean about twenty to four. I got home, called my wife [and told her] she should get ready, we were going for a walk. She went over to the window. Then a neighbor called me to the other side of the building.[8]

A moment later, Celecia heard shots, and his wife shouted to him that someone was being killed. Douglas was skeptical. To him, it sounded like just another military exercise. But when Josie ran to him, saying some people had been shot dead, he decided to investigate, a decision that was only reinforced when he heard another long string of explosions that sounded like gunfire.

Running to the window, Celecia looked across the street and could see two bodies, one of them a woman, slumped on the footpath next to the Shell Station. A number of men in civilian clothing were standing around them. Parked on the same side of the road as the petrol station was a Gibraltar Police car.[9]

By this point, Celecia believed that he was looking at the aftermath of the murder of two undercover police officers – a unique event for Gibraltar – something he made quite clear at the inquest:

I thought to myself, "I'm going to go for my camera." I went to the kitchen, got the camera . . . I thought they're probably going to take the bodies away and everything and I won't have a chance to get the photographs, so I started shooting.[10]

Celecia took fifteen pictures, from both his apartment and the street level, capturing for posterity the grotesque sight of McCann's and Farrell's corpses sprawled across the footpath. Caught on camera as well were the SAS men who killed them, the Gibraltar Special Branch officers deployed in the area, and a number of uniformed police. Distracted by the bodies on the ground, none of them tried to stop Celecia taking photographs.

Realizing that he possessed critical evidence, Celecia gave his film to the Gibraltar Police so they could copy the negatives. After waiting some time for the return of his property, Celecia finally asked the police to give the film back, only to be asked, "What film?" After pressing a little harder, he learned that "national security" precluded its return. The public release of his photographs would jeopardize the safety of the SAS men and police officers in them.

The government only relented after Celecia hired Christopher Finch and sued to get the pictures returned. In the end, he got them back, but the heads of each and every member of the security forces who appeared in them had been brushed out.

Douglas Celecia was lucky. He got his evidence back somewhat intact along with a £10,000 payment from the Gibraltar Police for permission to use the film at the inquest. Another player in the Gibraltar saga, Harry Debelius, was less fortunate. The *Times* correspondent, who had acted as Manyon's interpreter during the filming of *Death on the Rock*, had also interviewed Proetta. When the Gibraltar Police asked to borrow the tape recording of his conversation with her, Debelius had been happy to oblige. Yet upon inquiring when the tape and the notes he took would be returned, he learned that they had been "lost", another unfortunate coincidence.[11]

This was the tip of the iceberg as far as missing evidence went. During the inquest, the government's witnesses relied on their memories to recall events then six months past. They did not use nor did they produce in court any tapes of military, police, or MI5 radio communications. Nor did they offer the jury any notes or recordings made of the critical briefing Canepa held on March 5. Documentary evidence about the use of force consisted of just three pieces of paper, the rules of engagement and the documents the SAS used to take control of the operation and then return it to the police. And it seemed that no one had thought to videotape any of the ASU's members as they moved about the town. It was quite poor record-keeping, given the authorities' stated intention to carefully collect evidence to use against McCann, Savage, and Farrell.[12]

Then there was minimal effort by the Gibraltar Police to find witnesses to the shootings. Normally, when someone dies violently in the United Kingdom, the police establish an "incident centre" close to the death scene where they collect evidence and identify and interview people who saw the crime. This did not happen on the Rock. In the first hours after the shootings, various Gibraltar Police officers simply asked the crowds gathered around the bodies if anyone had seen anything.

Another peculiarity was the SAS's abrupt departure from the crime scenes. In the United Kingdom, a police officer or a soldier acting in a police role – like an SAS man – who discharges a firearm is *never* supposed to leave the shooting scene unless the senior police officer present gives him or her permission to do so. The only exception is if the person involved in the incident is injured.[13]

This did not happen in Gibraltar. Soldiers A, B, C, and D left the area after receiving instructions from Soldier E, their commanding officer. When they turned in their weapons and magazines at the Gibraltar Police headquarters for forensic testing, the Army lawyer who accompanied them to the Rock was with them. This same individual secured permission for his charges to leave the Colony from Gibraltar's Deputy Attorney General *without* their giving any statements to the police about their actions. It was not until March 15 – presumably after several intense sessions with legal counsel – that the SAS men spoke to British police who passed on their statements to the Gibraltar Police. Events like those made the soldiers look more like criminals fleeing the scene of a crime than men "assisting the civil power".

The Gibraltar authorities' inept behavior reached its peak during the autopsies. British law calls for a government appointed medical examiner to examine the body of anyone who dies a suspicious death. In the case of McCann, Savage, and Farrell's deaths, this was Professor Alan Watson.

Watson lived in Scotland and was on the medical faculty of the University of Glasgow. A senior pathologist, he had worked for the Gibraltar authorities before on other less complex, certainly less politicized deaths.

The Gibraltar Police and military authorities ought to have gone out of their way to provide Professor Watson with whatever assistance he needed in Gibraltar. Instead, the opposite took place. When the Scottish pathologist arrived at noon on March 7 at the Royal Navy Hospital morgue where the bodies were, he discovered the Gibraltarians had stripped the corpses. The morgue did not have an x-ray machine, and he was not given access to any others the hospital possessed. Nor did any of the local medical staff help him. Later, Watson discovered that the police photographer who was supposed to record his findings had done a wholly inadequate job. [14]

The Professor's problems continued when he returned to Glasgow to prepare his report. Despite repeated requests, the London Metropolitan Police forensics experts never provided him with copies of the ballistics and evidence reports they prepared for the Gibraltar authorities. Nor did they give him the results of tests he asked them to perform on blood samples taken from the Provisionals' bodies.

At the inquest, McGrory told the pathologist he found this lack of cooperation bewildering.

Watson said, "It is a puzzle to me too. I am just giving you the facts." But why didn't the police give him the reports he needed?

"I cannot answer that question." [15]

Despite these obstacles, Watson reached some definite conclusions about the Provisionals' deaths. McCann had been shot a total of four times. One bullet had smashed into his lower left jaw causing relatively minor injuries. It may have ricocheted off Farrell. The other three rounds caused the fatal injuries. Two had gone into McCann's back and exited from his chest, inflicting massive damage to his heart, left lung, and liver. The last had torn through the back of his head and shredded the left side of his brain.[16]

As for Farrell, she had been shot five times. Two bullets hit her in the face producing a total of five minor wounds there. The three bullets in her back had killed her. She died from massive trauma to her heart and liver as they ripped through and out of her body.[17]

Savage had been shot perhaps as many as eighteen times. After his autopsy, a local mortician had to invest a considerable amount of effort into making his corpse fit for burial. During his testimony, Professor Watson took fifteen minutes to read out the total list of his subject's injuries. There were twenty-nine wounds on the young man's body. At least five bullets had hit him in the chest and back, piercing his right lung. Others had broken his left leg, right arm and wounded him in the shoulders, abdomen, and left hand. The five which entered his skull and neck killed him. As in the case of McCann, their impact literally pulped his brain.[18]

McGrory tried to emphasize the overkill. "We don't want to use non-scientific expression, but he was riddled with bullets?" he asked.

"Yes. I try not to use these words. I concur with your word. Yes, like a frenzied attack, one would say," Watson replied.[19]

The Professor's comment made headlines (FRENZY OF THE SAS screamed the *Daily Mail*), but for the government, his analysis of McCann and Farrell's wounds were even more disturbing. In Watson's opinion, the wounds in their faces meant that they had been turned toward their killers when they received them. The bullets which hit them in the back had travelled upward through their bodies. This was particularly evident in Farrell's case.

When his turn with the witness came, McGrory seized on this point. "Could we return, without inconvenience to Your Honour and the jury, to Miss Farrell and the bullets to her back? Now they appear to have an upward trajectory?"

"That is right," replied the Professor.

"That would indicate to you she was down?"

"Yes."

"So the gunman would have to be [kneeling] to [inflict those injuries], or she was down?"

"Yes, that is not a very marked opening."

"Well, she was only five-foot-one."

"Yes."

McGrory continued, "So, the gunman would need to be very well down to get that, or she was down?"

Watson said, "Yes, she must have been going forward like this." He leaned forward quickly.

"Or down?"

"Or even down."

*"Or on her face?"*

"Yes."[20]

As for Savage, Professor Watson told the jury even more. This was thanks to one of the few efficient Gibraltar policemen on duty that day. This individual (later identified as Inspector Revagliatte) had drawn an outline around Savage's corpse and circled five strike marks present there as well. Three of them were where Savage's head had been. McGrory showed a photograph of this to Watson. Viewing the picture for the first time (the authorities had not provided him with a copy), the pathologist stated that he felt it would be reasonable to conclude that Savage had been shot in the head as he lay on the street.

"So the scenario that fits your evidence as an expert, and this [photograph], is that he is brought down, possibly from the back, and then four bullets [are] fired into his head?" McGrory asked.

"That is right. He may have had one of these in the face. He may have been facing [his killer], and as in the case of [Farrell], turned round, and fallen to the ground and had these others. Either scenario would fit."[21]

Yet what Professor Watson said outside the courtroom upset the British government the most. Asked by a reporter whether Savage's wounds had shocked him, he said, "Yes, it did, actually." In response to a question about whether the killings had been murder, he replied, "It has to be, doesn't it?" Then, qualifying his remarks, Watson added:

> Murder is an emotive word. If it was death by shooting, you have got to choose between accidental death, and murder, or suicide. You have got to keep an open mind. Of the three, it has to be homicide. It's just a matter of whether it was justifiable homicide.[22]

Those comments along with Watson's statement to a BBC reporter that he believed Savage was shot while lying on the ground set off a flurry of activity among the Thatcher Administration's partisans. Citing the usual unnamed government sources, the *Sun* informed its readers that the overkill in Savage's case had been quite deliberate and not frenzied. What better way was there to ensure a terrorist was not a threat than to surgically "[blow] his brains out"?[23] Meanwhile in Parliament, Conservative MP Harry Greenaway commented on Professor Watson's views by saying, "That was 'frenzied' conjecture on his part. He wasn't there so how would he know?" The thought that pathologists rarely observe the deaths they are called to investigate did not appear to have occurred to him.

Despite the damage control, it still had been a bad day for the British government. However, McGrory did not gloat. Speaking to one reporter, he said, "As soon as I saw the professor wanted to tell the truth, the rest was easy."[24]

Equally damaging to the government's case was the testimony of the forensic experts. In most inquests, these witnesses appear immediately after the pathologists testify. This is because their evidence compliments that from an autopsy. Yet in Gibraltar, normal operating procedure was flouted once more. Professors Watson and Professor Pounder, another pathologist McGrory brought to the hearing, testified about their findings on September 8. It was not until over two weeks later, that David Pryor, forensic scientist for New Scotland Yard appeared in the Coroner's Court.

Like Watson, Pryor encountered difficulties in doing his job, not the least of which being that the IRA operatives' clothing arrived at his laboratory, "in such a condition . . . that accurate determination of which was an entry site and which an exit site was very difficult."[25] Using the powder marks on Savage's jacket, he was able to say a pistol had been fired at him from about six feet away. His testimony about Farrell's clothing was much more significant. The powder burns on her jacket indicated that a pistol had been fired at her perhaps as close as three – perhaps even two – feet from her back. Pryor's finding contradicted Soldiers A and B's testimony that they had been six feet or more away from McCann and Farrell when they shot them. It did square with Carmen Proetta's memory of a big, blond gunman crouching down and firing from point blank range at the IRA members' prostrate bodies.

There evidence left many questions unanswered. But the greatest puzzle dealt with something more tenuous, the surveillance operation in Spain. Had the ASU's members been watched before they entered Gibraltar or had the Spanish lost them? That question centred around a set of missing witnesses and a document of dubious origins.

In the heady days immediately after the shootings, it had been the Crown's unofficial but quite extensively-leaked position that on March 6, the Spanish had indeed followed McCann, Savage, and Farrell right up to the gates of the Colony where members of MI5 had taken over the surveillance. By September 1988, the tale British Foreign Office and MoD spokesmen had told about "brilliant" Spanish police maintaining unbroken watch on the ASU's movements vanished like a soap bubble. In its place, Commissioner Canepa and the security forces' officials who followed him into the witness box had a new version of events for the jury.

As stories go, it was a simple one which many Gibraltarians must have had no difficulty in believing. When the IRA team flew into Malaga Airport on March 4, it seemed that the Spanish police had been a bit careless following them. After briefly spotting the Provisionals in the terminal, the undercover police lost all three of them. McCann and Savage were last seen climbing into a taxi, and Farrell simply disappeared. Despite a frantic three-day search up and down the Costa del Sol, the Spanish failed to track any of them down.[26]

So, the Gibraltar Killings had not really been the British government's fault. With no information coming in from the bungling Spanish authorities, the SAS men had to assume the worst, that Savage had driven a car-bomb into the Colony when he appeared there on March 6.

Unfortunately, a few people remembered the Spanish government's official statement on March 9 that the surveillance of the ASU outside Gibraltar had been continuous. Speaking on the record, Spanish police had also informed Tim McGirk of the *Independent* that they had kept such close watch on the IRA team that an undercover officer had even heard McCann and Savage discuss their planned attack as they sat drinking in a bar. And just before the inquest, Augustin Valladolid, the Spanish government's spokesman about the shootings, repeatedly stated in public that the Spanish police had made no mistakes; that the entire operation had been airtight.[27]

Equally inconveniently, the British Foreign Minister, Sir Geoffrey Howe, said the following about the Spanish effort when he addressed Parliament about the shootings on March 7:

Confident that the House will wish me to extend our gratitude to the Spanish authorities, without whose invaluable assistance the outcome might have been very different. This cooperation underlines once again the importance of the international collaboration in fight against terrorism.[28]

That was praise, not criticism and until the inquest, the only official description of the Spanish surveillance operation on record.

With Howe's statement hanging in the air, the most logical step for the British to take would have been to have a senior Spanish police officer testify about what had happened outside of Gibraltar. Yet despite the many assurances that one – later identified as Chief Inspector Tomas Rayo Valenzuela – would do just that, it did not happen. At the last minute, the Spanish government informed Pizzarello's court that Valenzuela would not testify at the hearing. Not a few people linked that particular "coincidence" to a visit Margaret Thatcher made to Spain a few days before the Spanish made that decision. The talks she had with Spanish premier Felipe Gonzalez were reportedly "very successful".[29]

What the Gibraltar Police offered in place of Valenzuela's testimony was a statement he supposedly gave them on August 8, 1988. It corroborated the story Canepa and the other witnesses told the inquest.[30] There had been no surveillance of McCann, Savage, and Farrell outside Gibraltar on March 6. Leaked to the media, it did an admirable job dispelling doubts. For example, *The Times*, which had been one of the first to state that the Spanish followed the Provisionals to the gates of Gibraltar, now solemnly told its readers that the Provisionals had not been watched that day.[31]

The problem was that Valenzuela's statement was unsworn and unsigned. When McGrory learned that Hucker and Laws planned to have it given to the jury, he informed the Coroner that he would be introducing as evidence affidavits from

208

Harry Debelius as well as two Spanish journalists who had interviewed the police involved in the surveillance operation. Unlike Inspector Valenzuela, these individuals were willing to appear in court and discuss their signed and sworn depositions.

That was not to be. Pizzarello refused to admit all the statements on the grounds that they were hearsay. It was a strange ruling since he did allow several government witnesses to testify about events that they had not actually seen. But that too may have been another Gibraltar coincidence.[32]

## Notes

1. I was greatly assisted in this portion of the book by an individual trained in forensic pathology.
2. Jack, "Gibraltar", p. 71.
3. Testimony of Sergeant Emilio, Acris, the Gibraltar Inquest, Day 15, 26 September 1988, Channel Four Television, p. 48.
4. Ibid. Nor did Sergeant Acris mark where the shells had been.
5. Testimony of Officer Q, the Gibraltar Inquest, Day 10, 9 September 1988, Channel Four Television, 1988, pp. 83-84.
6. Ibid.
7. Interview with Douglas Celecia, Gibraltar, June 1996.
8. Testimony of Douglas Celecia, the Gibraltar Inquest, Day 12, 21 September 1988, Channel Four Television, 1988. p. 48.
9. Ibid, p. 50.
10. Ibid, p. 51.
11. Telephone interview with Harry Debelius, Madrid, Spain, July 1996.
12. Multiple excerpts from the Gibraltar Inquest Transcript, Channel Four Television, 1988.
13. John Stalker, *The Stalker Affair*, Viking Penguin Inc, New York, 1988, pp. 41-42.
14. Testimony of Professor Alan Watson, the Gibraltar Inquest, Day 3, 8 September 1988, Channel Four Television, 1988, pp. 19-23.
15. Ibid.
16. Ibid, pp. 5-9.
17. Ibid, pp. 1-5.
18. Ibid, pp. 11-16.
19. Ibid, p. 34.
20. Ibid, p. 33.
21. Ibid, p. 35.
22. Bolton, p. 262.

23. "Why the Dogs Had to Die", *Sun*, September 9, 1988. Interestingly enough, the *Sun* admits that McCann, Savage, and Farrell were "shot in cold blood with no chance to surrender" and admits that perhaps such a fate is not "British justice".

24. Gordon McKibben, "Belfast Lawyer 'Key Actor' at IRA Inquest", *Boston Globe*, September 11, 1988.

25. Testimony of David Prior, the Gibraltar Inquest, Day 16, 27 September 1988, Channel Four Television, 1988, p. 3.

26. Gibraltar Police Witness Statement containing the Account of the Spanish Police Operation, Allegedly Given by Inspector Tomas Rayo Valenzuela, August 8, 1988.

27. David Leigh, Paul Lashmar, and John Hooper, "Spanish Police Explode MI5 'Rock' Story", *Observer*, February 19, 1989. Just as revealing, then there was the fact that Mrs Thatcher and MI5 sent telegrams of congratulations and thanks for a job well done to the Spanish immediately after the shootings.

28. Northern Ireland: IRA Terrorists, Gibraltar, British Information Services, March 8, 1988.

29. "Reading Between the Lies", *Private Eye,* 701, October 28, 1988, p. 25.

30. Gibraltar Police Witness Statement.

31. "Reading Between the Lies."

32. This was particularly true with Soldier E's testimony.

# CHAPTER FOURTEEN

### RIDDLES, BUTTONS, AND HACKS

"Gibraltar simply underlined the continuing British position on [covert operations]: reveal nothing, deny everything, even the hard evidence."
— J Bowyer Bell, *In Dubious Battle*

Mr O, the SAS, and the Commissioner may have been the stars of "The Bomb That Threatened the Gibraltar People", but there were other members of the cast as well. These "extras" came in two groups: those who saw the Provisionals die; and assorted technical experts.

In broad terms, the evidence of the first group, consisting of "Witnesses" H through N, "Officers" P, Q, and R, Inspector Revagliatte, his entourage, and Detective Constable Huart, supported the SAS. But there were inconsistencies both in their individual stories and the collective picture they formed of events on March 6.

First, despite Commissioner Canepa's claim that no one marked out the Shell Station as the place to conduct the arrest, a large number of people converged there over a very short period of time, before or just after the shootings. There were: Officers P, Q, and R, the armed policemen, who ringed the building; Detective Constable Huart who wandered onto the scene after leaving his post at the Spanish immigrations hut; Witness K (an MI5 officer who had been lurking by the Shell Station for some time); and Inspector Revagliatte and his three subordinates.

The sudden concentration of Gibraltar Police on Winston

Churchill Avenue was particularly odd given their complete absence from Landport Lane. According to the plan, there should have been at least one police officer there to formally arrest Savage after Soldiers C and D captured him. Yet this individual, if he ever existed, did not appear at the inquest.

The presence and participation of three armed policemen in the operation also suggested that three pairs of SAS men confronted the Provisionals. In fact, months earlier, an article in the supposedly well-informed *Sunday Times* stated there had been such a third arrest team – the gunmen Stephen Bullock and his wife encountered. Yet by September, these individuals had vanished from the story as well.

That raised two interesting questions about the nature of Operation Flavius. First, there had been a minimum of eight SAS troopers deployed on Gibraltar's streets on March 6, Soldiers A, B, C, and D and at least four more men at the airport. But the authorities had only used the first four to apprehend three supposedly fanatical, armed terrorists they believed had the ability to blow up the Gibraltar town centre and kill scores of people. Why confront McCann, Savage, and Farrell on an almost one-to-one basis when more manpower had been available?

The second issue was equally curious. Despite acting in a police role, the soldiers had *not* carried handcuffs or rope to bind the IRA members' hands. It is a generally accepted principle that armed police must carry some non-lethal means of restraint. On at least several occasions in Northern Ireland, the SAS has observed this rule, using rope or flexicuffs (plastic handcuffs) to tie up prisoners. But not in Gibraltar – there, they relied on police who, in at least Savage's case, were simply not there.

And Inspector Revagliatte's presence and actions near the Shell Station before and after the shootings were more than a little odd. He and the three officers riding in his car that day testified they had known nothing about Operation Flavius. Nevertheless, the SAS, MI5, and Gibraltar Police personnel who did, allowed them – four unarmed, uniformed police – to enter an area where undercover soldiers were about to confront a trio of what were believed to be suicidally dangerous terrorists armed with a massive radio-controlled car-bomb. After the shootings, despite having no idea who they were, Revagliatte had immediately approached the SAS men at the Shell Station. For an unarmed policeman to walk up to what appeared to be criminals who had just murdered two defenseless people seemed more like suspicious than "conspicuous" gallantry.

As for the MI5 witnesses, the small number of them who appeared at the inquest was mystifying. Only two – Witnesses I and N – were on or near Landport Lane and gave testimony about Savage's death. Only four – Witnesses H, I, K, L and M– had anything to tell the jury about McCann and Farrell's last moments. This, counting Witness N who said he was not in the area when the shootings happened – was a total of seven people from a mobile surveillance group consisting of twenty to thirty personnel. Where were the other watchers – off duty, asleep, shopping for souvenirs? The accounts of civilian eyewitness to Savage's death suggest at least two of them were within several feet of the IRA man when Soldiers C and D killed him. These individuals, if they existed, did not give testimony in Gibraltar.

Another question British taxpayers might have fairly asked was whether they were getting their money's worth out of the MI5 surveillance officers on the Rock. Witness J had been only fifteen feet from Savage when he spun around, his attention drawn by the gunfire cracking out to his north. She immediately turned away to avoid eye contact with him. Witness J claimed she did not see Soldiers C and D shoot the IRA man, nor did she hear the fifteen to eighteen rounds they fired into his body.

The soft-spoken woman explained this memory lapse as the result of having never heard shots fired before, not even during her training course. McGrory found this a little hard to believe, "Is that not a remarkable thing?" he politely inquired.

"It may be sir, but I did not hear them."[2]

If McGrory was unhappy with Witness J's memory, he must have been delighted with that of Witness I. When the military took control for the final time at 3:40 p.m., that MI5 officer had been standing on the lefthand side of Corral Road looking on as McCann and Farrell walked north toward the Shell Station. The surveillance specialist noticed that by this point Savage had turned back and was strolling up Landport Lane.

A police siren then sounded. The MI5 man could not tell from where. An instant later, he heard gunshots from the direction of the Shell Station and saw Soldiers A and B firing at McCann and Farrell. Witness I believed one of the soldiers had been standing on the road. This directly contradicted the testimony of SAS men who said they both opened fire on the Provisionals from behind and never left the footpath.

Yet it was the statement Witness I gave to the Gibraltar Police in May that briefly raised the spectre of handcuffs for Soldiers A and B rather than medals for their actions. Judging by his questions, McGrory had studied the document thoroughly.

" . . . In that statement, did you say that you saw the last few shots fired at McCann and Farrell, who had just fallen to the ground?" he asked.

"Yes, sir," the watcher replied.

"Now, of course, you would wish to make some slight amendment to that, would you?"

Witness I hedged, "No, sir, when I say they'd just fallen to the ground, as I've said to the Coroner, they were more to the ground than standing up. I would say they were on the ground."

"They were on the ground when the last few shots were fired?"

"I believe they were still moving when I saw the last few shots being fired."

"They could be on the ground and move for a while?"

"That's true."

McGrory tried again, "They were on the ground?"

And got nowhere. "They still moved."

"Oh, I know, but on the ground?"

"Almost on the ground, yes."

"You're now adding the word almost'?"

"Well, I'm saying is they weren't actually lying on the ground. They were hitting the ground when I saw the shots being fired."

The lawyer was exasperated, "I won't spend much more on it. I just want to remind you of what you had said in your first evidence to the learned Coroner. You saw them fire the last few shots at McCann and Farrell who had fallen – past tense *fallen* – to the ground. That's what you said."

"Yes, sir."[3]

McGrory did not have many moments like that during the inquest, but he did enjoy several. Besides those during Professor Watson's and Witness I's testimony, most came during his examination of several technical witnesses who appeared at the proceedings. Their evidence dealt directly with the foundation of the government's case: that the killing of the Provisionals was lawful, because at the time the SAS men believed they had the ability to set off a car-bomb at the assembly area. Under British law, such a belief justified the use of lethal force.

Yet this only applied if the existing circumstances made that belief reasonable. If it could be demonstrated that the circumstances made it *unreasonable*, the jury could conclude that the SAS men had never worried about a "button job", and that there were darker reasons for their actions that day.

The Belfast lawyer began his assault on the reasonableness of the button-job theory when questioning the first government witness who qualified as an expert on car-bombs. This was Allen Feraday, a scientist on the staff of the MoD's ordnance research establishment in Kent. Under examination by Coroner Pizzarello, Feraday, a man with "thirty-three years of experience" with explosives, confidently identified the device found by the Spanish police in Marbella as having the "artwork" of a Provisional IRA bomb. Quizzed by the Coroner

215

about the range of any "button" carried by the Provisionals, Feraday stated his views quite forcefully. A signal from the hand-held citizen's band "walky-talkies" the IRA was currently using *would* have reached the car at the assembly area. Because of that, Feraday would "happily assume" McCann, Savage, and Farrell could have set off an explosion from Landport Lane, Winston Churchill Avenue, or even further away.[4]

Yet under cross-examination, Feraday made a series of statements that damaged some of the good he had done for the SAS. Prodded by McGrory, he admitted that the standard antenna on Savage's car was not the type he would have used to set off a radio-controlled device. He also confirmed an important part of George Styles' contribution to *Death on the Rock*. Like Colonel Styles, Feraday had no knowledge of any incident where the IRA had triggered a radio-detonated bomb when they did not have direct line of sight to the target. Nor did Feraday know of any cases where the IRA had used a radio initiation device in a built-up urban area like Gibraltar.[5]

Then there was Soldier G, Operation Flavius's bomb disposal officer. He had made the key and fatal determination that the Renault 5 was a "suspect car-bomb." As it turned out, his judgment had been little more than a hunch. Soldier G had felt that the car's antenna looked out of place: it was old and rusty and did not match the "newishness" of the rest of the vehicle. Produced in court, the antenna looked quite unremarkable, a simple piece of bent wire.

A confident enough witness under examination by the Crown's lawyers, Soldier G wilted when McGrory questioned him about what could have been done to minimize the supposedly terrible threat Gibraltar faced that day.

"Once the three people were clear of the car and were clearly heading down to the frontier, why didn't you go back [to the assembly area] and unscrew that aerial?" he asked the witness.

Soldier G seemed caught off-guard. "I didn't think of that."

"If you had, their little transmitter would have been utterly useless to them. Isn't that so?"

"I think that is reasonable, yes."

McGrory pressed home, "When you had your discussion with your [superiors after returning to the command centre] . . . did it occur to nobody that the simple method of neutralizing the whole thing was just to unscrew it?"

"No, it didn't at all."[6]

A moment later, Soldier G corrected himself, informing the jury that unscrewing the antenna would have been very risky and might have made the receiver inside the car unstable with disastrous results.[7] The fact the SAS men's lawyer, Mr Hucker, had to prompt him to say that made the witness look something less than a bomb-disposal "expert."

Another very damaging admission in Soldier G's testimony had to do with communications. By 7:30 p.m. on March 6, an RAF bomb disposal team had examined and found Savage's car to be empty. There were literally dozens of ways this simple piece of information could have gotten to London. Gibraltar is well linked to the outside world by its telephone service. The British military units there have communications links to the MoD in London as well. The SAS, as a matter of rule, uses sophisticated tactical satellite communications radios. Yet appearing on BBC's radio news program *Today*, nearly twelve hours later, Ian Stewart, the British Armed Forces Minister, had somehow got it wrong, saying, "there was a car-bomb found in Gibraltar, which has been defused."[8]

Finally, while no one brought it up, the authorities in Gibraltar might have had a far more scientific option available to them for dealing with the supposed threat the Renault posed. By the late 1980s, the British military had developed a set of counter-measures for use against radio-detonated bombs in Northern Ireland. These techniques ranged from the simple: broadcasting signals up and down the radio spectrum used by

IRA engineers in an effort to prematurely detonate their devices to the quite sophisticated: flooding an area around a suspect bomb with electromagnetic noise to drown out a detonation signal. By the late 1980s, these techniques had forced the Provisionals to revert to using unjammable detonation systems, specifically timers and command wires.[9]

It is unknown whether this technology was available or employed in Gibraltar. If it had been, the British government's silence about it was understandable. The techniques in question were and remain shrouded in secrecy. However, there were legal reasons for not bringing up the issue as well. If the counter-measures had been available but not used, it would confirm that no one had seriously expected a radio-detonated car-bomb in the Colony. Just as important, an admission that the authorities had been jamming the radio spectrum around the assembly area would have reduced much of the drama the SAS men's final confrontation with the ASU.

Late in the inquest, McGrory called a technical expert of his own, Dr Michael Scott. Scott held degrees in electrical and electronic engineering and a doctorate in control engineering as well, far more impressive credentials than Feraday's. He also qualified as an expert on radio-controlled detonations, having testified and advised in two different trials of alleged IRA bombers.

In his evidence, Dr Scott emphatically disagreed with Feraday's stated belief that the ASU could have set off a car-bomb at the assembly area from Winston Churchill Avenue. Unlike his opposite number, he had carried out field work to back up his contention. Upon arriving in Gibraltar, Scott had obtained two ICOM walky-talkies similar to one Feraday had shown to the jury. Leaving one in the assembly area car park, he began walking north, pausing periodically to see if he could establish a voice linkage between the two radios. By the time he had reached the Shell Station, the quality of the link had degraded significantly.[10]

This fact raised serious questions about whether the IRA could have set off the hypothetical bomb at the assembly area. By the mid-1980s, the Provisionals were no longer relying on simple radio transmissions to cause explosions. Instead, their initiators used encoders. When activated, these devices transmitted a series of radio tones to the explosive device in question. If the signals matched the setting on the decoder attached to the bomb in question, it would go off. Getting a match required a high quality linkage – better than simple voice – and in Scott's opinion one that could not have existed between the assembly area and Winston Churchill Avenue.

Scott also had a few words to say about the entire concept of the button job. In the evidence they gave, the SAS men and Feraday had given the jury the impression that all the Provisionals had to do to cause instant mayhem was to press a single switch on a transmitter. This was not the case. Going for a button required several actions: turning the transmitter on, pressing its "send" button, and activating the encoder. The first two steps could be taken in advance. Yet doing so would leave the transmitter running down its battery and in a state where it could send a detonation signal if someone bumped into the person carrying it.[11] With the jostling that takes place on Gibraltar's crowded, narrow streets, carrying an initiator set in such a fashion was a risky enterprise – even for suicidally-minded terrorists.

Dr Scott's statements drew a heated response from Mr Hucker. The SAS lawyer's very first question to the witness was whether he would be willing to allow his "dear mother" to be near a car-bomb at the assembly area with his "worst enemy" at the Shell Station armed with a radio initiation device. In response, Scott replied that he hoped he would have the faith in his conclusions that would allow him to take such a risk.[12]

Thwarted on that gambit, the government lawyers commissioned tests of their own (ones they apparently felt were unnecessary before Dr Scott came on the scene). A team of British Army Signal Corps personnel rushed through the town, checking the quality of radio linkages at various points around the Rock. They reached conclusions that supported Feraday's original ones. Voice and tone communications were possible between the assembly area and Winston Churchill Avenue, but not guaranteed. The soldiers had used more powerful radios during their tests than Scott had, and it had taken several tries to get the desired linkage.[13] Recalled to the witness stand, Feraday then told the jury that the IRA also used these higher power radios and that one such transmitter had been in the arms cache allegedly discovered by Belgian police on January 21, 1988.[14] But judging by the way one member of panel (dubbed "Henry Fonda" by the Irish press in honour of the juror played by the film star in the courtroom drama *Twelve Angry Men*) bombarded him with questions, Feraday's credibility had been undermined in the eyes of at least one Gibraltarian.[15]

Nevertheless, the scientist did not retreat from his original position, that it was possible to detonate a car-bomb from the Shell Station. In effect, the duel over the credibility of the SAS's "sincere" belief in the button job had been fought to a draw.[16] Some of those following the proceedings wondered whether McGrory had:

gotten sucked into [the British government's] game of self-contained logic [and] allowed the Crown to dictate the nature and pace of the inquest, leaving a lot of damning evidence about what actually *happened* on the day insufficiently undermined in the minds of the jury.[17]

This would have included the fact the SAS men – "sincerely believing" the ASU members had devices on their persons that could set off a massive car-bomb at the press of a button – had shot repeatedly into their bodies and allowed them to fall to the ground.

This was all frightfully dull for the British tabloid reporters gathered on the Rock. They had come to Gibraltar to hear something exciting, not boring technical details about the capabilities of radio transmitters.

So to entertain themselves, some of the hacks purchased transmitters-receivers and begun conducting their own scientific trials. A typical one consisted of one participant shouting obscenities into his radio and getting similar ones in response.[18] Writing about such antics, Ian Jack later commented, "This was the English journalists' reconstruction of the SAS's role as executioners of the Irish Republican Army."[19]

## Notes

1. "The SAS in the Dock", *Sunday Times*, May 8, 1988. The paper refers to "two plain-clothes SAS men with four more in back-up roles."

2. Testimony of Witness J, the Gibraltar Inquest, Day 9, 16 September 1988, Channel Four Television, 1988, pp. 37-38.

3. Testimony of Witness I, the Gibraltar Inquest, Day 9, 16 September 1988, Channel Four Television, 1988, pp. 27-28.

4. Testimony of Mr Allen Feraday, the Gibraltar Inquest, Day 5, 12 September 1988, Channel Four Television, 1988, pp. 71-84.

5. Ibid.

6. Testimony of Soldier G, the Gibraltar Inquest, Day 6, 13 September 1988, Channel Four Television, 1988, pp. 1-19.

7. That explanation is also incorrect. Actually, the danger would have come from the possibility that touching the antenna would set off an anti-handling device. Yet Soldier G appeared not to have worried about this when he put himself in close proximity to the Renault, something Feraday said was very foolish behaviour.

8. Bolton, p. 190.

9. Urban, *Big Boys' Rules*, p. 113.

10. Testimony of Dr Michael Scott, the Gibraltar Inquest, Day 16, 27 September 1988, Channel Four Television, 1988, pp. 27-31.

11. Ibid, p. 26.

12. Ibid, pp. 32-33.

13. Furthermore, they did not use an encoder to establish the tone link but a simple tape recording of a single audio tone.

14. Testimony of Captain Mark Edwards and Allen Feraday, the Gibraltar Inquest, Day 17, 28 September 1988, Channel Four Television, 1988.

15. Interview with Ed Moloney, Belfast, June 1996.

16. In fairness, James Howland, an impartial, highly qualified American radio expert consulted by me, agreed with the British government's position. My view is that the entire debate over the bomb is irrelevant because the evidence shows that the British did *not* believe the Provisionals had one.

17. O'Higgins and Waters, "A Controlled Explosion of the Truth", p. 39.

18. Jack, "Gibraltar", pp. 15-16.

19. Ibid.

# CHAPTER FIFTEEN

## A NEAR RUN THING

"Who dares, gets away with it."
— "The Guns of Gibraltar", *Private Eye*, 1989

Besides the anonymous spies, police, and soldiers parading through Pizzarello's courtroom, witnesses with names showed up there as well. Most of these were government employees, ranging from Gibraltar Police officers to fingerprint specialists brought in from Scotland Yard. But mixed in with this mighty stream of British officialdom were a few individuals with claims to being independent witnesses to McCann, Savage, and Farrell's deaths.

What they said depended on who discovered them. The several Gibraltarians brought forward by the police saw nothing criminal happen on the streets of their town. Most had only watched fragments of the action by the Shell Petrol Station and on Landport Lane. To a man, they agreed that the SAS certainly did not fire into the IRA members' bodies after they fell to the ground.[1]

One of them, Constable James Parody, made a particularly good impression, even though he was not really an independent witness. A member of the Gibraltar Police, at the time of the shootings, he had been off-duty and relaxing in his apartment on Winston Churchill Avenue. Like Inspector Revagliatte, he told the court he had been unaware at the time of Operation

222

Flavius. When Parody heard the police siren blare, he ran to his window to see what was going on. From there, the young officer could see everything. According to him, Soldiers A and B shouted, "Police! Police!" before shooting the Provisionals.[2]

This was welcome testimony for the government. It corroborated the accounts of Officers P, Q, and R but differed from them on two counts. First, Parody and the undercover officers' clear memories of the shouts contradicted the evidence given by the men who killed McCann and Farrell. Soldiers A and B had not been certain they gave the couple orders to do anything. As Soldier A put it, "events overtook the warning". Second, Parody said the SAS men fired at the IRA operatives from the middle of the road, something both soldiers denied doing.[3]

Then there were the *Death on the Rock* witnesses. When called to the stand, Stephen Bullock repeated the account that he gave *This Week*. He had seen McCann, hands in the air, reel away from a gunman who fired at him from point-blank range. He had then heard gunshots after the two men he and his wife had been watching ran down Landport Lane in Savage's direction. His wife Lucinda gave similar testimony.

Josie Celecia also appeared. She too stood by what she had told *This Week*. Her evidence about hearing gunfire as an SAS man stood with his arms outstretched and pointing down toward McCann and Farrell's bodies painted a powerfully suggestive picture.

Hucker, the soldiers' lawyer, did his best to undermine it. First, he argued that Celecia had not heard shots from a soldier finishing off McCann and Farrell but the ones on Landport Lane that killed Savage. Second, he pointed out that she had changed one part of her account since *Death on the Rock*. On the programme, Celecia had claimed there had been more gunfire after the burst of four or five shots. She now did not believe there had been. As a final tactic, Hucker implied to the jury that the witness was unreliable because she could not identify the SAS men from the photographs her husband took. Since the authorities had brushed out each and every face of the police and soldiers in those pictures, that was hardly surprising.[4]

As for the idea that Celecia mistook the shots which killed Savage for additional ones fired at McCann and Farrell, she emphatically rejected it.

" . . . the bangs came from [by the Shell Station]?" McGrory asked her when it was his turn to examine the witness.

"Yes," Celecia replied.

"No question at all in your mind that the bangs were coming [from where Savage died] or anywhere near it?"

"No."

"Because, of course, you're very, very close to this. You are very close to what happened, aren't you?"

"Yes."

"Just across the road from them?"

"Yes."[5]

The Bullocks and Celecia, though, were sideshows. Carmen Proetta was the main event. The so-called "tart of Gib" had had a nasty summer waiting for the inquest. The British tabloids made certain of that. In the weeks following her appearance on *Death on the Rock*, reporters from those publications scoured Spain and Gibraltar for unsavory details of her private life.

Some of their "research" smacked of desperation, a desire to build a defense against the massive libel actions Carmen was bringing against their employers. One reporter checked into an expensive hotel on the Costa del Sol and proceeded to order up prostitutes on a half-hour basis. When the girls arrived at his room, he paid them for their time and showed each a picture of Proetta. But none of the real "tarts" knew her.

Several stories the tabloids published clearly were a continuation of their initial attack on Carmen's credibility as a witness. One appeared on May 29 in the *Mail on Sunday*. Titled

"Carmen Says No" it stated, "Government sources have now revealed that Mrs Proetta, a court interpreter, is refusing to repeat her story in court".[6] Meanwhile, articles appeared in other papers claiming that her children did not believe her and that her husband Maxie would contradict her when he testified.

The harassment intensified as the inquest drew closer. The Proettas received threatening and obscene phone calls. The family dog mysteriously disappeared. Their more "patriotic" neighbours stopped speaking with them. A "rat pack" from the tabloids began following Carmen day and night. Reporters belonging to it approached her young daughter when she went to school in an effort to get "dirt" on her.[7]

If this was intended to keep the Proettas from testifying, it did not work. Maxie took the witness stand on September 22, 1988. His account was simple. The couple was in the kitchen together. Maxie had been making himself a cup of tea. He glanced out the apartment window and saw a Gibraltar Police car travelling south from the border. It came to a screeching halt opposite the Shell Station and sounded its siren. Four men, three in civilian clothes and one in a police uniform, leaped from the car and rushed toward and jumped the barrier dividing the highway.

Looking over at the Shell Station, Maxie could see McCann and Farrell. They stopped walking when the siren rang out and had turned toward the police car. A man was standing on the road pointing a pistol at them. Another gunman was on the footpath behind the couple.

Farrell put her hands up. A shot rang out, and she collapsed. McCann tried to grab her, but more gunfire came, and he, too, fell to the ground. A second later, there was a final series of shots.

This version of events matched Carmen's in broad detail, but there were several differences, ones Maxie freely admitted when pressed by Hucker and Laws. He did not see the gunmen from the car fire at McCann and Farrell. And he felt that Farrell's actions before being shot were more self-defense than an attempt to surrender. In Maxie's opinion, the SAS men did not give either of the two time to surrender. Asked to explain why his evidence did not completely match that of his wife, he replied, "each person can put a different interpretation on what they see."[8]

Maxie also rejected an argument that the government lawyers repeatedly put forward: that he and his wife had not seen a car full of SAS men coming from the border but Inspector Revagliatte's car coming back from the roundabout on Winston Churchill Avenue. That suggestion was an important part of the authorities' defense because it provided an innocent explanation for the men jumping over the barrier. They had not been SAS men bent on murder, but police arriving on the scene *after* the shootings. The Proettas had mixed things up.

Unfortunately, there was a problem with that theory. It did not make sense. In Maxie's inelegant words, " . . . if [Revagliatte's] car drove by . . . instead of stopping next to the shooting, [and] . . . went round the roundabout and came back, I think it would be stupid."[9]

The next day, it was Carmen's turn. Under examination by Pizzarello, Hucker, and Laws, she gave an account of the shootings slightly at odds with what she said on *Death on the Rock*. The key difference was her lack of absolute certainty that the SAS men shot McCann and Farrell on the ground. Carmen had seen them fall and seen the soldiers pointing their automatics at the bodies. But she did not see smoke or flame from the pistols or the weapons ejecting shell casings.

The government lawyers pounced on this issue, pointing out that she expressed no such doubts when talking to *This Week*. To that, Carmen responded, "If you see people with guns [and hear gunfire], you presume it's coming from them. You don't get guns in people's hands every day in Gibraltar".[10]

She also gave ground on whether she had seen McCann and Farrell surrender.

" . . . You said on television, 'They were giving themselves up'?" Hucker asked.

"That's the impression I got, but they weren't given a chance."

The lawyer seemed to want a definitive answer to a subjective question. "Were they surrendering, yes or no?"

Carmen hedged, "For me, the signal of hands up can mean surrendering. It can mean shock, or it can mean something else. I could see, but I can't think for somebody else."[11]

That was the sum total of the qualifications Carmen made to her evidence. As in his examination of Maxie, Hucker strongly suggested that she mistook Inspector Revagliatte and his men for a team of soldiers coming from the border. Carmen rejected that. Laws also tried to imply that there was something suspicious about her testimony because she gave her account first to *This Week* and not to the police.

"At all events, you didn't give a statement to the police till after you'd spoken to the television company and given your . . . affidavit [to them], if I can so describe it?" Laws demanded.

"I wasn't asked."

"No, but that's the position as a matter of timing."

"I'd have loved for [the police] to come and ask me and I would have given [my] statement straightaway. It would have been out of my mind."

With barbed sarcasm, the lawyer asked, "It is not far from Rodney House [Proetta's apartment building] to the police station?"

"And it is not far from the police station to Rodney House," the witness sweetly replied.[12]

The courtroom tittered. Carmen had brought out a fact that Laws conveniently neglected to mention, the distinct lack of enthusiasm behind the Gibraltar Police's effort to identify

227

witnesses to the shootings until after *Death on the Rock* had been broadcast. Since Carmen was Commissioner Canepa's *stepsister*, their failure to promptly talk to her after the programme aired was more than a little odd.[13]

The rat pack, of course, did not mention that in their stories. They were interested in more important things, like Carmen's appearance. The photographs of her which appeared in British newspapers the day she testified focused on her legs. The articles that accompanied those pictures often had a leering tone that implied that Carmen was a "shady lady" and not to be trusted. For example, the *Daily Mail* breathlessly reported:

[Proetta] was dressed for stardom. The black linen dress, buttoned up the front, exposed the flash of elegant leg covered in black stockings. She balanced on black stiletto heels, and a wide, wide patent leather belt encircled a small waist.[14]

The owner of that "elegant leg" had hardly fallen apart giving her evidence, but that was not the way her "friends" on Fleet Street reported it. The headlines ran "I Could Have Got It Wrong, says Carmen" (*Daily Mirror*), "Carmen Doubt on Surrender" (*Today*), and "Carmen Has Her Doubts" (*Daily Star*).[15]

As it turned out, there was a good reason why the Proettas and Josie Celecia could not say with certainty that the SAS men finished McCann and Farrell off on the ground. It came several days after "glamorous Carmen's" appearance at the inquest during the testimony of London Metropolitan Police forensic expert David Prior. According to him, on a clear day, it would have been quite possible to miss the flash and smoke of the soldiers' pistols firing. That was something very few British newspapers, tabloid or broadsheet, cared to report.

A relatively large number of witnesses testified that they saw McCann and Farrell die. But despite the fact that there had been up to thirty people near Savage when he was shot, only three civilian eyewitnesses gave significant testimony about his death.[16]

228

The first of these was was Robyn Arthur Mordue, a British catering manager who had been on holiday in Gibraltar on March 6 and had not appeared on *Death on the Rock*. Pizzarello introduced him by saying, " . . . the sooner we get rid of him, the better I think".[17] The Coroner probably made that comment because the witness had come in from England, at government expense. However, there might have been another reason for his rather testy-sounding statement. Mordue tended to give answers that favoured the side of whoever was asking them at the time. The result was a "ping-pong match" between McGrory, Hucker, and Laws where "the ball" (Mordue) went through his evidence ten times.

The gist of Mordue's testimony was that he had just finished lunch at the Gibraltar Arms and been on his way to the beach. As he strolled along Landport Lane, Savage came walking toward him. Suddenly, someone pushed a woman riding a bicycle into Mordue, and both he and the girl fell to the ground.[18] As they did, he could hear shouts of "Stop! Police!" and "Get down!" Gunfire rang out, and Mordue saw Savage collapse.

"You are falling down; you fell down; the shots are still going on?" Pizzarello asked the witness.

"That is correct."

"You get to the ground, and the shooting stops for a bit?"

"A couple of seconds."

"You are still struggling to get up?"

"That is correct."

"You hear more shots?"

"That is correct."[19]

At the inquest, no one saw or ever suggested that Savage got up or tried to get up after Soldiers C and D brought him down. Therefore, it followed that the second burst of shots Mordue heard came while the IRA man lay on the ground. Mordue may have witnessed even more than that. At one point, he told the court that he had shouted out, "He's a madman. He's going to kill us all!" to the woman riding the bicycle. That was the type of thing someone might say if he saw a gunman shooting at point-blank range at a man lying on the ground.

The jury also got to hear from Diana Treacy. One additional detail came out when she gave the jury her account of seeing Savage dash past her pursued by a gunman who shot him in the back without warning. The young woman testified that she saw and heard a maximum of five shots striking the IRA man as he fell onto his back.[20] Soldiers C and D had hit Savage a minimum of sixteen times. This meant at least eleven bullets struck him as he lay on the ground.

Cross-examining Treacy, Hucker strongly attacked her memory of events, correctly saying that no other witness testified to seeing the IRA man running. What he did not point out was that with the exception of Mordue, all these other witnesses had been SAS men or MI5 surveillance officers.[21]

Finally, there was Kenneth Asquez, who eclipsed Carmen Proetta as the most controversial figure of the inquest. Called to the witness stand on September 23, 1988, the young bank clerk looked desperately unhappy, as if he would have given anything not to be there.

It quickly became apparent why. Guided by Pizzarello, Asquez haltingly told the jury that he had made up his statement about seeing a gunman with his foot on Savage's throat firing shots into his head. Supposedly, he wrote it out in response to "pestering" from Major Bob Randall, the man who sold *This Week* a videotape of the aftermath of the killings. According to Asquez, the retired British Army officer phoned constantly and promised him money if he would give an interview to the reporters. In order to get Randall "off his back", Asquez concocted what Laws called his "base and lying accusation".[22]

His retraction delighted the rat pack. The headings of the

tabloids' articles about Asquez reflected that. "I Told Lie after Lie", screamed the *Sun*. There were similar stories in the rest of the popular press. Strangely enough, most ran next to large pictures of Carmen Proetta, making it look at a glance like the "SAS smear girl" had done the retracting.[23]

Even the mainstream British media accepted Asquez's about-face almost without question. Typical was BBC One Television which informed its viewers that "Kenneth Asquez has admitted he was lying". Meanwhile, Mrs Thatcher's backbenchers joined the feeding frenzy. MP Jerry Hayes thundered that *This Week*'s use of Asquez's statement was "at best . . . sheer incompetence . . . at worst a conspiracy". His colleague, Bill Walker, was equally blunt, saying "the whole thing was blown up to discredit the SAS and the Security Services".[24]

It was a defining moment. The inquest would go on, but the British public's attention had switched away from what happened on March 6, 1988, to whether *This Week* should have used Asquez's unsigned statement. Roger Bolton and the rest of *Death on the Rock*'s makers had replaced the SAS in the dock. Trial by television had become trial *of* television.[25]

Few people asked the obvious question. Had Asquez told the inquest the truth, or was his original statement the truth? There are several indications that the latter was the case.

First, there was the unlikeliness of the witness's claims. How could Asquez have believed that a false story about seeing an SAS man murder Savage would help him? Such an explosive account could not fail to generate further interest in him as a witness, the last thing he supposedly wanted. Simply telling Randall the "truth", that he saw nothing, would have been the best way to avoid being drawn into the case. Yet Asquez did not take that eminently sensible step.

Second, three other people were in the car with Asquez on March 6. None of them appeared at the inquest. No one ever offered any reason for their absence.

Third, there was the matter of Major Randall. Dubbed "the TV pest" by the tabloids, he was in America on vacation when Asquez testified. Before departing on his trip, Randall had telephoned the Gibraltar Police and asked if he would be needed as a witness. Despite knowing what was about to happen, the police told the Major to go ahead and enjoy his holiday.[26] Contacted by Chris Oxley, *Death on the Rock*'s producer, Randall sent him an affidavit flatly denying the allegations against him. After the inquest Asquez continued to shrink away from his claim that the Major pestered him.[27] After the inquest concluded, he wrote a letter to a local Gibraltar newspaper denying that he ever accused Randall of pressuring him into giving a false account of Savage's death.[28]

Finally, for a "pack of lies", Asquez's handwritten statement contained several definite facts: an SAS man on Landport Lane *had* held up an identity card, worn a black beret, and shouted something like "Stop. It's okay. It's the police".[29] Those details were *not* public knowledge. Yet Asquez knew them. Coroner Pizzarello wanted to know how.

"The trouble is, Mr Asquez", he told the witness, "that this question of the beret, the ID card, and words to the effect of 'Stop! It's okay. It's the police,' have only . . . come out for the first time in this court, [after] you made [your original] statement. Can you try to explain that a little further?"

Asquez was evasive. "No. As I said before, I'm a bit confused. My thoughts are vague from that time."[30]

The witness was also quite eager to avoid admitting that he was a liar. That became apparent when McGrory examined him.

"Is the vital part of [your] statement that the man with the black beret had his foot on the dying man's throat?" McGrory read from a copy of it. "He shouted 'stop' and . . . then fired three or four more shots." He showed Asquez the document. "Do you see that part of the statement? Did you make it up?"

"Probably", came the weak reply.

McGrory did not accept that. "Of all the people present in this room, only you know whether you made it up or not and what you are saying." He pointed to the jury. "These are eleven of your fellow citizens of Gibraltar. Tell them whether it's true or not!"

Asquez squirmed. "I can't say 'yes' or 'no'." I was probably still confused."[31]

Responses like that suggest Asquez told the truth the first time. Someone may have forced him to change his evidence at the inquest. Gibraltar is a very small, tightly-knit community with a pronounced dislike for people who threaten its "Britishness". Asquez saw that attitude in action against the Proettas. Sticking by a statement that damned at least one SAS man as a murderer could have proven very costly for someone in his position. It might have meant winding up as the second "tart of Gib". Like Carmen Proetta, it seems he had seen something he was not supposed to see. Like her, he paid a high – but different – price for talking about it.

After the last witness testified, the inquest was at its end. Unlike a criminal trial, there were no summations of evidence by the rival interested parties. The Coroner's Rules did not allow that. Only Pizzarello had the right to address the jury about the facts of the case. What the rules did allow was for Laws and McGrory to make submissions to the Coroner about what instructions the jury should receive.[32]

Laws spoke first, making a detailed presentation about the use of force and the concept of self-defense. Along with the dry legal reasoning, the Crown's counsel made one astonishing request. He asked Pizzarello not to allow the jury to return a verdict of unlawful killing on the grounds that there had been criminal intent behind the planning of Operation Flavius. In his opinion, there was no evidence of such behavior on the part of the senior British intelligence officials and military officers who had sent the SAS to the Rock. But at no time did he acknowledge that the PII certificates had made obtaining such evidence impossible.

What the government lawyer was willing to entertain was the possibility of Soldiers A, B, C, and D facing the consequences for their actions in Gibraltar by themselves. He said to Pizzarello:

If you [feel] that there [is] material to go to the jury as to whether there was an unlawful killing by the soldiers themselves – murder done – that could be the only category of unlawful killing [the jury] could be properly asked to consider. As I say . . . [the jurors] may only be properly concerned with whether there was murder done by any of those immediately engaged in the act of shooting the terrorists.[33]

What the SAS men felt about Mr Laws' submission is unknown but can be imagined.

Then it was McGrory's turn. He made the most of the opportunity, eloquently arguing against Laws' submission. McGrory contended that there *had* been a high-level plot to murder McCann, Savage, and Farrell, a conspiracy which began when the British government decided to use the SAS against the IRA members.

" . . . I'm saying to your honour [that decision] was wholly unreasonable and led to a lot of what happened afterwards . . . And it started a whole chain of unreasonable decisions which led to the three killings which I submit were unlawful and criminal killings . . . " he stated.

"In other words, conspiracy to commit murder?" the Coroner asked.

"Precisely . . . It's my submission that the choice of the SAS is of great significance . . . If the killing of the ASU was in fact contemplated by those who chose the SAS, as an act of counter-terror, or vengeance, that steps outside the rule of law, and it was murder . . . and that's a matter for the jury to consider."[34]

On September 30, 1988, having heard counsel for both

234

parties speak, Pizzarello instructed the jury. In general, the summation of the evidence he gave to them was fair and comprehensive, with two exceptions. One had to do with Mordue. The Coroner instructed the jury that that witness's evidence had been that the SAS men fired no shots at Savage while he was on the ground, a grossly incorrect statement. More seriously, Pizzarello skirted around the most damning evidence against the soldiers, that given by pathologist Alan Watson. Yet he did tell them that under five circumstances, they could return a verdict of unlawful killing. One of those was if they believed there had been a high level plot to take McCann, Savage, and Farrell's lives. It was Paddy McGrory's last victory.

At 11:28 a.m., the jurors retired to deliberate. At 5:00 p.m., Pizzarello called them back and asked if they had reached a verdict. The answer was yes but not with the necessary majority. Apparently, the Coroner's patience was wearing thin, because he told the panel members that they were now at "the edge" of the reasonable amount of time they had to reach a verdict. Pizzarello did not explain why he felt five and a half hours was an adequate period to evaluate the testimony of nearly eighty witnesses who had given evidence over a period of eighteen days.[35]

After receiving that admonition, the jury returned to its deliberations. At 7:15 p.m., its members filed back into the courtroom. Just two hours before, they had been split 8-3 in favor of finding McCann and Farrell's deaths lawful and 7-4 the same way on Savage. The count was now 9-2 in all three cases, sufficient for a finding of lawful killing.[36] It was, as one local caustically observed, "a very Gibraltarian verdict."[37] The jury had ratified the SAS's actions but only by the slimmest majority possible. Even with all the advantages the British government had enjoyed in Gibraltar, it had been a near run thing.

But in the eyes of the law, a verdict was a verdict. That evening Mr Laws held a small victory party for his assistants at El Patio, a Gibraltar restaurant he liked. During the meal, a member of the rat pack walked up to his table. The reporter shouted out, "Yarggggh! Stop! Police! Or police! Stop! Or words to that effect!" He then fired three well-aimed shots from a water pistol into the lawyer's face. Laws was not amused. It was a fitting end to a very black comedy.[38]

## Notes

1. These witnesses were Charles Walker, Robert King, and Manola Cruz.
2. Testimony of Officer James Parody, the Gibraltar Inquest, Day 15, 26 September 1988, Channel Four Television, 1988, pp. 6-32.
3. Ibid.
4. Testimony of Josie Celecia, the Gibraltar Inquest, Day 12, 20 September 1988, Channel Four Television, 1988, pp. 37-42.
5. Ibid, p. 44.
6. "Carmen Says No", *Mail on Sunday*, May 29, 1988.
7. Bolton, p. 4.
8. Testimony of Maxie Proetta, the Gibraltar Inquest, Day 13, 22 September 1988, Channel Four Television, 1988, p. 22.
9. Ibid, p. 20.
10. Testimony of Carmen Proetta, the Gibraltar Inquest, Day 14, 23 September 1988, Channel Four Television, 1988, p. 87.
11. Ibid, p. 83.
12. Ibid, pp. 92-93.
13. O'Higgins and Waters, "A Controlled Explosion of the Truth," p. 43.
14. Miller, "The Damage Was Done", pp. 23-24.
15. Ibid.
16. "Minutes which led to IRA deaths", *Independent*, May 13, 1988. There was a basketball game going on in a playground not far from where the SAS shot Savage. Two teenagers told the *Independent* that after hearing "Stop! Police!" they saw an SAS man fire into the IRA man's prostrate body. Yet for some reason, these individuals did not appear at the inquest.
17. Testimony of Robyn Mordue, the Gibraltar Inquest, Day 13, 22 September 1988, Channel four Television, 1988, p. 40.
18. This "someone" was presumably one of the MI5 watchers who did not appear at the inquest.
19. Mordue, pp. 68-69. This exchange came the final time Mordue ran through his evidence. I believe it is the most credible because Pizzarello, the neutral party, extracted it.
20. Testimony of Diana Treacy, the Gibraltar Inquest, Day 16, 27 September 1988, Channel four Television, 1988, pp. 80-82.
21. "In Review: Gibraltar" the *Sunday Times*, September 18, 1988. Besides this, the lawyer also tried to cast doubt on Treacy's recollection that the SAS man who shot Savage held his pistol in his left hand. Both Soldiers C and D had claimed they were right-handed. Yet while no one noticed it, Treacy had

support on that particular issue from an unlikely source, the *Sunday Times*. In one of its many articles about the killings, the paper published a sketch of the supposed way Savage died, shot after whirling around in reaction to Soldiers C's and D's challenge. In the illustration, Soldier C is firing his Browning automatic *left*-handed.

22. Testimony of Kenneth Asquez, the Gibraltar Inquest, Day 14, 24 September 1988, Channel four Television, 1988, p. 17.

23. Such as the *Daily Express*'s "Why I Lied by TV Trial Witness", *Today*'s "TV Drove Me into Web of Lies over Shooting", The *Daily Record*'s "It Was Lies, Says Provo Shootings Witness".

24. "TV in Dock", *Sun*, September 24, 1988.

25. Windlesham and Rampton, pp. 141-145. In 1989, the Windlesham-Rampton Inquiry, an independent commission established by Thames Television, to investigate the making of *Death on the Rock* found with several minor exceptions that it had been a "trenchant" piece of journalism and had been made in good faith.

26. Bolton, p. 11.

27. The affidavit was given to Asquez, who read it and testified in response to it. However, the document could not be read out in court because Major Randall was unavailable to be cross-examined about its contents.

28. Bolton, pp. 267-268. Upon return from his vacation, Randall had publicly challenged Asquez to repeat his accusation outside of court.

29. Asquez's handwritten Statement, undated.

30. Testimony of Kenneth Asquez, Day 14, the Gibraltar Inquest, September 24, 1988, Channel Four Television, 1988, p. 5.

31. Ibid, p. 36.

32. Hucker allowed Laws to speak for him.

33. Summation of Mr John Laws, the Gibraltar Inquest, Day 18, 29 September 1988, Channel Four Television, 1988, p. 7.

34. Summation of Mr Patrick McGrory, the Gibraltar Inquest, Day 18, 29 September 1988, Channel Four Television, 1988, p. 14.

35. O'Higgins and Waters, "A Controlled Explosion of the Truth", p. 42.

36. Ibid.

37. Interview with an anonymous source in Gibraltar, June 1996.

38. Niall O'Flynn, "Laws the target in 'SAS' Prank", *Sunday Press*, October 2, 1988.

237

# CHAPTER SIXTEEN

## ROUGH "JUSTICE"

"I am serving a life sentence for being nosey."
  — Michael Timmons

Nearly eighteen months later, on February 5, 1990, Pat Kane, Michael Timmons, and Seán Kelly's trial opened in Belfast. The three men went into the courtroom hoping to be acquitted on all the charges facing them. That was not simply blind optimism on their part. Just a month before, Mr Justice McCollum had found four Casement defendants not guilty of falsely imprisoning and inflicting grievous bodily harm on Corporals Wood and Howes. Many in Northern Ireland's legal community interpreted those verdicts as the judiciary's signal that there had been enough prosecutions arising out of the Andersonstown murders.[1]

But before that, there had been an ominous development. At Kane's and Kelly's preliminary hearing, the Department of Public Prosecutions (DPP) filed murder charges against the two men. As with Timmons, the DPP did not argue that Kane and Kelly actually killed anyone. Instead, it viewed them in law as accessories to the murder of the soldiers.

This was an application of the "common purpose" doctrine. Expressed in simple terms, that British legal principal holds that if: A and B go out to commit a crime, and A kills someone during it, B is guilty of murder provided he or she contemplated

238

that murder was one possible outcome of the "joint criminal enterprise".[2]

Common purpose normally applies to situations where the defendants planned a crime before committing it. But Kane, Timmons, and Kelly had not met, contemplated, or set out to break any law the day of Kevin Brady's funeral. They had not even known each other until after being arrested.

To get around those hurdles, the DPP devised an interpretation of what took place on March 19, 1988, to fit a "common purpose" case. The actions leading up to Corporals Wood's and Howes's deaths were not the outcome of panic but elements of a plan that was generated spontaneously as events unfolded at Casement Park. In the DPP's eyes, the actions of people there would reveal whether they participated in this plan and the range of crimes they contemplated as possible results of their taking part.[3]

It was a clever approach. Some individuals in Casement Park had known what they were doing. They had seen and taken an opportunity to "stiff" (kill) two British soldiers. But these had been IRA men, something that Kane, Timmons, and Kelly had never been. Yet that did not matter. The prosecutors argued that the defendants "must have" known that the IRA would kill Wood and Howes. Because they knew that, all three men's actions outside and in the park damned them as murderers.

In Kane's case, the prosecution contended that he had been the "man in green" the news video showed at the back of the group pushing Corporal Wood into Casement Park. The helitele film showed this person kick or stamp on one of the soldiers after they were beaten to the ground.

Besides this photographic evidence, several RUC officers testified about Kane's statements during his interrogations at Woodburne RUC barracks. Taken at face value, Kane's admissions there "proved" that he had opened and closed the gates to admit Corporal Howes and helped Henry Maguire force Father Reid from Casement Park.[4]

239

As for Timmons, the DPP accused him as well of helping to push Corporal Wood into the park. In the heli-tele film, he "closely associated" himself with the savage beating the crowd gave the soldiers. Even more damaging for Timmons were his statements to the police that he kicked one of the corporals and helped strip him. Besides this, the heli-tele film showed Timmons "associating" himself with putting Wood and Howes over the wall. Then there was his admission that he ran a few yards after the taxi carrying them away. For the Crown, that act was the final link in the chain connecting Timmons to the joint enterprise to commit murder.[5]

Unlike Kane and Timmons, Seán Kelly had not given the DPP any incriminating statements to use against him. The only evidence the prosecuting attorneys had was the heli-tele film and the press video footage and photographs the police had seized.

Yet in the Crown's eyes, those slender strands of evidence formed a rope strong enough to hang Kelly. The media photographs and video "proved" that he took part in the attack on the soldiers' car and pushed Corporal Wood into Casement Park. In this footage, Kelly could be seen wearing a blue jacket with a broad stripe down the arms. The Crown prosecutors argued that an identically-dressed figure was present inside the park. This man, someone two RUC officers testified they believed had Kelly's athletic walk, helped close the gates and took part in dropping Wood and Howes over the wall to the IRA.[6]

Kane's and Timmons's efforts to defend themselves did not go well. Neither made a good witness. Cross-examining Timmons, the government lawyers ridiculed his claim that he entered Casement Park out of sheer "nosiness". By the time they were through with him, he looked, at the very least, like a ghoul, at the worst, a man with a conveniently faulty memory.[7]

Kane's humiliation was just as complete. The prosecutors extracted an admission from him to admit that he had not been able to hold several of the jobs that he had worked at and been unemployed since the age of twenty-six. He got no mercy because of his disabilities. Far from it, at one point, a prosecuting lawyer mockingly asked him if he was blind as well as deaf.[8]

Watching his co-defendants being cut to pieces on the witness stand made a deep impression on Seán Kelly. He had nothing to gain and everything to lose by exposing himself to cross-examination. His barrister, Desmond Boal, believed that he had no case to answer and recommended that he not take the stand. With that advice, Kelly refused to give evidence.[9]

Kane's and Timmons's disastrous performances in the witness stand were not the only reverses the defendants suffered. Justice Carswell also refused to throw out the highly incriminating statements made by them. Despite this, by the trial's end, the defendants' families remained confident their loved ones would be acquitted.

But Mr Justice Carswell shattered their hopes. On March 30, 1990, he found Pat Kane, Michael Timmons, and Seán Kelly each guilty of two counts of murder, false imprisonment, and infliction of grievous bodily harm. There was a deafening silence as he read out the verdicts. Even the police and the prosecutors in the courtroom seemed stunned by the scope of the judgment.

In his over fifty-page long analysis of the case, Justice Carswell decided in favor of prosecution on nearly every contested fact. In Kane's case, the video evidence was enough to convince him that the defendant probably was the "man in green". Yet what doomed Kane was Carswell's decision to accept the incriminating statements that he made to the RUC. If those were true, it followed that Kane's denials were lies. As such, they were evidence of an effort to "cover up guilty acts and guilty knowledge".[10]

As for Timmons, who admitted that he had been in

Casement Park, Justice Carswell rejected the defendant's explanations for his actions and accepted those the prosecution offered. He found that while rushing toward the soldiers' car, Timmons had not whirled and put his hands out to hold people back. Far from it, he had been trying to stop photographers from taking pictures of what was taking place. Similarly, the defendant had not joined the group around Corporal Wood out of misguided "nosiness" but enthusiastically participated in forcing him into Casement Park.

More significantly, the judge rejected Timmons' claim that he only admitted to kicking a soldier and helping strip the man so that he could get bail. It did not matter that the heli-tele tape failed to show the defendant assaulting anyone. In Carswell's opinion, that event could have taken place when the helicopter's camera panned away from the wall where Wood and Howes were lying.[11]

Then there was Seán Kelly. Justice Carswell felt he could see the young man "attacking" the driver's side door of the soldiers' car. The judge also believed that Kelly was visible in the group that pushed Corporal Wood toward Casement Park. Finally, he "saw" the defendant standing near the taxi that took the corporals to Penny Lane. For Carswell, Kelly's failure to mention any of these "facts" in the single statement that he gave to the RUC exposed it as a "farrago of untruths and half-truths".[12]

As to whether Seán Kelly had been in Casement Park, Justice Carswell had difficulty with the police's claim that he was easily recognizable in the heli-tele film. In his judgment, he wrote, "I should have some reservations about accepting [that] identification . . . because of the quality of the film". Fortunately for the prosecution, the judge believed it was "legitimate and necessary to examine together all the facts which might point to [Kelly] having been one of the group inside Casement Park".[13]

One of those facts, of course, were the "lies" in the defendant's statement. The other had been Kelly's refusal to testify on his own behalf. Article 4 of the Criminal Evidence Order (Northern Ireland) of 1988 allows a judge to draw an inference of guilt against defendants who remain silent in face of "firm evidence" against them. That is precisely what Mr Justice Carswell did with young Seán Kelly.[14]

But even if Kane, Timmons, and Kelly did everything they were accused of, how could it add up to murder? Justice Carswell found that question easy to answer. Kane was a killer because he knew that he was at an IRA funeral and "must have" known the IRA would kill any British soldiers or loyalists it captured. The judge felt if this was not "crystal clear" at first, it "must have" been after the soldiers were stripped of their clothing. Because under interrogation Kane admitted that he knew "something bad" was going to happen and he still remained in Casement Park, he "must have" been part of the common purpose to murder the soldiers. Concluding, Justice Carswell ruled:

> He may not have known precisely what was going to happen to the soldiers, but I am satisfied that he knew that their death was one of the likely eventualities . . . I therefore hold that he possessed the necessary *mens rea* (guilty mind) for murder.[15]

He used similar logic against Michael Timmons and Seán Kelly. All three men received the mandatory penalty, a life sentence on each count of murder. With the word "life" ringing in their ears, the defendants hardly noticed it when the judge sentenced them to two ten-year sentences for inflicting grievous bodily harm on the corporals and two fifteen-year terms for falsely imprisoning them as well.

One year later, the Northern Ireland Court of Appeal considered the safety of the convictions of Kane, Timmons, and Kelly. The Court restricted itself to assessing Justice Carswell's findings of fact. It did not consider his interpretation of the law

243

of common purpose. Not surprisingly, the judges upheld the convictions. In Pat Kane's case, they even found him guilty of kicking the other soldier, something he supposedly admitted to while under interrogation at Woodburne RUC barracks.[16]

Ruling on Michael Timmons' plea, they damned him further. In the Court's opinion, Timmons "must have" known that Wood and Howes were Protestant gunmen or soldiers when he helped push them into Casement Park. He "must have" known what would happen to them there. Yet he kept on pushing. In the judges' eyes, that act and that knowledge together was enough to constitute murder.[17]

Seán Kelly fared somewhat differently. Acting on his appeal, the Court found that Justice Carswell erred when he found that Kelly took part in the attack on the soldiers' car. It also determined that the judge was mistaken when he identified the young man as standing near the taxi that took Wood and Howes to their deaths. Those findings should have made Kelly's conviction unsafe. Yet unlike Justice Carswell, on the strength of the video evidence alone, the appeals judges felt they could positively identify Kelly as "the man in blue". Therefore, they felt it was not necessary to draw an inference of guilt against him because of his silence in the courtroom. Kelly was still guilty of murder but now for different – and less controversial – reasons.[18]

To many, the three's convictions were a miscarriage of justice, for many reasons. First, Justice Carswell had grossly overextended "common purpose" doctrine to find the trio guilty of murder. At the very most, the Crown proved that the defendants took part in a conspiracy to imprison and assault the soldiers in Casement Park. Nevertheless, the judge convicted them of murder. This was despite the fact that they did not know the actual gunmen and were nowhere near Penny Lane when the killings took place. Under Justice Carswell's logic, had the IRA held Wood and Howes for ransom for two years and killed them only after the British government failed to pay it, the defendants still would have been guilty. As noted Queen's Counsel Peter Thornton observed in his legal opinion about the case, "This cannot be right. It stretches the meaning of [common purpose] beyond its natural limit".[19]

Besides this, the Northern Ireland judiciary's application of the common purpose doctrine was inconsistent. In March 1991, Mr Justice MacDermott tried Kevin McCaughley on murder, grievous bodily harm and other charges. McCaughley had driven the taxi that took the soldiers to Penny Lane. Once there, the heli-tele captured him on film hitting one of them. Yet MacDermott acquitted the taxi driver on the murder charge because he felt McCaughley might not have had the necessary *mens rea* for a killer. That belief did not prevent MacDermott from ruling against Kane's, Timmons', and Kelly's appeals, earlier in the month.[20]

There was one further problem with the common purpose conviction. To establish whether the defendants thought the corporals' deaths were a possible outcome of the joint enterprise they supposedly had joined, Justice Carswell should have used a subjective test. In simple terms, the law required him to consider what Kane, Timmons, and Kelly thought *at the time* they took the actions that incriminated them. Yet in his judgment, the judge wrote:

. . . one has to look at what was taking place . . . [The soldiers] were clearly being assaulted as they were being pushed along, and the inference was that they were being taken out of the way to be dealt with . . . A person in Casement Park who had not been told what was to happen to them might have supposed that they were to be taken off for interrogation. But it must have been obvious that those who were in charge in Casement Park were active IRA members or supporters. Any person seized by them in such circumstances . . . could have no significant chance for survival.[21]

Those are the words of a man who seems to be looking at events objectively, with benefit of hindsight, not someone trying to understand what a defendant thought at the time the crime took place. Justice Carswell did not appear to consider the hysteria and fear that Michael Stone had created just three days before Kevin Brady's funeral, except to justify his belief that Kane, Timmons, and Kelly "must have" known the soldiers would be killed.[22]

The judge might not have reached those conclusions had he heard testimony from Dr Andrew Coleman. A forensic psychologist, Coleman believed the dense crowding, noise, hysteria, and sense of being under attack triggered a psychological state of "de-individuation" in the people on Andersonstown Road. In an interview with the author, he explained that:

> immersion in a large group can diminish an individual's . . . personal accountability and lead to irrational, impulsive, uncharacteristic behavior. In this state of so-called *de-individuation*, people behave foolishly, irresponsibly, and in ways they would not behave while alone . . . [Their behavior] is not subject to normal, rational restraints, and [is] somewhat akin [to being drunk].[23]

De-individuation would have gone a long way toward explaining Timmons' "nosiness", behavior the judge refused to believe was innocent because it was too bizarre. It might have also explained why Kane might kick or stamp on a soldier without having "murder in mind". In South Africa, at that time a state hardly known for upholding human rights, Coleman's testimony saved several defendants from the gallows for participating in riots that ended in murder. Yet in Northern Ireland, before Kane's, Timmons', and Kelly's trial, another judge had ruled expert psychological evidence inadmissable, and Mr Justice Carswell honoured the precedent set by his peer.[24]

Psychological testimony would have particularly helped Pat

Kane. Doctors examining him had verified his near total illiteracy and ultimately determined that he had an IQ of 70 and the emotional maturity of an eleven-year-old. They also found that he suffered from a state of high anxiety as well, a psychological condition that might lead him to say anything in order to get out of a hostile police interrogation. Yet without the benefit of this information, Justice Carswell found that "[Kane] was deliberately trying . . . to give an appearance of being more unintelligent than he is."[25]

As for Timmons' and Kane's "confessions", Justice Carswell had apparently been unwilling to believe that the detectives could have manipulated the two men into making false statements. But before he dismissed their allegations, he might have done well to consider the case of David McConnell, another man put on trial for his actions at Kevin Brady's funeral. As with Kane and Timmons, the authorities accused him of taking part in the murder of Wood and Howes. The DPP based that charge on admissions McConnell made to the police: that he had seen one of the corporals wearing a belt only a British soldier would have; that he had smashed a window on the soldiers' car; and that he had taken all of the actions he did with the belief that the two men would be murdered.

Unfortunately for the DPP, neither soldier had worn the belt McConnell described. Film of the incident did not show him breaking any window on any car. By themselves, of course, those facts prove nothing, except that people in the custody of the RUC sometimes confess to crimes that they have not committed. That may have been the reason why Mr Justice McCollum dismissed the murder charge against McConnell on the grounds that he did not "realize he might be charged with murder, and . . . contemplate the significance of what he was saying".[26] The possibility that this might have taken place with Kane and Timmons does not seem to have occurred to Justice Carswell.

Justice Carswell missed or disregarded an even stronger

warning that there was a problem with at least one of the confessions. In convicting Kane, he had drawn heavily on the admissions that the defendant's written statement contained. Yet one of the most incriminating statements within that document, that Kane pulled Father Reid away from the soldiers, is false. As the heli-tele film clearly shows, Kane did not force the priest away from Wood and Howes. Someone else did. While this happened, the "man in green" Carswell believed to be Kane was standing near the park gate, nowhere near the soldiers.[27] Kane had confessed to something that did not happen.[28]

Be that as it may, Kane made it easy for the judge convict him by denying that he had ever been in Casement Park. This was despite the fact that the "man in green" resembled Kane and that man's actions and the ones Kane claimed he took in his early statements to the police matched closely. The BBC programme *Rough Justice* stressed this while arguing his innocence.

If Kane had been in Casement Park, he lied about it on the witness stand. Why? It might be because while being held at Woodburne RUC barracks, he allegedly named a number of prominent IRA men as being inside Casement Park.[29] That statement could have been used to charge *them* with murder. People in Republican West Belfast who implicate the IRA in crimes do not enjoy happy lives in or out of prison. Insisting that he stayed outside Casement Park might get Kane convicted, but it would discredit his incriminating comments about seeing IRA men take part in the murders. If that is the reason why Kane lied -- if he lied at all -- besides being a victim of the British legal system, he was a victim of the IRA. The "brave soldiers of the People's Army" ran away and let an innocent man go to jail for their crimes.

Kane's ordeal lasted nearly nine years. In early 1997, feeling the pressure from an intense campaign mounted by his family, friends, and a galaxy of human rights groups, Sir Patrick Mayhew, the Secretary of State for Northern Ireland, referred the case back to the Appeal Court. On May 27, 1997, its judges ruled that they would consider testimony about Kane's low IQ and mental state, evidence that had been inadmissible at his original trial. Four weeks later, speaking for his fellow judges, Lord Justice McCollum stated:

> The court has come to the conclusion that if the trial judge had had the benefit of hearing [this testimony] it would have had a considerable influence on his consideration of the . . . reliability of the confessions made by [Kane] . . . We are not satisfied that the judge would have admitted [Kane's] confession or relied upon it if he had the benefit of [the psychological] evidence. Accordingly, we regard the conviction as unsafe and quash it.[30]

For Pat Kane, it was finally over. He was free. But it is not over for Michael Timmons and Seán Kelly. They remain in prison, their best hope being an early release.[31] Yet if paroled, they would still bear the taint of their "crimes". As Seán Kelly put it: "The words 'convicted murderer' are like the letters 'PhD,' they follow your name wherever you go."[32]

## Notes

1. *The Casement Trials*, p. 14.
2. *Upholding the Rule of Law? Northern Ireland: Criminal Justice under the {Emergency Powers" in the 1990*, The Haldane Society of Socialist Lawyers, London, 1992, pp. 52-53.
3. Ibid.
4. Ibid, pp. 55-58.
5. Ibid, pp. 61-62.
6. Ibid, pp. 64-65.
7. Transcript of Regina V Kane and Others, 1990.
8. Ibid.
9. Interview with Seán Kelly, Maze Prison, Belfast, November 1996.
10. *The Queen V Patrick Gerard Kane . . .* , p. 25.
11. Ibid, pp. 26-41.
12. Ibid, p. 43.
13. Ibid, p. 45.
14. Ibid.
15. Ibid, pp. 24-26.

16. *Upholding the Rule of Law?*, p. 59.

17. *The Queen versus Patrick Gerard Kane* . . . Summary Judgment, Her Majesty's Court of Appeal, pp. 16-24.

18. Ibid, pp. 26-34.

19. Peter Thornton, QC, *The Queen V Patrick Gerard Kane, Michael John Timmons, and Seán Kelly*, Opinion, London, 1996, p. 31.

20. *The Casement Trials,* p. 29.

21. *The Queen V Patrick Gerard Kane* . . . , p. 24.

22. Thornton, p. 27-28.

23. Interview with Andrew M Coleman, Reader in Psychology, University of Leicester, United Kingdom and defense consultant during the Casement Trials, November 17, 1998.

24. *The Casement Trials,* p. 21.

25. *The Queen Versus Patrick Gerard Kane* . . ., p. 20.

26. *The Casement Trials,* p. 32-33.

27. "Murder in Mind", *Rough Justice.* Father Reid also told *Rough Justice* that neither of the two men who followed him out of the park (Maguire and Kane) was the person who dragged him away from the corporals.

28. I would like to stress here that I made every attempt to interview Justice Carswell on this case. He declined to speak with me (citing a policy in Northern Ireland where judges do not comment to the press about cases). I also attempted to interview the prosecutors in this case, but they refused to be interviewed (providing no explanation for their decision).

29. Transcript of Regina v Kane and Others.

30. "Joy as Man is Cleared on Appeal of Murder", *Irish Times*, June 21, 1997.

31. "Stone's Graveyard Visit", *Belfast Telegraph.* In what could only be described as a grotesque display of insensitivity to the families of his victims, in March 1997, the British government permitted Michael Stone to visit Milltown Cemetery to lay flowers at a relative's grave. One might have thought Stone had forfeited his right to visit that graveyard but apparently not.

32. Interview with Seán Kelly.

# CHAPTER SEVENTEEN

## THE SHADOW OF DOUBT

"Truth will come to light. Murder cannot be hid for long."
 – William Shakespeare, *The Merchant of Venice*

Meanwhile, Felix Pizzarello might have ruled the matter of the deaths of Daniel McCann, Seán Savage, and Mairéad Farrell closed. Yet it was far from over. As Paddy McGrory observed: "If you enter into a conspiracy and large numbers of people know about it at several levels . . . leakages will happen."[1]

So they have. One of the first appeared in November 1988. Speaking in Dáil Éireann, Dick Spring, the leader of the Irish Labor Party, revealed that he had obtained a copy of the operations order Commissioner Canepa drew up on March 5 for the police part of the arrest attempt.[2] One page of the secret document listed Inspector Luis Revagliatte as being the commander of two firearms teams assigned to the operation.[3] No one had disclosed that fact at the inquest. Had someone done so, they would have had to accept the following dubious propositions:[4]

1. Although Officers P, Q, and R, policemen listed as being Revagliatte's subordinates on the operation order had known about Operation Flavius, the Inspector had not.

2. Despite being listed as P, Q, and R's supervisor, the fact

251

Revagliatte and those officers arrived at the Shell Station almost simultaneously was a simple coincidence.

3. Revagliatte's decision to have his car's siren switched on the very moment the SAS moved to arrest McCann and Farrell had nothing to do with the arrest attempt.

To this date, the Gibraltar Police have refused to explain the contradiction between Revagliatte's testimony and the operations order, preferring to hide behind the Official Secrets Act.

Another fact revealed by the operations order had to do with the credibility of Constable James Parody, the "independent" witness who testified to hearing the SAS men warn McCann and Farrell to surrender. Canepa's order listed Parody's brother, Harry, as being one of the three undercover officers on the scene at the Shell Station ("Officer P"). That was not a fact Hucker, or Laws shared with the jury, perhaps because it would have made Parody look even less like the disinterested witness the government made him out to be.

Details that came to light near the end of the year also explained the curious behavior of Robin Mordue, the vacationer who witnessed the SAS kill Savage and who had caused Coroner Pizzarello such frustration. At the hearing, Mordue had seemed desperately eager to please everyone and changed his story repeatedly about whether he had seen the soldiers shoot Savage while he was on the ground.

But Mordue may have had good reason for this erratic performance. Before flying down to Gibraltar to testify, he had been barraged at work and home with threatening phone calls. The callers, men speaking in upper-class English accents, told Mordue that he was a "bastard" and that he should stay away from the hearing. What scared him the most about this was that apart from his family and a few select friends, only the Gibraltar Police had his unlisted home number.[5]

There were also the peculiar circumstances surrounding the

testimony of Victor Adams, a Yorkshire mining engineer who had been on holiday in Gibraltar. He had been close enough to the shootings on Winston Churchill Avenue for a ricochet to wound him. Taken to a local hospital, Adams had given the police a statement there before being discharged.[6] Months later, at the inquest, he and his wife were of no help to the government or McGrory, claiming to have seen nothing.

Then there was an overlooked statement in a news story written by James Keegan, defense correspondent for the *Daily Telegraph*. The article appeared on April 30, 1988, two days after the broadcast of *Death on the Rock*. Drawing on the usual faceless "official sources", Keegan wrote:

Gibraltar Police vehicles may have used their sirens after the shootings. *The car carrying the SAS team would certainly not have done so beforehand* [author's italics].

The fact that Keegan's sources told him the siren had gone off after the shootings was curious. At the inquest, everyone agreed that it had been before. Telling Keegan otherwise might have been an early attempt to disguise the role Revaliatte played in Operation Flavius. But the part about "the car carrying the SAS team" was even more startling, since the soldiers who testified in Gibraltar told the Coroner that they had arrived on foot at the Shell Petrol Station.[7]

The reason for this little discrepancy seems clear. Back in April, whoever briefed Keegan could not have known the official line at the inquest would be. Admitting that a car had been used must have seemed harmless. But it tended to confirm Proetta was telling the truth about seeing the SAS men arrive at the Shell Station in a Gibraltar Police car.

Still another development had to with the credibility of star government witness, Alan Feraday. His testimony about the capabilities of the IRA's radio detonator equipment had played a key part in persuading the jury that the SAS men's actions on March 6 had been reasonable. In his "expert" opinion, *if* there

253

had been a radio-detonated car-bomb at the assembly area and *if* the IRA members had been armed with the right equipment, they *could* have set it off from where the soldiers shot them or even from inside Spain.

Yet in September 1993, the appeals court in London quashed the conviction of a man jailed on Feraday's testimony for supplying radio-detonation equipment to Syria. Among other things, the appellate judge found the witness to be "extremely dogmatic" and said that he had admitted under cross-examination that he had "no experience of the operational use of [such] equipment".[8] Mark Twain might well have been thinking of Feraday when he said that "an expert is just some guy from out of town".

Besides these details, the "serious press" belatedly realized the significance of the fact that a number of actions attributed to McCann, Savage, and Farrell had to have been performed by other members of the IRA. A simple comparison of the activities of "John Oakes", "Brendan Coyne," and "Katherine Smith" (the aliases the IRA team members used) with the known actions of McCann, Savage, and Farrell made this quite evident.

On Friday, March 4, using the Oakes identity, Savage supposedly hired a red Ford Fiesta, the car the Spanish police discovered parked just outside of Gibraltar a few hours after the shootings, from the Autoluis Agency. Then, on Saturday, from Avis Car Rentals, Savage obtained the white Renault 5 which he drove into Gibraltar on Sunday. This time, the name he signed on the rental contract was Coyne, the alias he had used to enter Spain.

For this sequence of events to be accurate, Savage had to have been in two places at once. He did not leave Belfast until the afternoon of March 3, the same time "Mr Oakes" had checked into the Hotel Al Andalus in Torremolinos.[9] Flight IB657, the aircraft McCann and Savage came into Spain on, did not even arrive at Malaga Airport until 8:05 p.m. on Friday, March 4, eight hours *after* Savage supposedly picked up the red Fiesta.

It got even better. Luis Cardon, the proprietor of Autoluis, remembered Oakes as being tall with a long, thin face and fair, curly hair, definitely not McCann or Savage. The clerk at Avis Car Rentals working that Saturday, who signed over the Renault to Coyne, described him as missing two fingers from his right hand, a handicap that Savage did not have. And according to the clerk who rented "Katherine Smith" the white Fiesta, his customer did not look like Farrell.

What this pointed to was obvious. The IRA bombing team had not consisted of just McCann, Savage, and Farrell, but had at least two, possibly three other members.[10] Two of these people, a man and a woman, had been in Spain weeks before McCann, Savage, and Farrell showed up there. They had flown into Valencia in February, presumably checked the explosives hidden there, and set to work performing the logistical tasks and reconnaissance that a strike in Gibraltar required. At times, all the Provisionals had shared the same aliases, a ruse intended to ensure that any witnesses' descriptions of them did not match.[11]

Who were these extra people? In the immediate wake of the killings, the tabloid press named Evelyn Glenholmes, an alleged Provisional bomber, as "Mary Parkin". News stories appeared with headlines like *"Evil Evelyn"* and *"Find this Woman!"* in the columns of the *Sun, Daily Mirror* and similar publications. Yet when asked by a member of the regular or "broadsheet" press the reason why the tabloids nominated Glenholmes as the fourth member of the bombing team, the brutally frank response was: "Because we have a nice photograph of her, and she won't sue."[12]

It was the somewhat more respectable *Sunday Times* which came up with a more serious Parkin "candidate", Siobhán

O'Hanlon. From a staunchly Republican North Belfast family, she had recently left prison after serving a sentence for being in a bomb-making factory.[13] Extremely short, with fair hair, O'Hanlon closely resembles the various witnesses' description of "Mary Parkin". And there was a link between her, McCann, and Savage. The police had arrested all three in 1982 for conspiring to blow up the RUC band in Belfast.[14] Still one more connection can be found in the notices section of the March 7, 1996 issue of *An Phoblacht/Republican News*. Among all the commemorations of the eighth anniversary of McCann, Savage, and Farrell's deaths, one reads: "In proud and loving memory of Volunteers Mairéad Farrell, Dan McCann, and Seán Savage, who were murdered by the SAS in Gibraltar on March 6, 1988 – Siobhán O'Hanlon."[15]

The British government did not stay silent about the other members of the ASU out of embarrassment over letting them escape. Had that been the case, "Mary Parkin" and the role she played in the incident would have never come to light. In early 1989, two news reports published in the *Irish Times* and the *Independent* offered a possible explanation.

Citing interviews with senior members of the Spanish police, the journalists' stories would have been explosive had they not had to do with Northern Ireland, a place the British public was always sick of hearing about. The white Renault 5 had come into Gibraltar on Saturday, March 5, *not* Sunday, March 6. Speaking to Heather Mills and Tim McGirk, journalists for the *Independent*, a very high-ranking Spanish police officer said, "We told the British that we were 90% certain that [the Renault] contained no bomb".[16]

That would explain why no one saw Savage drive the Renault across the border into the Colony on Sunday. They didn't see it, because it didn't happen. He walked in with McCann, Savage, and Farrell after driving in the red Fiesta (the one found just north of the border). And either the British had allowed a car that could have been loaded with over a hundred pounds of primed high explosives sit all Saturday in Gibraltar, or they had known from the very start that the Renault did not contain a bomb.

The Spanish police may have lied, but there is reason to think this is not the case. According to the authors of *Phoenix: Policing the Shadows,* "Mary Parkin" had been in Gibraltar on March 5. Surveillance teams had watched her reconnoitre the area around the Convent. Afterwards, she had gone into a nearby Catholic chapel and was seen lighting a candle before leaving the Colony.[17]

"Parkin" had travelled to the Rock several times between late 1987 and early 1988. All these previous trips had been on days the changing-of-the-guard took place. Why would she break this routine just to look around the Colony one last time? Her presence in Gibraltar on March 5 would be quite understandable, however, if she had driven the blocking car in that day.

This interpretation of events solves one of the riddles of the affair: why Commissioner Canepa held his special meeting for Operation Flavius's key participants in the dead of night on Saturday. The appearance of the blocking car by the Convent on Saturday afternoon would have been the clearest indicator possible that the Provisionals' attack on Gibraltar was going ahead.

But of all the developments that came to light, the ones dealing with the surveillance operation in Spain did the most damage to the British government's credibility.

First, in December 1988, the *Observer* revealed the contents of an affidavit sworn out by Julian Manyon for the Windlesham-Rampton Inquiry, the independent investigation of *Death on the Rock* Thames Television had commissioned. According to Manyon, during his April 1988 meeting with Army public relations chief Brigadier Sam Sowan and MoD publicity man Hugh Colver:

I . . . put to them the account I had received from the

Spanish authorities about the surveillance operation . . . namely that [Savage's car] had been under surveillance as it arrived at the Gibraltar border whereupon British surveillance had taken over. Mr Colver and [Brigadier]] Cowan indicated that this was correct.

Yet when the MoD gave evidence to the inquiry, Brigadier Cowan said, "Categorically that Spanish surveillance was never discussed". However, after Manyon's affidavit, Colver admitted that it had. The MoD than asked the Windlesham-Rampton inquiry for permission to "correct" its evidence.[18]

Next, journalists learned the simple fact that the checking-in process at a Spanish hotel entails the traveler filling out a card with the details of his or her passport on it. Each day, hotels send these cards to nearby police barracks where they are entered into a registry. McCann and Savage booked into the Hotel Escandinavia in Torremolinos on Friday night, March 4. They were travelling under false passports known to both the Spanish and British governments.[19] Furthermore, the proprietor of the Escandinavia remembered sending his son off the next afternoon to deliver the registration cards to the Torremolinos police.[20] Unless the Spanish failed to take the very basic step of checking their own records during the manhunt, they could not have failed to locate McCann and Savage. By late afternoon or early evening on Saturday, the Spanish police would have known where the IRA men were staying.[21]

There were also the assorted statements that members of the Spanish government made before and after the inquest. Between late 1988 and into 1989, Chief Inspector Miguel Martin Pedraz, head of the police union whose members included the officers who took part in the operation, emphatically stated – on the record – that McCann, Savage, and Farrell had been under constant surveillance while in Spain. Pedraz, who said he knew the details of the case "inside and out", stressed that both the British and the Spanish were aware

258

that the three were unarmed and did not have a bomb with them when they set off for Gibraltar that last Sunday.[22]

Other members of the Spanish police informed journalists that they had been certain McCann, Savage, and Farrell were not dangerous on March 6 because they never took possession of the explosives from the IRA team supporting them in Spain. Somebody from that part of the ASU, "Parkin", "Oakes", or someone else, had picked up the "gear" from the Valencia arms cache. Whether he or she was under surveillance at that time is unknown. However, the same Saturday night "Katherine Smith" made arrangements to rent the white Ford Fiesta from the Marbessol in Marbella, two British intelligence officials, one from the police and the other from MI6, checked into a hotel only fifty yards away from the rental agency.[23] Their sudden appearance there was no coincidence. If the British and Spanish police knew which car the IRA team was going to pick up, they may have put a radio-tracking device on it. The Marbella hotel would have been an ideal staging point from which to do that.

In any case, the British certainly used the hotel as an observation post to see who collected the white Fiesta. And when "Katherine Smith" drove the car away from the Marbessol, she led them and presumably the Spanish police straight to the Marbella garage where the red Fiesta and the explosives were waiting.

The behavior of the Spanish government made this more than merely plausible. Madrid did not silence the outspoken Inspector Pedraz. And in December 1988, at a secret ceremony, twenty-two Spanish police officials, participants in Operation Flavius, received special awards from the Ministry of the Interior. It was hardly the action of a government displeased with its security forces. It did resemble one of a country desperately trying to preserve the morale of its police force while not undermining an ally.[24]

Stronger confirmation that McCann, Savage, and Farrell had

not been lost came on March 16, 1989. That day, Jose Luis Corcuera, Spain's Minister of the Interior, gave a press conference for Spanish journalists at his country's embassy in London. According to one of those present, "He said 'We followed the terrorists. They were completely under our control. We did not lose them.'"[25]

Rafail Vera, Spain's director of state security at the time of the shootings, was also present at the briefing. The answer he gave to a question about why he did not protest the British allegations of Spanish incompetence was quite instructive, "Not always by keeping quiet does one agree with what is being said".[26]

The British government's "gyrations" about the Valenzuela statement did not help its credibility either. Not every journalist who received a leaked copy of that document trusted it implicitly. Looking into its origins, several of them discovered a surprising fact. Twice, the Spanish government, in response to a formal request for evidence, had provided the British with a signed and sworn deposition given before a Malaga judge by Inspector Valenzuela about the surveillance operation in Spain.[27] Yet what was provided to the Coroner's Court had been the unsigned and unsworn translation of a statement allegedly made by the Spanish policeman to Detective Inspector Correa.

When this piece of information hit the newspapers in May 1989, it touched off a minor diplomatic war. The British Foreign Office insisted that Valenzuela had never sworn out a statement before a judge, that the only one he gave had been to the Gibraltar Police. In the Colony, Coroner Pizzarello was unable or unwilling to provide the original of this document (which was supposedly signed and in Spanish). Meanwhile, in Madrid, the Spanish government continued to categorically state that its version of events was correct.[28]

Next, Ed Moloney broke a little bit of news about Valenzuela and the nature of the entire Spanish effort against the IRA. Members of the Foreign Intelligence Brigade of the

Spanish police directorate had told him that they, not the Malaga police, had orchestrated Madrid's end of the counter-terrorist operation. Inspector Valenzuela and his subordinates had only learned about the IRA plot a few days before March 6 and played only a supporting role in the surveillance of the ASU.[29] Since the British authorities knew this, their decision to get a statement from Valenzuela, the "bit player", was odd to say the least. And the *Sunday Times'* decision to treat the document as gospel truth while lashing out at *This Week* for broadcasting Kenneth Asquez's unsigned statement was more than a little hypocritical.

Following this, after weeks of denying that any sworn statement existed, the British government announced that there had been one after all and that the document prepared by Inspector Correa had been a simple working draft of it. The Foreign Office did not explain why it failed to deliver this critical deposition to Coroner Pizzarello in time for the inquest.[30] On May 28, 1989, in a bizarre twist, after promising that the statement would made available to the public, the Foreign Office announced that someone at the British Embassy in Madrid had "lost" it. It was not until early June that the diplomats there "found" the document. Perhaps not surprisingly, it was identical to Correa's so-called "working copy".[31]

Yet, as Harry Debelius learned, Inspector Valenzuela had not sworn to the statement's accuracy, *only that he had made it.*[32] By then, the British public had grown heartily bored with the whole thing. Apart from a small number of "lefties" and "wets", few cared.

And the allegations continue. In March 1998, almost ten years to the day that the SAS shot McCann, Savage, and Farrell, well-placed sources in Gibraltar made two claims to Brendan Anderson of the *Irish News*. The first was that the authorities filmed the Provisionals on closed-circuit television when they crossed the border into the Colony. To borrow the *Sunday*

*Times'* expression, if true, that fact "destroys" the story that the IRA's arrival in Gibraltar took the British by surprise.[33]

The second allegation had to do with the conduct of the inquest. British intelligence agents bugged a room used by the jury at that proceeding. Why they would do such a thing, and what impact it might have had on the inquest is unknown. But if it happened it would make a mockery out of the claim that a "deep and abiding" respect for the rule of law drove the security forces' actions in Gibraltar.[34]

## Notes

1. Mary Campbell, "Spanish Silence Police Honoured for IRA Watch", *Irish Times*, March 15, 1989.

2. Dáil Éireann, Parliamentary Debates, November 16, 1988.

3. Gibraltar Police Operations Order, No. 88, enclosed as Appendix D of the British Irish Rights Watch Report, "The Deaths on Gibraltar."

4. Jack, "Gibraltar", p. 80.

5. *Private Eye* #, 708, February 3, 1989, p. 5.

6. "Gibraltar Team Flies to See New Witness of IRA Deaths", *The Times*, May 9, 1988.

7. The Gibraltar Inquest Transcript; *Private Eye* #, 712, Saturday, April 1, 1989, p. 7.

8. Richard Norton-Taylor, "Businessman Cleared of Terrorist Bomb-making Charge", *Guardian*, September 29, 1993.

9. Jack, "Deaths that Cannot Be Buried Away", *Observer*, May 28, 1989.

10. Andy Pollak and Geraldine Mitchell, "Six Linked to IRA's Gibraltar Operation", *Irish Times*, May 10, 1989; Tim McGirk and Heather Mills, "SAS Shootings Allowed Others to Escape", *Independent*, May 23, 1989.

11. Interview with Brendan O'Brien, Dublin November 1997. The number of IRA personnel involved with the Gibraltar operation from its inception in late 1987 was closer to thirty than three.

12. David Miller, "The Truth on the Rocks", *Magill*, February 1989, pp. 11-12.

13. Urban, *Big Boys' Rules*, p. 143.

14. Ibid, p. 144. She was acquitted on that charge.

15. That is supposition of course. Back in 1988, O'Hanlon vehemently denied having anything to do with the Gibraltar operation and bitterly complained that by naming her as "Parkin", the press had set her up for assassination. She may have been telling the truth. But the Republican Movement is relatively small, and there are not many women in it who have the ties to McCann, Savage, and Farrell that O'Hanlon did.

16. Tim McGirk and Heather Mills, "Spanish Police Contradict British Line on IRA Deaths", *Independent*, May 23, 1989.

17. Holland and Phoenix, p. 135.

18. David Miller, "The Damage was Done", *Magill*, April 1989, p. 18.

19. "Intelligence Experts Stalked IRA's Movement", *Independent*, May 23, 1989. Just how much the British knew about the IRA's plans is illustrated by the fact that two days before McCann and Savage appeared in Spain, MI5 had already passed their photographs on to a Spanish police command post in Marbella.

20. John Hooper and Peter Murtagh, "Questions Linger Over Rock Shooting", *Guardian*, March 25, 1989.

21. Translation of "Internal Communication of the Intelligence Section of the General Directorate of Police", undated. According to this document, the Spanish police located McCann and Farrell on March 4 which indicates that they were never lost.

22. Geraldine Mitchell and Andy Pollak, "Spanish Unease Over IRA Surveillance Claim", *Irish Times*, April 25, 1989.

23. "Intelligence Experts Stalked IRA's Movement."

24. John Hooper and Peter Murtagh, "Anti-terror Officers Win Awards", *Guardian*, March 14, 1989.

25. John Hooper and Peter Murtagh, "Spain Rejects Gibraltar Evidence", *Guardian*, March 16, 1988.

26. Ibid.

27. Harry Debelius, untitled and apparently unpublished, dated September 28, 1988.

28. David Leigh, Paul Lashmar, and John Hooper, "Madrid Angry at UK 'Lies' on IRA Deaths", *Observer*, May 21, 1989.

29. Ed Moloney, "Spain Undermines British Version of the Gibraltar Killings", *Sunday Tribune*, March 19, 1989.

30. Tim McGirk, "Gibraltar Statement Was Not Given to Inquest", *Independent*, June 1, 1989; Geraldine Mitchell and Andy Pollak, "Gibraltar Report Withdrawn but not Denied", *Irish Times*, April 26, 1989.

31. "FO Reveals Gib Document", *Observer*, June 4, 1989.

32. Harry Debelius, draft story, untitled, May 1989.

33. Brendan Anderson, "Gibraltar Story is Still Unfolding", *The Irish News*, March 4, 1998.

34. Ibid.

# CHAPTER EIGHTEEN

## DEATH IN THE AFTERNOON

" . . . the victim is condemned to die once it enters the arena, there is no chance of living against the surprises and superior skills of the matador."
  – Paddy McGrory at the Gibraltar Inquest

In 1994, a short novel about the Gibraltar killings appeared on the market in the United Kingdom. One of a popular action series featuring the SAS, it was badly written, and the author's apparent belief that the killing of three unarmed people was a triumph absolutely mystifying. Yet for all its faults, on the inside cover of *Soldier R SAS: Death on Gibraltar*, there is a perfect description of the British government's account of what happened on the Rock:

[This] is a work of fiction based on a factual event . . . [Only] the real names of the three IRA terrorists shot dead . . . have been retained . . . many [other] events have been either partially reinvented or invented in their entirety.[1]

That particular "work of fiction" is a story of errors, miscalculation, and incompetence that led to tragedy. By mistake, MI5 assumed that when McCann, Savage, and Farrell entered Gibraltar, they would be armed and have a car-bomb with them, one they could detonate simply by pressing a button. By mistake, Soldiers A, B, C, and D received information that made them think that bomb was at the assembly area and the IRA members were about to trigger it. By mistake, the Gibraltar

Police switched on a siren just as the SAS men were closing in on the Provisionals, a siren that made Daniel McCann look back over his shoulder and see Soldier A. It was regrettable but unavoidable, and there was no malice to any of it. The soldiers had believed their lives and others had been in danger so they took the action they did. It was all a mistake.

If that was all there was to it, there would be no reason for doubting the authorities' account of the incident. But because there is more to it, that comforting, soothing story about good-intentioned mistakes leading to unavoidable deaths is a lie, a crime, and an integral part of a conspiracy to pervert the course of justice.

That is a very harsh judgment to draw about the actions of men and women charged with the responsibility of protecting their country from a determined, skillful, and ruthless paramilitary organization. It is not something to be put forward lightly. Yet blindly accepting McCann, Savage, and Farrell's deaths as accidents requires setting aside of too many facts that point in another direction.

How many facts would that be? It is not a question of a few inconvenient details; the British government's story simply doesn't hold water.

First, there are the deceptions it contains. When instructing the inquest jury, Coroner Pizzarello had the following advice about falsehoods, "Even a lie has its uses. A lie . . . does not prove anything in itself, but it is a good indicator and can lead to inferences being drawn".[2]

What inferences can be drawn from the larger lies told about the Gibraltar killings? What do the fictitious stories about car-bombs and gun battles on the Rock prove? Not much, except that someone in Gibraltar felt it was imperative to implant a lasting false impression of events there in the public's minds. What does the vicious assault on Carmen Proetta's character suggest? It suggests that she was regarded as a dangerous witness whose credibility had to be damaged. Why did the British government conceal the fact that Canepa's order listed Inspector Revagliatte as a critical player in Operation Flavius? Because it needed his "coincidental" presence near the Shell Petrol Station to justify the killings as an accident. Why did Witness N claim that she did not hear fifteen gunshots fired just yards away from her by two unsilenced pistols? Because saying she heard (and saw) nothing was a simpler perjury than claiming that Soldiers C and D did not shoot Savage on the ground. To paraphrase the old Latin saying, *res ipsa loquitur*, these things speak for themselves.

Most important of all, why did the British government try to admit into evidence an unsigned, unsworn translation of a statement that Inspector Valenzuela allegedly made about the Spanish surveillance operation, a statement he has both denied and acknowledged as his? Why did the British authorities stoutly deny they ever received a *sworn* statement from Valenzuela about the surveillance and then admit later that they had? Why, in the case of the document ultimately produced at the British Embassy in Madrid, did Valenzuela only attest to the fact that he had given the statement, not that it was accurate version of the Spanish police's activities? And why did the British government choose not to share that fact with the media and public? None of this makes sense unless the account contained in the Valenzuela "statement" is false. The document containing that version of events was never really intended to be evidence for the inquest. Its target was the press. Its mission was to overturn the publicly acknowledged fact that the Spanish police follow the Provos right up to the gates of Gibraltar.

That the SAS, MI5, and Thatcher Administration officials lied to the British public about Gibraltar is not surprising. Lying is regrettably necessary in the political and intelligence worlds. Unfortunately, people who live in those domains sometimes confuse their own interests with those of their country. When that happens and when they have permission to lie to protect "national security", sooner or later they give themselves permission to lie to protect themselves.[3]

But beyond ignoring the falsehoods, accepting the British version of the killings means believing the following:

– Stephen and Lucinda Bullock lied or were mistaken about seeing the two gunmen on Smith Dorrien Avenue

– Josie Celecia lied or was mistaken about seeing a man standing over McCann and Farrell's bodies and then hearing gunshots coming from there

– Carmen Proetta lied or was mistaken about seeing three gunmen emerge from a Gibraltar Police car and shoot McCann and Farrell; Maxie Proetta's similar account was equally mistaken or perjured

– Diana Treacy lied or was mistaken about seeing an SAS man shoot Savage in the back without warning

– Robin Mordue lied or was mistaken about seeing Savage fall to the ground after being shot and hearing more gunfire after that

– Witness I lied or was mistaken about seeing Soldiers A and B shoot McCann and Farrell after they fell to the ground

– The British authorities' failure to evacuate the area around Savage's "car-bomb" until well after the shootings was a simple oversight on their part

– The Gibraltar Police's almost complete destruction of the crime scenes was purely accidental

Simply put, if all of this is true, Soldiers A, B, C, and D were the unluckiest men in the world.

Finally, rising above the lies and "coincidences", there is a yawning gap between what the soldiers testified they did and what the physical evidence says about McCann's, Savage's, and Farrell's deaths. In less politically-charged circumstances, people in the United Kingdom and the United States have been convicted of murder on discrepancies like those alone.

In McCann's and Farrell's cases, it is simply a matter of counting the wounds on their bodies and comparing that reality with Soldiers A and B's stories. The government pathologist, Professor Watson, told the inquest jury that Farrell had been first shot twice in the head while facing her killer. These bullets produced several non-fatal wounds. She had only died from the heart and liver damage caused by the three rounds then fired into her back.

As for McCann, four bullets struck him, one in the jaw; another two in the back, lacerating his heart, liver, and left lung; and the final entering the back of his head and shredding his brain. To the pathologist, the shots in the back appeared to have come while he was on or near the ground and the one to the back of the head after that.

The men who caused all this damage, Soldiers A and B, testified they did so in the following sequence: after McCann glanced over his shoulder and locked eyes with Soldier A, the SAS man immediately put a round into his back. Seeing Farrell make her threatening movement, he shot her there as well. Shifting back to McCann, he fired three more shots, two into the Provisional's back and one into his head.

Soldier B's actions mirror-imaged those of his partner's. He fired first at Farrell and then turned his gun on McCann before firing a final burst into Farrell. Soldier B said he had let off a total of seven shots and did not miss with any of them. But he could not remember how many times he had hit each Provisional.

The problem with this is that the numbers do not add up. If Soldiers A and B were telling an accurate and truthful story, McCann should have had five bullet tracks in his body. He had only four. Farrell should have had six or seven. There was evidence of only five.

Perhaps Soldiers A's and B's aim was not as good as they thought. Two of the petrol pumps at the Shell Station bear strike marks and a ricochet hit Victor Morgan, a British tourist strolling north of the Shell Station with his wife.[4] If the soldiers missed three times that brings their "hits" down to nine. This corresponds to the number of bullet tracks in McCann's and Farrell's bodies.[5]

If Soldier A was being honest about shooting McCann four times, his partner could not have hit him at all. If he was telling the truth about shooting Farrell at most once in the back, that meant Soldier B was responsible for four of the five bullets that hit her – the two in her face and two of those in her back. To accomplish this, the SAS man would have had to have fired bursts of shots from two completely different positions almost simultaneously – first from the road at Farrell's head while she was looking at him and then from the footpath into her prone body. But Soldier B was adamant that he fired at her only from behind and stayed on the footpath at all times.[6]

As for Savage, Soldiers C and D claimed that they shot him fifteen times, another odd discrepancy in numbers since Watson identified sixteen separate bullet tracks through his body. The commandos admitted they both hit Savage in the head twice but vehemently denied firing at him after he collapsed. Yet this is exactly what Professor Watson believed had happened, that at least some of the rounds struck the IRA man's head while he was on his back. That possibility takes on added likelihood when combined with one of the pieces of evidence that the Gibraltar Police did not see fit to destroy, the bullet strike marks inside the silhouette drawn around Savage's body. There were three of them right where his head had lain and a few feet to the right, there had been several shell casings. Browning automatics eject their brass that direction and distance which suggests a pistol was not far from Savage's head when it fired. So perhaps Kenneth Asquez told the truth when he said he saw a gunman standing on Savage's chest, shouting, "Stop! It's okay. It's the police!" and shooting him.[7]

If the British government's version of events is false, what did happen on the Rock on March 6, 1988? That question is likely to remain unanswered. As Mr O himself said at the inquest:

It is very, very rare for the whole picture to be known. Almost invariably all is known are fragments, and we have to put together an assessment of the most likely course of events based on what we have available.[8]

Following this procedure, it is possible to construct an explanation for events on March 6. This assessment may not be completely accurate but is far more *reasonable* than the British governments' presentation. This is because it does not rely upon a spectacular series of coincidences to work.

The first step in developing this scenario is determining the British government's intentions toward the Provisionals. There are three clues to this.

First, McCann, Savage, and Farrell were dedicated, skilled members of the IRA who had shown by their actions they would never stop taking part in violence. The British government had reason to wish each of them dead. McCann and Savage were veteran bombers and close-quarter killers responsible for the recent murder of two RUC Special Branch officers. Farrell was a highly popular activist and quite valuable as a symbol for the Republican Movement. All three were on a bombing mission that would have produced mass casualties similar to, if not worse than, Enniskillen.

Furthermore, at least some elements in the British intelligence community believed that the IRA was going to blow up Gibraltar to demonstrate its revolutionary credentials to Colonel Quadaffi.[9] The Libyan dictator certainly would have relished the fact that his explosives had been put to good use against a British target relatively close to his own country.

The second clue is that the British sent a military assault unit to deal with the ASU. By its own officers' testimony, this force

– the SAS – has killed twenty-five percent of the individuals it has targeted for arrest. That percentage puts its soldiers among the ranks of the most lethal policemen in the world. In contrast, for years, officers of the London Metropolitan Police Special Branch and the RUC have managed to avoid killing most of the IRA men they have tried to arrest. Why were they not sent to Rock instead of the SAS? In Northern Ireland, courts are entitled to draw an inference of guilt when a suspect does not answer reasonable questions. It is only fair to apply the same standard to the British government's decision to hide behind the PII certificates and refuse to explain its decision to commit the SAS to Operation Flavius.

Finally, there is what came out at the inquest, namely, the soldiers' irrational and unreasonable certainty that they were facing a radio-detonated car-bomb and Inspector Ullger's statement that the ASU had to be let in for Operation Flavius to work.

Together, these facts suggest that the British government was carefully constructing an opportunity to "legally" use lethal force against the Provisionals. Such an event did not require an elaborate conspiracy behind it. The IRA would put their heads in the noose for the British. If everything went according to plan, they would enter Gibraltar on Monday night or early Tuesday morning with the car-bomb and carrying weapons. Once the Provisionals were on the wide open space of the airstrip, the jaws of the trap would close. Using the claim that the IRA team might be carrying "buttons", the SAS could easily justify immediately shooting them dead. The fact that the Provisionals would have had a car-bomb with them would erase any doubt in the public's mind that killing them was necessary. No one would ask whether they could have been arrested under less dangerous circumstances.

Given that intent, the confrontation the British government planned to have with the IRA was something like a bullfight.

McGrory made that point to Coroner Pizzarello, drawing on Earnest Hemingway's *Death in the Afternoon*. In that classic essay about the *corrida* (bullfight), Hemingway had written:

[It] is not a sport in the Anglo-Saxon sense of the word. It is not an equal contest or an attempt at an equal contest. Rather it is a tragedy, the death of the bull, which is played, more or less well by the bull and the man involved and in which there is danger for the man but certain death for the animal.[10]

The analogy is clear. From beginning to end, Operation Flavius was a carefully-scripted event controlled by the matador, in this case MI5 and the SAS. The ASU was the bull.

There would have been two motives for that sort of spectacle. First, killing McCann, Savage, and Farrell would permanently remove from the IRA's ranks three highly-skilled, committed activists. Second, it would send a simple message to the Provisional units in Europe and England: they could be killed just as easily as they were in Northern Ireland. What happened in Gibraltar was a warning to the IRA, not law enforcement.

This simple plan miscarried. Short of a major judicial inquiry by the British government, the reason why will remain a mystery. Yet enough data exists to develop a sequence of events that explains how three corpses came to lie on Gibraltar's streets.

Few would argue that by March 6, the IRA's plan to car-bomb the Royal Anglians was not thoroughly compromised. Using telephone taps, informants, and surveillance both in Spain and Northern Ireland, the British pieced together a comprehensive picture of the Provisionals' intentions. They were simple: the ASU would place a blocking car in the assembly area by the Convent and replace it with a timer-detonated car-bomb on Monday night or early Tuesday morning.

Confirmation for this assessment would have come from

MI5's familiarity with the IRA. Contrary to what he claimed at the inquest, Mr O certainly knew that the Provisionals have never much worried about killing civilians if they believe doing so is unavoidable. The very fact that they were planning to let off a massive car-bomb in Gibraltar after the "disaster of Enniskillen" was proof of the IRA's lack of concern about the consequences of their actions. Mr O also knew full well that the Provisionals are not suicidal by nature. As British army Brigadier General James Glover once wrote, "a safe method of escape is the dominant feature in [IRA] tactics".[11] Using a radio-detonated car-bomb in Gibraltar would have forced at least one IRA member to remain behind in the Colony to set it off and face the consequences for doing so. Not using a blocking car would have risked the possibility of being unable to carry out the attack. The IRA has often displayed comical incompetence, but this sort of behavior, which Mr O claimed he expected, pushes the "Paddy factor" too far.

So on Sunday, the SAS and MI5 were expecting the IRA to bring a blocking car into Gibraltar. Or if the Spanish police were telling the truth, they had already seen one come in on Saturday. Given the story in *Phoenix: Policing the Shadows* about "Mary Parkin" visiting the Rock on March 5, that seems more likely.

In either case, the authorities knew that the Provisionals might put in additional appearances on the Rock before finally driving the car-bomb in on Monday night. If the blocking car had not come on Saturday, parking one at the assembly area would have been reason enough for the IRA team to make a visit. If the blocking car was already there, they might have entered Gibraltar simply to look the target area over and test it for surveillance. This would not have disturbed the MI5 officers running Operation Flavius. They had no reason to be upset. The Spanish police had been keeping McCann, Savage, and Farrell under constant watch and had informed the British they were not bringing explosives into Gibraltar. Knowing this, MI5 was content to give the ASU a round trip ticket.

Yet to guard against the unexpected, the trio had to be carefully monitored while in the Colony. That would have been the MI5 watchers' job, but the SAS would have been on the streets as well – to provide firepower and extra manpower for the surveillance and let the soldiers familiarize themselves with their targets for Monday night.

But somehow, far too late, the Provisionals realized that they were in a trap. Someone watching them gave the game away. The guilty party could have been one of Canepa's men (Officer P who had made eye to eye contact with Savage?) or even one of the MI5 officers. The most likely culprits, though, are the SAS men, members of a military unit known to be inept at passing its members off as civilians. The specific soldiers who compromised the operation probably were Soldiers C and D. By their own testimony, they received orders to move away from the assembly area after identifying McCann, Savage, and Farrell from Trafalgar Cemetery. Only minutes after the SAS men complied with those instructions, their commanders began pressing the police to authorize "the military option" despite the fact only two other soldiers – A and B – were left in the area to make an arrest. Why pull Soldiers C and D back at such a critical moment? Could it have been because their superiors had a sinking feeling that the two SAS men's attempt to pass as civilians had not fooled the Provisionals?

If McCann, Savage, and Farrell finally realized they were under surveillance, their response would have been to abort the attack. That is standard operating procedure for the IRA under such circumstances. Better to scrap the mission than risk the lives of the volunteers. They could just walk out of Gibraltar, and a different ASU could try there again some time in the future.

Or the Provisionals might have had no idea of what was

going on but just looked like they did. For all their expertise, the intelligence people watching them could not have known for sure. All they could have been certain of was that their targets were acting like they knew they were under surveillance. As each minute ticked by, the trio were getting closer and closer to the Spanish border. If the ASU left Gibraltar and did not return, the months of effort the authorities had spent to get into position to legally eliminate them would be for nothing. McCann, Savage, and Farrell would fly back to Belfast and, after a rest, go back to killing. If that happened, the men running Operation Flavius could look forward to quite a "handbagging" from Mrs Thatcher.

So the SAS were sent into action. The available evidence from the civilian eyewitnesses suggest that the following events took place after the decision to exercise the military option was made.

First, Operation Flavius's controllers picked a site to conduct the attack. Their selection of the Shell Station over the airstrip may have reflected eagerness on the SAS's part to come to grips with the Provisionals. An alternate explanation would be that the petrol station was closed on Sunday and would have been a less crowded and therefore safer place than the airport to deal with the ASU.

Next, the SAS detachment commander sent more men to the scene. There were, after all, only four soldiers in the area to confront McCann, Savage, and Farrell. So three SAS men at the border piled into one of the Gibraltar Police cars being used by MI5 that day and sped south as reinforcements. Meanwhile, Soldiers C and D, who had been positioned near the playground on Smith Dorrien, received orders to stand by to assist their fellow soldiers but not to move until after the action began.

Unfortunately, Savage complicated things by splitting away from his companions and walking back south. His doing so seems to have caught the authorities off-guard. Soldiers A and B and the men coming from the border were committed against McCann and Farrell. The possibly compromised Soldiers C and D were the only men left to move on Savage.

Once the SAS men's car halted opposite of the Shell Station, its occupants jumped out, leaped over the fence dividing Winston Churchill Avenue, and ran up to McCann and Farrell. Just as the soldiers confronted the Provisionals, Inspector Revagliatte's siren blared. The police's triggering it may have been intentional, a signal for the soldiers or a device to startle McCann and Farrell into their "suspicious movements". Or it might have been a genuine mistake.

In any case, by then, Soldiers A and B had drawn their pistols, and one of them had moved out onto the roadway. McCann and Farrell, their attention drawn by the sirens, turned in that direction. Seeing as many as four armed men facing them, they put their hands up. Seconds later, at least two of their assailants – one on the road – gunned them down. Once they were on the ground, at least one SAS man put "the battlefield practice" of shooting them in the head into effect. A moment after that, Soldiers C and D, finally let off the leash, ran Savage down and sent him to "the final court of justice" as well.

The dark area of this scenario is the soldiers' intent. Immediately after the killings, Carmen Proetta saw the blond gunman who shot McCann and Farrell on the ground have a short but heated argument with several men who arrived on the scene by car. This discussion might have had had to do with tactics – the stupidity of administering a *coup de grace* to two people in broad daylight. But the argument might have occurred because someone clearly did want the Provisionals arrested that day.[12]

Whatever the case, McCann, Savage, and Farrell were dead.

But in a bullfight, it is not enough to simply kill the bull. One must kill well, with style, grace, and genuinely court death from the animal while doing so. This the audience expects of the matador for:

> A killing is judged by . . . the manner in which the man goes in to kill rather than by the immediate results. To kill the bull with a single sword thrust is of no merit at all . . . unless the man passed over and had his body within reach of the horn at the moment he went in.[13]

Those conditions simply did not exist when the SAS men shot the Provisionals. There would be no roar of approval from the crowd, no admiring articles in the newspapers for killing three unarmed people. So an image of danger was manufactured. This process began twenty-three minutes after the shootings when Savage's blocking car became a "suspect car-bomb", and the evacuation of the Gibraltar town centre commenced. It continued back in London when the British media got their first "exclusives" about the shootings. By the time the truth came out on March 7, the damage had already been done.

What about the Gibraltar Police's role in all of this? It seems unlikely that Commissioner Canepa and his men entered into a conspiracy before the fact to murder McCann, Savage, and Farrell. Not because policemen never break the law, but because it is absurd to believe MI5 would have trusted Canepa, a minor colonial official, with a plan to eliminate three members of the IRA. The idea that the MoD would have given Canepa genuine control of ordinary soldiers, let alone an SAS unit, is equally ludicrous. The good Commissioner's real role in Operation Flavius was that of a rubber stamp, dutifully signing away his authority when "advised" to do so. As for the actions of the Gibraltar Police *after* the killings, the image of a dustman dutifully sweeping up the mess, "the help" left behind, comes to mind. The only question about the police's performance is when incompetence driven by the belief that what happened on the Rock was not a crime ended and obstruction of justice began.

In the end, the British people should regard the Gibraltar killings as a tragedy but not because the world lost something when the Provisionals died. McCann, Savage, and Farrell's families and friends have a right to feel a sense of loss, but the people they almost killed have no such obligation. Nor should the British public be angry because the IRA team was not given "a sporting chance" to carry out the bombing. No, the reason for regretting Operation Flavius's outcome is because killing the IRA operatives the way they were killed was *murder*. And Margaret Thatcher bears ultimate moral – if not criminal – responsibility for that outcome. She had sent the SAS to Gibraltar. She was the one who had publicly stated "that those who choose to live by the bomb and the gun . . . cannot in all circumstances be accorded exactly the same rights as everyone else."[14]

Thatcher's statements set the stage for what happened on the Rock, events that were not only criminal but unnecessary. The British government could have had the Spanish police arrest the ASU for conspiracy and possession of explosives. Or if Spanish justice was too unreliable, the Gibraltar Police could have arrested the trio for possessing false passports when they entered the Colony. That was a charge McCann, Savage, and Farrell could not have beaten.[15] Yet instead of working for that easy and legal objective, the SAS and MI5 took a course of action that presented the IRA with a first-class propaganda victory. By failing to prevent Michael Stone's attack on the mourners at Milltown Cemetery, the British authorities in Northern Ireland doubled that victory. By not allowing common sense to govern a number of the Casement Park prosecutions, they redoubled it. An atrocity in Gibraltar had been prevented but at the price of undermining the rule of law. As Hemingway put it when he saw a cowardly matador "assassinate" a bull:

> I could see the bull had to be killed to make the bullfight; I was pleased that he was killed with a sword, for anything to be killed with a sword was a rare enough business; but the way that he was killed looked like a trick . . . This is the bullfight, I thought, the end is not so good.[16]

Sitting in their cells in the Maze Prison, Seán Kelly and Michael Timmons would feel "the end is not so good" is an understatement. Their families, those of Michael Stone's victims, and those of Corporals Wood and Howes probably do as well.

## Notes

1. Shaun Clarke, *Soldier R SAS: Death on Gibraltar*, 22 Books, Rochester, Kent, United Kingdom, 1994.

2. Statement of Mr Felix Pizzarello, the Gibraltar Inquest, Day 19, 30 September 1988, Channel Four Television, 1988, p. 16.

3. Dan Raviv and Yossi Melman, *Every Spy a Prince: The complete History of Irrael's Intelligence Community,* Houghton Mifflin Company, Boston, p. 284.

4. Victor Adams was only scratched and bruised as a result. Testifying at the inquest, he was unable to give any help to either the government or to Paddy McGrory.

5. O'Higgins and Waters, "A Controlled Explosion of the Truth," pp. 39-40.

6. Ibid.

7. Ibid.

8. Testimony of Mr O, the Gibraltar Inquest, Day 2, 7 September 1988, Channel Four Television, p. 8.

9. O'Brien, p.151 and other sources.

10. Ernest Hemingway, *Death in the Afternoon*, Charles Scribner's Sons, New York, 1932, p. 16.

11. Brigadier General James Glover, "Northern Ireland: Future Terrorist Trends", British Army, 1978. This was originally a classified report. It became public after someone stole a copy from the Royal Mail and provided it to the Republican Movement.

12. Interview with Stephen Bullock. When I spoke with Mr Bullock, he

commented about the fact that the SAS men, Soldiers C and D "put their heads together" before running after Savage. It seems at least possible that they were surprised by the shootings and had to pause before deciding to back up their comrades by killing Savage.

13. Hemingway, pp. 245-246.

14. Geraghty, 1993 edition, p. 313.

15. They could have also requested the Irish government or the governments of other countries through which McCann, Savage, and Farrell travelled to arrest them on similar grounds.

16. Hemingway, p. 234.

# EPILOGUE

## UNFINISHED BUSINESS

"The past is never dead. It's not even past."
  – William Faulkner

The Thatcher Administration may have intended Gibraltar to be a message to the Provisionals, but that message fell on deaf ears.

The IRA's activities on the British mainland are proof of that. On September 18, 1989, a bomb ripped through Deal Barracks in Kent, killing ten Royal Marines, music students but as Gerry Adams put it, "marines first, musicians second".[1]

The following year, the attacks on British military towns and personnel continued. Between February and June of 1990, Provo "sleeper" units on the mainland killed two servicemen and injured twenty-nine soldiers and civilians.

On June 25, 1990, the IRA switched its focus back to the "ruling class" with a bomb that smashed the Carlton Club, a posh London refuge for Tory MPs. The blast wounded over twenty people. Five days later, Mrs Thatcher lost another close, personal friend when Ian Gow MP closed the door of his car, setting off the trembler-switch-0detonated explosive device an ASU had hidden inside it. Just weeks after that, an IRA gunman shot up the Staffordshire home of retired Gibraltar Governor, Sir Peter Terry. Although badly wounded, Terry survived. His wife escaped with minor injuries. The couple had paid a heavy price for the governor's off-hand comment in Gibraltar that "even in this remote place, there is no place for terrorists".[2]

Then at the height of the Gulf War, on February 7, 1991, the Provos mortar-bombed Number 10 Downing Street, almost killing Prime Minister John Major. The IRA had planned the attack with Mrs Thatcher in mind, but she had left office just months before. The opportunity to teach "the Tory war mongers" a lesson had been too good to waste, so the operation went forward anyway. It was a stellar triumph for the IRA's bombing campaign, now a permanent feature of life in Britain, unbroken except by cease-fire.

That was not to say that the Provos could bomb at will on the mainland. Between 1988 and 1997, British police, working with MI5, arrested dozens of IRA operatives thwarting scores of terrorist attacks. And they managed to do it and kill only one man, Diarmuid O'Neill, in the process.[3] In an arrest operation in 1993, one Provisional had been carrying an armed bomb when police confronted him.[4] In another arrest in 1994, the "target" had explosives *and* a pistol.[5] Yet somehow, the police took both "armed, ruthless, and fanatical terrorists" alive, something that the SAS was unable to do in Gibraltar.

Meanwhile, in Northern Ireland, the SAS continued to fight the "non-war" against terrorism. In April 1990, in Kinnego, Armagh, soldiers from the regiment killed Martin Corrigan, a veteran member of the Irish People's Liberation Organization, a splinter from the INLA. Six months later, the SAS returned to Loughgall, scene of its 1987 triumph over the IRA's East Tyrone Brigade. This time, just two Provisionals, Desmond Grew and Martin McCaughey, fell into the net. Both died in a hail of gunfire as they moved assault rifles from one arms cache to another.[6]

The next "battlefield" for the soldiers was Strabane. On November 12, 1990, an INLA gang opened fire on the home of a UDR reservist. SAS men staked out around the house killed one of the would-be assassins, Alexander Patterson, before the INLA men discovered that they had been shooting at an empty building. The bloom came off that particular triumph when it later emerged that Patterson might have been a police informant, killed in yet another SAS mistake.[7]

After that, it was the IRA's turn again. On June 3, 1991, Peter Ryan, Lawrence McNally, and Tony Doris, members of the East Tyrone Brigade, drove into the small town of Coagh. They intended to murder a local UDR man. They never got the chance. A group of SAS troopers raked their car with over three hundred bullets. It crashed and burst into flames. By the time the fire died down, all three IRA men had been incinerated.[8]

The Coagh episode brought the total number of deaths that the East Tyrone IRA had suffered between 1983 and 1991 to twenty-one. Yet the Brigade carried on. On February 16, 1992, one of its ASUs machine-gunned the Coalisland RUC barracks. Afterwards, the IRA men fled in a truck to the car park of St. Patrick's Catholic Church, just north of the town. They intended to hand over their weapons to another group of Provisionals waiting there. But teams of SAS men had been hiding around the church. When they stopped shooting, the building was in flames, and the IRA had four fresh martyrs to bury: Kevin O'Donnell, Seán O'Farrell, Patrick Vincent, and Peter Clancy.

With that, the ambushes stopped for a time. Perhaps someone in the British government listened when O'Donnell's father said, "The IRA has the 'No Vacancy' sign up in East Tyrone since they killed my son and the other brave lads".[9]

As this twilight war raged, the McCann, Savage, and Farrell families continued their effort to extract the justice they believed that they were due. On March 1, 1990, they submitted claims for compensation against the MoD. Two weeks later, the British Foreign Office issued statements barring their legal action. The justification was simple. Daniel McCann, Seán Savage, and Mairéad Farrell had died in Gibraltar, territory outside the United Kingdom. British laws on compensation did not apply to acts committed there. Later the same year, the High Court struck out the relatives' lawsuit.[10]

With no more legal avenues open to them in Britain, the families next filed a claim with the European Commission on Human Rights. They argued that by killing McCann, Savage, and Farrell, the British government had violated Article 2 of the Convention on Human Rights, "the right to live". On September 3, 1993, the Commission declared the case admissible for consideration. Seven months later, it issued its report. By a majority of eleven to six, the Commission held that there had been no violation of the Convention.[11]

To the British government's horror, that finding did not conclude the matter. Despite its ruling, the Commission referred the case up to the European Court of Human Rights, a panel of nineteen jurists drawn from the member countries of the Council of Europe. On February 20, 1995, in Strasbourg, France, this distinguished body heard pleadings from the relatives, interested human rights groups, and the British government about the case. In late September, almost seven years to the day after the Gibraltar Inquest concluded, it issued its ruling. The Court found that the deaths of McCann, Savage, and Farrell were a violation of their right to live.

Republicans in Ireland interpreted this as total victory. BRITISH GOVERNMENT FOUND GUILTY, JUSTICE AT LAST blared the headline of the *An Phoblacht/Republican News*. Speaking to the *Irish Times*, Niall Farrell, Mairéad's brother and spokesman of the Gibraltar Three's families, was jubilant:

This was the . . . the Council of Europe bringing the British establishment to court. That we even got to the court was a huge victory; that we won is tremendous not only for us, but for all those other families who have lost people in shoot-to-kill incidents. It will give them a lot of hope.[12]

In Britain, the mood was one of outrage. There was loose talk about withdrawing from the European Court of Human Rights' jurisdiction or at least ending the right of individual citizens to petition to it.

Yet in truth, if the Court's decision was a victory for the IRA and the relatives, it was a hollow one. It found for the plaintiffs by the narrowest margin possible, ten to nine.[13] And because McCann, Savage, and Farrell died while preparing to commit an act of terrorism, the jurists ruled that their families were not eligible for any damages, only £38,700 for their legal costs.

Most important, the judges rejected the families' claims that there had been a conspiracy to kill their loved ones, that the SAS men who killed McCann, Savage, and Farrell had broken the law, and that the laws of Britain and Gibraltar were fundamentally flawed. Instead, their ruling had two bases: the British authorities failed to allow for the possibility that their intelligence assessments might be wrong, and the SAS men's "automatic recourse to lethal force" had been excessive.

In effect, the Court found Britain guilty of negligent homicide. Ruling that way was a far cry from agreeing with the McCanns, Savages, and Farrells that the British had "blood on their hands". But for the SAS men involved, it still rankled. Speaking through the usual unnamed sources, they let it be known that they felt "betrayed" with the Court's decision.[14] But the soldiers wanted their admiring public to know that they took comfort in the fact that there would be no payment of compensation to relatives of what one British MP described as "terrorist scum".

For a time, it seemed even possible that Britain would not pay the legal costs it owed to its adversaries. Yet short of withdrawing from the European Convention on Human Rights, a treaty that it had helped to draft, Britain had no choice but to pay up. On December 24, 1995, just days before the three-month deadline set by the European Court of Human Rights expired, John Major's government paid the costs. One tabloid described the act as a "Christmas present for terrorists".[15] Speaking for his and the other families, Niall Farrell stated:

> This is a clear indication that the British government now accepts the verdict of the highest human rights court in Europe that they unlawfully killed, or in plain English murdered, our loved ones.[16]

Hardly. In London, MoD and Foreign Office press officers assured the public that the payment did not constitute an admission of guilt. And the words of Michael Heseltine still hung in the air. Asked by BBC Radio, in light of the ruling whether there would be any changes to SAS training or counter-terrorist policy, the Deputy Prime Minister had been succinct:

> We shall do absolutely nothing . . . We will pursue our right to fight terrorists, to protect innocent people, wherever we have jurisdiction. And we will not be swayed or deterred in any way by this ludicrous decision of the Court.[17]

Yet even after the European Court of Human Rights' "ludicrous" ruling, the Gibraltar killings still remain a contentious issue. On October 5, 1995, Niall Farrell announced that his and the other families would be petitioning the United Nations' Special Rapporteur on Extra-judicial, Summary, or Arbitrary Executions to investigate the case. Showing perhaps a naive faith in the powers of that international body, he stated:

> We simply want the whole truth. The UN, we hope, can get to the bottom of this scandal, which we firmly believe leads to the heart of the British Establishment.[18]

For him, like so many others, it will never be truly over.

## Notes

1. J Bowyer Bell, *The Irish Troubles: A Generation of Violence 1967-1992*, St Martin's Press, New York, 1993, p. 760.
2. Heather Mills, "Sudden Death and the Long Quest for Answers", *Independent*, September 8, 1995.
3. Richard Ingrams, "The Police Should Admit They Were Wrong (even the

IRA Has Done That), *Observer*, September 26. 1996. Members of the London Metropolitan Police Firearms Unit shot O'Neill to death in disputed circumstances.

4. "Police Arrest IRA Suspect Carrying Bomb," *San Francisco Chronicle*, July 15, 1993.

5. Stewart Tendler and Kate Alderson, "Yard Holds Two after Semtex Find," *The Times*, February 23, 1994.

6. Geraghty, *Who Dares Wins*, p. 279.

7. Jack Holland and Henry MacDonald, *INLA: Deadly Divisions*, Torc, Dublin, 1994, p. 318.

8. Ian Burrell, "Army Goes to War over SAS Man's Revelations," *Independent*, August 8, 1997. Six years later, Adrian Weale, a military historian and former intelligence officer, wrote about the ambush in his history of British special forces. According to the source that he consulted, the IRA men had been under continuous surveillance which began even before they armed themselves. Showing that it had learned something from the *Death on the Rock* debacle, the MoD had Weale's publisher censor that statement from the book.

9. Ibid.

10. "IRA Families Lose Cash Fight", *Daily Telegraph*, June 1, 1991.

11. *Deaths on Gibraltar 1988*, p. 20.

12. Dick Grogan, "Farrell's Brother Says Ruling Shows Shootings on the Rock Were Murder", *Irish Times*, September 28, 1995.

13. Donncha O'Connell, "Strasbourg Ruling Not Clear Cut", *Irish Times on the Web*, September 28, 1995.

14. Hugh McManners, "SAS Tells of its Relief over Gibraltar Killing", *The Times*, October 1, 1995.

15. Andrew Sparrow and Stephen Olfield, *Daily Mail*, December 27, 1995.

16. Arthur Leathley, "£40,000 Paid to Death on the Rock Families", *The Times*, December 27, 1995.

17. *The Deaths on Gibraltar 1988*, pp. 21-22.

18. Heather Mills, "UN set to investigate Gibraltar shootings", *Independent*, October 5, 1995.

# POSTSCRIPT

As of August 1, 1998, Seán Kelly and Michael Timmons are no longer inmates at the Maze Prison. Prior to a complete release on license, they now reside in a half-way house. Unless successful in future appeals, both men – in the eyes of the law – remain convicted murderers.